Knight's Cross

HOLDERS OF THE

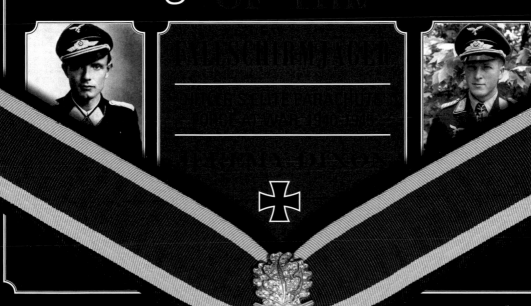

Schiffer Publishing Ltd

4880 Lower Valley Road • Atglen, PA 19310

Type set in Minion Pro

ISBN: 978-0-7643-4892-1
Printed in China

Published by Schiffer Publishing, Ltd.
4880 Lower Valley Road
Atglen, PA 19310
Phone: (610) 593-1777; Fax: (610) 593-2002
E-mail: Info@schifferbooks.com

For our complete selection of fine books on this and related subjects,
please visit our website at www.schifferbooks.com.
You may also write for a free catalog.

This book may be purchased from the publisher.
Please try your bookstore first.

We are always looking for people to write books on new
and related subjects. If you have an idea for a book, please
contact us at proposals@schifferbooks.com.

Schiffer Publishing's titles are available at special discounts for
bulk purchases for sales promotions or premiums. Special editions,
including personalized covers, corporate imprints, and excerpts can
be created in large quantities for special needs. For more information,
contact the publisher.

CONTENTS

(Author's collection)

ACKNOWLEDGEMENTS

This is my third book on the subject of the Knight's Cross and it's dedicated to John Preece and his wife Barbi. John has not only helped with proof reading the book but has given me helpful advice and encouragement from the beginning. It's so important to have support from both friends and family and I would like to take this opportunity to thank them.

I would like to thank my parents and my sister for their encouragement and also various friends which include, Julie Cheetam, Jared Copeland-Gregory, Ann Driscoll, Dan Fraser, Lorraine Horsnell, Candy and Nick Isles, Tracy Jackson, Sue Keen, Linda and Steve Kingsford, Sophie McLoughlin, Nathan Pearce, Jo Robinson, David Ross, Lee Smith, Anne Taylor and Ben Tipp. I also need to thank the owners of the Wehrkundearchiv who gave me permission to use photographs from their collection, and two other contributors of photographs who would like to remain nameless.

I would also like to thank the publishers, Schiffer for accepting my manuscript and for producing another excellent publication.

Jeremy Dixon
Dartford, July 2014

An early wartime Luftwaffe recruitment poster, representing aggression with the swooping eagle that denotes triumph. The caption "Mit unsern Fahnen ist der Sieg!" means "Victory! Follows our banners." (Author's Collection)

INTRODUCTION

The German word for paratroopers is *Fallschirmjäger*. The word *Fallschirm* means "parachute" and *jäger* is literally "hunter," which refers in this context to light infantry. They played an important role during World War II and, together with the German Mountain troops (*Gebirgsjäger*), they were perceived as the elite infantry units of the German Armed Forces (*Wehrmacht*).

The German *Fallschirmjäger* troops in World War II were the first paratroopers to be committed in large-scale airborne operations. The Allies called them the "Green Devils."

The idea of airborne troops is far from new and dates back as far as the ancient Greeks. Even parachutes, as toys have existed for hundreds of years, but it was not until the late-19th century that the idea of a "para-chute," without a rigid framework evolved. The first types of parachutes were used during the First World War as a life-saving device, at first used for observation balloon crews. Early types were of the static line variety, in which a rope attached to the aircraft pulls the parachute out of its container. The ripcord, which proved a major benefit for pilots and crew, was not invented until 1919.

The first serious parachute experiments were conducted by the Russians and Italians. The Germans were interested but didn't have an air force, and were forbade one under the terms of the Treaty of Versailles. However, when Adolf Hitler came to power in January 1933 things began to change. Hitler denounced the Versailles Treaty and reintroduced conscription and rebuilt Germany's air force with the help of a former First World War fighter ace, Hermann Göring.

Göring was so impressed by the demonstration in Russia he became personally committed to the creation of Germany's first parachute unit. As the Bavarian Prime Minister, he ordered the formation of a specialist police unit in 1933, the *Polizeiabteilung z.b.V. Wecke,* was devoted to protecting Nazi Party officials. The organization of these units was entrusted to *Polizeimajor* Walther Wecke of the Prussian Police Force. In July 1933, the unit was *renamed Landespolizei Wecke z.b.V.* (State Police Wecke – z.b.V. meaning "for special duties"). On 22nd December 1933, the unit became the *Landespolizei General Göring*. It carried out normal police duties for the next two years under the command of Göring's adjutant *Polizeimajor* Friedrich Jakoby,

On 16th May 1940, Hitler decorated ten officers of the Sturmabteilung Koch with the Knight's Cross for their part in the assault on Eben Emael and the bridges over the Albert Canal on 10th May 1945. The photograph was taken at Führer Headquarters "Felsennest," approximately thirty miles southwest of Bonn. Left to right: Hauptmann Walter Koch, Oberleutnant Rudolf Witzig, Oberleutnant Gustav Altmann. Other officers present are Oberleutnant Otto Zierach, Oberarzt Dr. Rolf Jäger, Leutnant Egon Delicia, Leutnant Helmut Ringler, Leutnant Joachim Meissner, and Leutnant Gerhard Schacht. Not present was Leutnant Martin Schächter, who remained in hospital after being wounded during the fierce fighting at Kanne. (Author's Collection)

but it was Göring's intention to ultimately produce a unit that would match the *Reichswehr*.

In March-April 1935, Göring transferred the *Landespolizei General Goring* into Germany's first dedicated airborne regiment, giving it the military designation Regiment *General Göring* on 1st April 1935. The unit was incorporated into the newly formed Luftwaffe in October of the same year. Göring ordered that a group of volunteers be drawn for parachute training. These volunteers would form the first parachute battalion; they would be the future parachute troops or *Fallschirmjäger*. In January 1936, 600 men and officers formed the 1st Battalion of Regiment *General Göring*, commanded by *Major* Bruno Bräuer. Germany's parachute arm was officially born on 29th January 1936 with an

Order of the Day calling for recruits for parachute training at the Stendal Parachute Training School, west of Berlin. NCOs, officers and other ranks of the Luftwaffe were required to successfully complete six jumps in order to receive the Luftwaffe Parachutist's Badge.

In 1938, Göring's new battalion was transferred to the 7th Air Division. By September 1939, with Germany at war, the Luftwaffe now had full parachute rifle battalions with support troops – these were the first German airborne divisions. The army had put together a full infantry division specially trained in air-landing techniques. The paratroopers however were trained to jump by parachute or land by glider and seize important objectives such as airfields or bridges ahead of advancing forces and holding them until relieved.

Paratroopers had surprise and speed and could land behind enemy lines and attack from the rear. They were soon given the status of elite fighting troops and with their combination of surprise and speed; the paratroopers were the best and quickest way and least costly means of winning a battle. The air-landing troops would be flown by transport aircraft along with their heavy equipment and would then land on ground already seized by the paratroopers.

During World War II, the Luftwaffe formed a variety of airborne light infantry units. The *Fallschirmjäger* units made the first airborne invasion when invading Denmark on the 9th April 1940. In the early morning they attacked and took control of Aalborg Airport, which played a key role as a refuelling station for the Luftwaffe in the subsequent invasion of Norway. The *Fallschirmjäger* participated in many of the famous battles of the war and as well as seeing action in Denmark and Norway they also took part in the invasion of France, Belgium and the Netherlands in 1940. One of the most notable actions that the *Fallschirmjäger* troops took part in was the aerial assault on the Belgian fort of Eben-Emael.

The Battle of Fort Eben-Emael took place between 10th May and 11th May 1940, and was part of the German invasion of the Low Countries which included France and Belgium. An assault force of *Fallschirmjäger* troops, under the command of *Hauptmann* Walter Koch, was tasked with assaulting and capturing Fort Eben-Emael, a Belgian fortress whose artillery dominated several important bridges over the Albert Canal that German forces intended to use to advance into Belgium. While some of the German assault force attacked the fortress itself and disabled the garrison, others simultaneously captured three key bridges over the Canal.

The battle was a decisive victory for the German forces, with the airborne troops landing on top of the fortress in gliders and using explosives and flamethrowers they captured the fortress. The Belgian garrison surrendered at 12:30 on 11th May and had suffered a total of sixty men killed and forty wounded. The Germans lost only six soldiers and nineteen wounded, and they had captured more than a thousand Belgian soldiers.

The airborne assault on the three bridges and Fort Eben-Emael had been a great success for the *Fallschirmjäger*. The capture of the bridges and the destruction of the artillery in the fort allowed infantry and armour from the 18th Army to bypass other Belgian defences and enter Belgium. As a result of their success, seven *Fallschirmjäger* soldiers were decorated with the Knight's Cross, including the commander of the assault force *Hauptmann* Koch.

In May 1941, a very different battle took place in which the troops of the *Fallschirmjäger* played a major role. The invasion of Crete stands as a landmark in the history of airborne warfare. Until that time all airborne operations had been used in a tactical and operational context to seize key objectives, such as during the Balkan campaign and in the seizure of the Belgium Fort Eben-Emael. The German invasion of Crete remains the only operation in history in which a major strategic objective was assaulted and secured by airborne troops. The planning of the invasion was conceived by *Generalmajor* Kurt Student, the commander and champion of the *Fallschirmjäger* troops.

At dawn on 20th May, Germany invaded Crete. It was the most spectacular air assault of the war as 22,750 troops of the *Fallschirmjäger* and glider units landed along the northwestern coast of the island. It was the first time in history an entire invasion force was moved by air. The British had 28,000 troops to defend the island as well as 14,500 Greek troops. The Germans suffered heavy casualties during the first day of fighting. Part of the pressure was relieved after the second wave landed much later in the day to the east around Heraklion and Retimo.

Within ten days, the Germans had won the island, but they had suffered heavy losses, almost 6,500 troops, of which 3,352 were killed or missing in action. Almost a third of the Junkers Ju 52 aircraft used in the operation were damaged or destroyed. The British and commonwealth forces suffered almost 2,500 casualties, about 1,700 were killed and almost 12,000 were taken prisoner. The Royal Navy lost three cruisers and six destroyers sunk, as well as an aircraft carrier, two battleships, six cruisers and seven destroyers were badly damaged, with the loss of over 2,000 men. The RAF lost forty-seven aircraft and hundreds of Greek soldiers and Cretan civilians died during the fighting.

The German airborne troops were well equipped but their operational planning was flawed due to poor intelligence. The lack of surprise had been lost and resulted in the high casualty rate. Had the Germans not had adequate air cover from von Richthofen's 8th Air Corps then the battle would have been lost. As a result of the huge losses suffered by the *Fallschirmjäger* in Crete, it was forbidden to mount any large-scale operations in the future. Hitler told Student on 19th July 1941 that, "the day of the paratrooper was over." The men of the *Fallschirmjäger* had fought bravely nonetheless and a total of twenty-four Knight's Cross were awarded as a result of individual acts of bravery. There would be small-scale operations for the paratroopers during the rest of the war but they would mainly serve as elite infantry force. Crete was dubbed the "*Graveyard of the Fallschirmjäger.*"

Later Germany's paratroopers took part in the Balkans Campaign, and in the bloody fighting at Monte Cassino. The Battle of Monet Cassino, sometimes known also as the Battle for Rome was a costly series of four assaults by the Allies against an Axis held line. The intention was a breakthrough to Rome. At the beginning of 1944, the western half of the Winter Line was held by German forces, they held the areas of Rapido, Liri and Garigliano valleys and some of the surrounding peaks and ridges. Together, these features formed the Gustav Line. Overlooking Monte Cassino was an abbey, which had been founded in the year 529. It was left unoccupied by the German defenders, but they had manned some positions set into the steep slopes below the abbey's walls.

The Allies feared that the abbey formed part of the Germans' defensive line, mainly as a lookout post and decided to bomb it. The Americans dropped 1,400 tons of bombs on the abbey, it was left in ruins. The rubble left by the bombing now provided excellent defences and had to be assaulted a total of four times by Allied troops.

Finally on 18th May 1944, the Battle of Monte Cassino was over, the Allies had driven the Germans from their positions, but at a high cost. The Allies suffered approximately 55,000 casualties and the Germans suffered 20,000 killed or wounded. The *Fallschirmjäger* troops had fought well and there were many stories of bravery during the fighting and twenty-four new Knight's Cross holders of the *Fallschirmjäger* were created during the fighting.

AWARDS

KNIGHT'S CROSS WITH OAKLEAVES, SWORDS AND DIAMONDS

The Knight's Cross with Oakleaves, Swords and Diamonds was instituted by Hitler on 15th July 1941. The Diamonds could only be awarded to previous winners of the Swords. Every recipient of the Diamonds was presented with his award personally by Adolf Hitler and only one was awarded to a member of the *Fallschirmjäger*. With the Diamonds came a lavish document, printed on high grade parchment in gold. The Diamonds were hand crafted by a jeweller using real diamonds set in the Oakleaves and on the handles of the Swords. However, some pieces feature diamonds on the Oakleaves only, while others have the Swords hilts set with stones too.

Recipients would receive two sets, one with genuine diamonds, the other for everyday use with imitation stones. The contemporary copies obtained as extra sets by the recipients were usually solid silver types as per the ordinary Swords and Oakleaves, as opposed to the hollow award pieces.

KNIGHT'S CROSS WITH
OAKLEAVES AND SWORDS

Instituted by Hitler on 28th September 1941, the Knight's Cross with Oakleaves and Swords could only be awarded to previous winners of the Knight's Cross with Oakleaves. The Swords were presented to each recipient in a small case. The Swords was attached below the Oakleaves crossed at a forty degree angle, with the right Sword overlapping the left. The reverse side mounted band clip was slightly larger than the one attached to the Oakleaves and the clip. Each Sword measured 24mm in length; the entire Oakleaves with Swords clasp was 24.83mm wide, 27.58mm high and weighed nine grams.

There were six members of the *Fallschirmjäger* who were recipients of the Swords, not including the one recipient of the Swords and Diamonds.

KNIGHT'S CROSS WITH OAKLEAVES

Instituted by Hitler on 3rd June 1940, the Knight's Cross with Oakleaves was worn above the original Knight's Cross and held in place by means of a silver loop that would also secure the neck ribbon. It could only be awarded to previous winners of the Knight's Cross. The decoration consisted of a cluster of three oak leaves with the center left superimposed on the two lower leaves. The original clasp had the digits .800 or .900 added, like the Knight's Cross to show it was made from .800 grade silver and it measured 2cm in diameter. The official manufacturer of the Oakleaves was exclusively the firm *Gebrüder Godet und Co.*, in Berlin.

Hitler would frequently make the presentations of the Oakleaves to the recipients himself in order to congratulate them personally. There were thirteen recipients from the *Fallschirmjäger* of the Knight's Cross with Oakleaves not including the recipients who also won the Swords and the Diamonds.

THE KNIGHT'S CROSS

The Knight's Cross of the Iron Cross was instituted by Hitler in September 1939, and is probably one of the most recognizable decorations of World War II. The first Knight's Cross was presented on 30th September 1939. It was a unique award since it had not been in existence prior to that time. Hitler had ordered that the Knight's Cross was to be awarded to all ranks, and in fact 1,676 NCOs and enlisted men won the award.

The Knight's Cross was basically the same design as the Iron Cross except it was larger. It measured 48mm x 48mm with a silver ring on top which measured 6mm. At the top of the cross there was an elongated ribbon top which went through the silver ring and this is where the ribbon went that was used to hold it in position around the recipient's neck. The decoration was presented in an elongated black leather-like case, which contained the decoration and a folded length of neck ribbon. Most were presented to each recipient by their divisional commander, corps commander etc. With the Knight's Cross came an impressive-looking citation presented in a red leather binder and stamped with an embossed German Eagle in gold on the front cover and signed by Hitler.

The most common Knight's Crosses were produced by the manufacturer Steinhauer and Lück, and their crosses were stamped with the digits "800," indicating .800 grade silver, on the reverse side. These digits can also be found on the band clip.

A total of 130 members of the Fallschirmjäger were awarded the Knight's Cross; a total of 110 received only the Knight's Cross and not the higher grades. Twenty-one recipients were NCOs – about 16%.

GERMAN CROSS IN GOLD

Introduced by Hitler on 28th September 1941, to bridge the gap that existed between the Iron Cross 1st Class and the Knight's Cross. The German Cross in Gold was a completely independent award, many who received the German Cross never got the Knight's Cross while there were Knight's Cross winners who never received the German Cross.

There was a cloth version made and it was introduced because the metal version was heavy and bulky and would stick out in confined spaces of an aircraft or tank. The cloth version would be sewn on in exactly the same place on the tunic as the original and was officially introduced on 5th June 1942.

The German Cross was worn in the center of the pocket on the right hand side of the uniform tunic. It took precedence over all other decorations on the tunic except the Blood Order. There were approximately 24,190 awarded during World War II and they are highly prized by collectors today.

THE IRON CROSS

The Iron Cross was originally instituted in 1813 and was reinstituted in 1870 without change. When Germany entered World War I, the Kaiser reinstituted the award again on 5th August 1914. In World War II, Hitler reinstituted the Iron Cross once again on 1st September 1939. Its basic design remained unchanged and it was awarded to all ranks. The only changes were instead of Oakleaves, the swastika now appeared on the front and the date was changed from 1914 to 1939. The Iron Cross 2nd Class was given with a ribbon attached and during World War II the colour changed from black and white to the same as the Knight's Cross: black, white and red stripe. The exact number awarded during World War II is unclear, but approximately 3,000,000 2nd Class awards were presented and around 450,000 Iron Cross 1st Class were awarded.

BAR TO THE IRON
CROSS 2ND CLASS

The Bar to the Iron Cross was awarded to those who had received the 1914 Iron Cross 2nd Class, for actions during World War I. The award was fixed to a black ribbon with two white stripes. Its design was that of the national eagle with outstretched wings mounted on a bar bearing the date 1939. It measured 29mm to 31.4mm across and 30.5mm to 31.5mm in height. It was worn in the second buttonhole of the tunic.

BAR TO THE IRON
CROSS 1ST CLASS

The Bar to the Iron Cross 1st Class was awarded to those who had received the 1914 Iron Cross 1st Class. It was given a pin-back clasp identical in design to the 2nd Class Bar, but was slightly larger. It measured 43.8mm to 45mm across the wingspan, and 30mm to 31mm in height. It was worn on the left breast pocket immediately above the 1914 Iron Cross 1st Class.

LUFTWAFFE PARACHUTIST BADGE

Instituted on 1st January 1935 by Hermann Goring. It was awarded after having completed the instruction course for paratroopers or having made five qualifying jumps.

LUFTWAFFE GROUND ASSAULT BADGE

Instituted on 31st March 1942. It was awarded for participation in three assaults, or having been wounded or having earned an award during the assault.

EASTERN FRONT MEDAL OR MEDAL
FOR THE WINTER CAMPAIGN IN RUSSIA

Instituted on 26th May 1942. This campaign medal was awarded to those who participated in fourteen days of combat or performed thirty combat sorties or served sixty days in the combat zone or were wounded in the line of duty between 15th November 1941 and 26th April 1942.

AFRIKA CUFF TITLE

Instituted on 15th January 1942. This was an award made from cloth and worn around the cuff of the recipient's tunic. It was awarded for at least one of the following: six months service in North Africa; invalided out as a result of a tropical disease; served at least three months in North Africa and had been wounded while serving there.

(Private source)

KRETA CUFF TITLE

Instituted on 16th October 1942. It was awarded for one of the following: Taking part in a parachute or glider landing on Crete between 20th-27th May 1941; taken part in air operation over Crete or seen active service in the sea around Crete.

NARVIK CAMPAIGN SHIELD

Instituted on 19th August 1940. It was awarded for the participation in the Battle of Narvik on 9th April 1940.

COMMEMORATIVE MEDAL
OF 13TH MARCH 1938

Instituted on 1st May 1938. It was awarded to those who participated in the march into Austria (*Anschluss*).

COMMEMORATIVE MEDAL
OF 1ST OCTOBER 1938

Instituted on 18th October 1938. It was awarded to those who participated in the annexation of the Sudetenland or Bohemia and Moravia.

GERMAN DEFENCES MEDAL
(WEST WALL MEDAL)

Instituted on 2nd August 1939. This was awarded to those who took part in the building of the fortifications along Germany's border or being stationed on the border before May 1940. It was reissued on 10th October 1944 when the defences along Germany's border were being strengthened.

WOUND BADGES

Instituted on 1st September 1939.

Wound Badge in Black – awarded for being wounded once or twice or being injured during an air raid or by frostbite in the line of duty.

Wound Badge in Silver – awarded for being wounded three or four times in fighting or in an air raid or serious injury in the line of duty.

Wound Badge in Gold – awarded for being wounded five times or more during combat or during an air raid or being wounded extremely serious (loss of a limb, loss of eye-sight) in the line of duty.

ARMED FORCES (WEHRMACHT) LONG SERVICE AWARD

Instituted on 16th March 1936 in four grades:
Silver Medal – having been a member in the Armed Forces for 4 years
Gold Medal – having been a member in the Armed Forces for 12 years
Silver Cross – having been a member in the Armed Forces for 18 years
Gold Cross – having been a member in the Armed Forces for 25 years

RECIPIENTS

HERBERT KARL ABRATIS

(21.03.1918 – 15.03.1945) *Major*

Knight's Cross: Awarded on 24th October 1944, as *Hauptmann* and *Führer* of the 2nd Battalion of the 1st *Fallschirmjäger Regiment* for actions in Italy. In February 1944 he took part in the defensive battles of Cavalry Mountain where he and his battalion helped prevent the Allies from breaking through to the Via Casilina. On the night of the 16th March 1944, he led his company to Cassino where they repulsed an attack by New Zealand forces, preventing the city from falling

His promising career was cut short when he died as a result of being shot in the neck. Some sources give the date as the night of 28th/29th March 1945, but Scherzer gives the date as 15th March 1945. His remains have never been recovered (Author's Collection)

(Author's Collection)

Herbert Abratis was born on 21st March 1918, in Babienten, Sensburg and volunteered to join the Luftwaffe in March 1936. He was assigned to the 11th Anti aircraft Regiment in Königsberg and served as a battery officer from September 1938. He was commissioned as a *Leutnant der Reserve* on 1st March 1939, and in February 1940 he was attached to the Döberitz Infantry School. He transferred to the staff of the 7th Air Division in April 1940, joining the 1st Company of the 1st *Fallschirmjäger Regiment*. He saw action during the Norwegian campaign and then later in Crete as a Platoon Leader. He was promoted to *Oberleutnant* in December 1941, and was awarded the Iron Cross 1st Class in Russia. In December he took command of the 7th Company of the 1st *Fallschirmjäger Regiment* and in September 1943 he was promoted to *Hauptmann* and took part in the fighting near Ortona, Italy.

Promoted to *Major* on 1st January 1945, he took command of the 53rd Parachute Anti-tank Battalion in February 1945, before assuming command of the 27th *Fallschirmjäger* Regiment eleven days later. On 28th March 1945 his unit was engaged in defensive fighting in the breach in the Oder Front south of Stettin-Rosengarten.

OTHER AWARDS		PROMOTIONS	
31.10.1940	Armed Forces Long Service Award 4th Class	30.09.1937	Reserve-Offiziersanwärter
00.00.1940	Parachutist Badge	01.10.1937	Gefreiter
19.06.1941	Iron Cross 2nd Class	01.04.1938	Unteroffizier
27.08.1942	Iron Cross 1st Class	01.10.1938	Wachtmeister
00.00.1942	Luftwaffe Ground Assault Badge	01.03.1939	Leutnant der Reserve
00.09.1942	Eastern Front Medal	27.08.1939	Leutnant (active)
00.00.1942	Wound Badge in Silver	01.12.1941	Oberleutnant
15.03.1943	German Cross in Gold	01.09.1943	Hauptmann
00.05.1943	KRETA Cuff title	01.01.1934	Major

HEINZ PAUL ADOLFF

(29.06.1914 – 17.07.1943)   *Major der Reserve*

(Wehrkundearchiv)

Knight's Cross: Awarded posthumously on 26th March 1944, as *Hauptmann der Reserve* and while *Führer* of the 1st Parachute Engineer Battalion in Sicily.

Paul Adolff was born in Backnang, Baden-Württemberg, northeast of Stuttgart and he began his military service in October 1935, joining the 17th Motorized Pioneer Battalion. He was commissioned as a *Leutnant der Reserve* in May 1939 and after completing the parachute-rifleman course in Wittstock in July 1940, he became a member of the German parachute troops. He served during the French campaign as Platoon Leader with the 7th Parachute Pioneer Battalion, winning both classes of the Iron Cross. He later took part in the Balkan campaign, the airborne invasion of Crete and in the bitter fighting in Russia. He was promoted to *Oberleutnant der Reserve* on 2nd July 1941, and fought with great bravery in Russia, winning the German Cross in Gold. On 25th January 1943, Adolff was promoted to *Hauptmann der Reserve* before taking his unit into action in the southern sector of the Eastern Front.

Adolff parachuted into Sicily in July 1943, where he was commander of two companies and was able to prevent the Allies from taking the bridge near Simeto. However the British forces fought back and the German defenders on the bridge had to abandon their posts. When his last 88mm Flak gun was put out of action Adolff knew he had to blow up the bridge. He drove a truck loaded with two bombs onto the bridge in order to detonate them – two attempts were made which failed. On 17th July, Adolff tried a third time to detonate the bombs, and as they exploded he was severely wounded and died later the same day.

OTHER AWARDS		PROMOTIONS	
28.10.1939	Armed Forces Long Service Award 4th Class	01.05.1939	Leutnant der Reserve
00.00.1940	Parachutist Badge	02.07.1941	Oberleutnant der Reserve
02.06.1940	Iron Cross 2nd Class	25.01.1943	Hauptmann der Reserve
27.06.1940	Iron Cross 1st Class	00.00.1944	Major der Reserve
00.00.1942	KRETA Cuff title	-----	-----
19.03.1942	German Cross in Gold	-----	-----
00.09.1942	Eastern Front Medal	-----	-----

GUSTAV ALTMANN

(13.04.1912 – 20.02.1981)   *Major*

Knight's Cross: Awarded on 12th May 1940, as *Oberleutnant* and *Führer* of Assault Group "Stahl," for actions in France. He was part of the Air Landing Assault Battalion *Koch* during the opening phase of the Battle of France and the attack on Fort Eben-Emael, in May 1940.

Gustav Altmann was born on 13th April 1912, in Britz, Eberswalde, and entered the Police Training School at Kiel

(Wehrkundearchiv)

Altmann was captured by British forces on 22nd May 1941 during the invasion of Crete, and didn't return home until after the war. It was whilst he was a prisoner-of-war that he learned of his promotion to Major. He died on 20th February 1981, in Reinhardshagen, Weckerhagen. (Wehrkundearchiv)

in April 1931. He then joined the Wecke State Police Group in 1933, and went on to become a member of the *General Göring Regiment* on 1st October 1935. In September 1937, he attended the Officer's Training School in Berlin and was commissioned as a *Leutnant* on 17th December 1937. He took command of the 11th Company of the *General Göring Regiment* and in September 1938 he took command of a company in the 1st *Fallschirmjäger Regiment,* Stendal. On 1st April 1939, he was promoted to *Oberleutnant* and was seconded to the "Friedrichshafen Trials Battalion," which was the cover name for the Koch Assault Battalion.

During the invasion of France, Altmann's Assault Group was tasked with the taking the Belgian Bridge at Veldwezelt and holding it until reinforcements arrived. Altmann led a group of ninety-one men who were crammed into nine gliders in the assault. It succeeded at the cost of eight dead and over thirty wounded. Gustav Altmann and eleven other German officers received the Knight's Cross for this feat,

His actions in Crete were acknowledged in a Wehrmacht Communiqué of 9th June 1941:

"During the battle for Crete, the paratrooper units under the leadership of Major (Walter) Koch, Hauptmann (Gustav) Altmann and Oberleutnant (Alfred) Genz have distinguished themselves exceptionally by boldness and heroic courage. In harsh fighting, the paratrooper units under the leadership of Generalmajor (Eugen) Meindl, Oberst (Richard) Heidrich, Oberst (Bruno) Bräuer, Oberst (Hermann-Bernhard) Ramcke and Oberst (Alfred) Sturm have established the decisive conditions for the conquest of Crete."

OTHER AWARDS		PROMOTIONS	
01.10.1935	Police Long Service Award 4th Class	01.04.1932	Polizei-Wachtmeister
00.00.193_	Parachutist Badge	01.10.1934	Trupp-Wachtmeister
02.10.1939	Armed Forces Long Service Award 4th Class	01.05.1935	Oberwachtmeister der Landespolizei
12.05.1940	Iron Cross 2nd Class	01.10.1935	Oberjäger
13.05.1940	Iron Cross 1st Class	01.12.1936	Feldwebel
-----	-----	17.12.1937	Leutnant
-----	-----	01.04.1939	Oberleutnant
-----	-----	16.05.1940	Hauptmann
-----	-----	24.08.1942	Majo

HELMUT ARPKE

(20.03.1917 – 16.01.1942)   *Oberleutnant der Reserve*

Knight's Cross: Awarded as a *Feldwebel* on 13th May 1940 while attached to the Assault Group *Stahl* part of the Air Landing Assault Battalion *Koch,* during the opening phase of the Battle of France under the command of *Oberleutnant* Gustav Altmann. In May 1940 Arpke had led his company in action near Veldwezelt and his squad had been responsible for cutting the fuses leading to the explosive charges on the bridge while under heavy fire. Arpke and his squad put out of action a heavy machine-gun bunker and captured all the barricades on and in front of the bridge.

A propaganda postcard of Helmut Arpke by the acclaimed German war artist Wolfgang Willich. (Author's Collection)

(Author's Collection)

Helmut Arpke was born on 20th March 1917, in Graudenz and joined the Luftwaffe in October 1935 and attending various NCO courses he joined the 1st Battalion of the 1st *Fallschirmjäger Regiment* in September 1939. He took part in the invasion of Poland and after his promotion to *Feldwebel* in May 1940, serving as a platoon leader and winning the Iron Cross 1st and 2nd Classes for actions near Veldwezelt. In 1941 he saw action in Crete and during the autumn he was transferred to the Russian Front with the 1st *Fallschirmjäger Regiment.*

During the bitter fighting at the Neva he was killed while leading the 3rd Company of the 1st Assault Regiment near Schaikowka, on 16th January 1942. He was posthumously promoted to the rank of *Oberleutnant der Reserve*

OTHER AWARDS		PROMOTIONS	
00.00.193_	Parachutist Badge	01.10.1936	Gefreiter
01.10.1939	Armed Forces Long Service Award 4th Class	01.10.1937	Unteroffizier
12.05.1940	Iron Cross 2nd Class	01.05.1940	Feldwebel
12.05.1940	Iron Cross 1st Class	01.11.1940	Reserve-Offiziersanwärter
-----	-----	15.02.1941	Oberfeldwebel
-----	-----	17.06.1941	Leutnant der Reserve
-----	-----	01.04.1942	Oberleutnant der Reserve

JOSEF BARMETLER

(11.03.1904 – 20.02.1945)   *Major der Reserve*

(Wehrkundearchiv)

Knight's Cross: Awarded on 9th July 1941 as *Oberleutnant* and Commander 7th Company, 1st *Fallschirmjäger* Assault Regiment in recognition of his bravery and skill during heavy fighting in Crete.

Josef Barmetler was born in Kempten, Bavaria on 11th March 1904. He entered the Reichswehr in April 1924 and served for ten years in the infantry. In August 1939, he was assigned as a *Leutnant der Reserve* with the 316th Infantry Regiment and saw action in Poland. In December, he served as acting commander of the 2nd Company of the 316th Infantry Regiment where he remained until June 1940. After he completed airborne training and was transferred to the Luftwaffe and took over as commander of the 7th Company of the 1st Parachute Air Landing Regiment. He took part in the airborne invasion of Crete in May 1941, leading his company during the battle for Hill 107 and in the destruction of the enemy's anti-aircraft guns on the hill as well as supplying support for the infantry. On 25th May, he was seriously wounded during fierce fighting on the hill held by New Zealand troops. He was recommended for the Knight's Cross by his battalion commander and as a result of his wounds he was evacuated to hospital. In October, his unit transferred to the Russian Front where he was acting commander of the 2nd Battalion of the 1st Parachute Air Landing Regiment. He was wounded on 29th November 1941 and had to be evacuated to hospital. This was his second very serious wound of the war. In December 1943, finally recovered from his wounds he returned to active duty, joining the staff of the 2nd Battalion of the 6th *Fallschirmjäger Regiment.* He served in Russia and had to return home in early-1945 due to his wounds. He died at home, in Kempten, of his wounds on 20th February 1945.

OTHER AWARDS		PROMOTIONS	
02.04.1936	Armed Forces Long Service Award 4th to 3rd Class	01.06.1926	Oberschütze
00.00.1940	Parachutist Badge	31.09.1927	Unteroffiziersanwärter
00.00.1940	West Wall Medal	01.11.1927	Gefreiter
22.06.1940	Iron Cross 2nd Class	01.10.1929	Oberjäger
18.06.1941	Iron Cross 1st Class	01.10.1931	Unterfeldwebel
00.12.1941	Wound Badge in Silver	01.10.1933	Feldwebel
-----	-----	01.05.1937	Leutnant der Reserve
-----	-----	01.01.1940	Oberleutnant der Reserve
-----	-----	25.07.1941	Hauptmann der Reserve
-----	-----	01.06.1944	Major der Reserve

KARL-HEINZ BECKER

(02.01.1914 – 03.10.2002)   *Oberst*

(Wehrkundearchiv)

Knight's Cross: Awarded on 9th July 1941 as *Oberleutnant* and Commander 11th Company, 1st *Fallschirmjäger Regiment* for actions during the invasion of Crete.

Knight's Cross with Oakleaves: Awarded on 12th March 1945, to become the 780th recipient, as *Oberstleutnant* and Commander 5th *Fallschirmjäger Regiment* for actions on the Western Front..

Karl-Heinz Becker was born on 2nd January 1914, in Schwedt, Angermünde and entered the *Landespolizei "General Göring"* in October 1934. After attending many training courses he was soon commissioned as a *Leutnant*. He served as a platoon leader with various companies and in May 1937 was made deputy commander of the 5th Company of Regiment "Hermann Göring." In October 1938, he was transferred to the General Göring glider battalion and this became the 1st *Fallschirmjäger* Regiment. In August 1940, he assumed command of the 11th Company and took part in the operation against Rotterdam's airport where he distinguished himself – winning the Iron Cross 1st Class. He participated in the Crete campaign, where his company attacked British positions in Heraklion at 23:05 on 20th May 1941, and defeated the garrison there, leading to the capture of the city and the surrender of the Greek commander on 29th May.

In the autumn and winter of 1941, he saw action during the bloody fighting at the Neva. In July 1942, he was made regimental adjutant of the 1st *Fallschirmjäger* Regiment and continued to see action. Wounded on the Eastern Front in January 1943, Becker was promoted to *Hauptmann* in May and later assumed command of the 5th *Fallschirmjäger* Regiment. Becker and his adjutant were named in the Wehrmacht communiqué on 29th July 1944 during the fighting for St. Lô. In January 1945, Becker led his regiment at Faymonville, Belgium against the 1st U.S. Infantry Division, a far superior force. His troops however managed to hold back the American tanks, preventing the complete capture of the German forces his unit saw action during the Ardennes offensive and he subsequently led the unit back through the West Wall in the final weeks of the war, and was captured by the Allies during the last week of April 1945.

OTHER AWARDS		PROMOTIONS	
00.00.193_	Parachutist Badge	01.04.1935	Fahnenjunker-Wachtmeister
10.10.1939	Armed Forces Long Service Award 4th Class	01.06.1935	Fahnenjunker-Oberwachtmeister
15.10.1939	Iron Cross 2nd Class	21.12.1935	Fähnrich
31.05.1940	Iron Cross 1st Class	01.04.1936	Oberfähnrich
07.02.1943	Wound Badge in Black	02.08.1936	Leutnant
29.06.1944	German Cross in Gold	01.06.1939	Oberleutnant
06.02.1945	Luftwaffe Close Combat Clasp in Silver	11.04.1942	Hauptmann
-----	-----	24.05.1943	Major
-----	-----	01.10.1944	Oberstleutnant
-----	-----	20.04.1945	Oberst

ERICH BEINE

(26.06.1914 – 06.02.2004) *Major*

Knight's Cross: Awarded as *Hauptmann* and *Führer* 3rd Battalion, 12th *Fallschirmjäger Assault Regiment* on 18th November 1944, for his success in pushing back the enemy during a tank attack in the Florence area of Italy. Beine saw further action in Italy until his capture by British troops on 3rd May 1945, and remained in Allied captivity until April 1946.

(Wehrkundearchiv)

(Wehrkundearchiv)

Erich Beine was born on 26th June 1914, in Dörentrup, Lippe and joined the Luftwaffe in April 1936. He joined, in May 1939, the 7th Company of the Luftgau Signals Regiment 1 in Kraussen and in July he had transferred to the parachute troops, He was commissioned as a *Leutnant* in April 1941 and joined the I Battalion of the 1st *Fallschirmjäger* Regiment and took part in the airborne invasion of Crete. He later transferred to Russia where he saw action in northern sector near Vyborgskaya and Zhaikovka, where he won the Iron Cross 1st Class. In February 1942, he assumed command of the 5th Company, 12th *Fallschirmjäger* Assault Regiment and saw action in Italy, where on 19th March 1944 he distinguished himself in battle and in July was praised by his corps commander, *General der Flieger* Alfred Schlemm for his leadership during a success counterattack. He saw heavy action and fought with guts until the last days of the war in Italy as commander of the I Battalion of 12th *Fallschirmjäger Regiment*. He was captured by British troops on 3rd May 1945 and became a prisoner of war, being released on 16th April 1946. Beine died on 6th February 2004 in Braunschweig.

OTHER AWARDS		PROMOTIONS	
28.11.1939	Commemorative Medal of 1st October 1938	01.04.1937	Gefreiter
24.03.1940	Wound Badge in Black	01.04.1938	Obergefreiter/Unteroffizier-Anwärter
15.04.1940	Armed Forces Long Service Award 4th Class	01.09.1938	Unteroffizier
28.06.1940	Iron Cross 2nd Class	01.10.1939	Feldwebel
03.10.1940	Parachutist Badge	01.10.1940	Oberfeldwebel
25.02.1942	Iron Cross 1st Class	01.11.1940	Offiziers-Anwärter
26.09.1944	Luftwaffe Ground Assault Badge	15.04.1941	Leutnant
24.11.1944	Wound Badge in Silver	22.12.1942	Oberleutnant
19.04.1945	Wound Badge in Gold	16.02.1944	Hauptmann
-----	-----	01.05.1945	Major

KARL BERGER
(31.10.1919 – 22.01.2001)   *Oberleutnant der Reserve*

(Wehrkundearchiv)

Knight's Cross: Awarded on 7th February 1945 as *Leutnant der Reserve* and Commander 10th Company, 15th *Fallschirmjäger Regiment* for his outstanding bravery during numerous combat operations in the West.

Karl Berger was born in Colmar, Elsaß on 31st October 1919 and he volunteered for the parachute troops in December 1940. He took part in parachute training but failed to see action during the invasion of Crete, much to his disappointment. It wasn't until April 1943 that he finally saw action, when he joined the III Battalion, 4th *Fallschirmjäger* Regiment as platoon leader. The first action of the war was in Russia where he won the Iron Cross 2nd Class and in early-1944 he transferred to Sicily where he again fought with great bravery and was awarded the Iron Cross 1st Class. He was a platoon leader and then a company commander and finally as adjutant of the III Battalion of the 15th *Fallschirmjäger* Regiment. From Italy he moved to Normandy. His battalion took part in the capture of Hill 122 near Foré de Moncastre. Later he once again distinguished himself during action on 11th July and was mentioned in the Wehrmacht Communiqué of 29th July 1944. He ended the war as part of the 17th SS-Panzer Grenadier Division *"Götz von Berlichingen,"* seeing action in the defensive fighting in the Harz Mountains. Berger died in Munich on 22nd January 2001, at the age of eighty-one.

OTHER AWARDS		PROMOTIONS	
07.05.1941	Parachutist Badge	01.10.1940	Gefreiter
04.02.1942	War Service Cross 2nd Class + Swords	25.03.1941	Unteroffizier-Anwärter
09.07.1943	Iron Cross 2nd Class	01.09.1941	Oberjäger
01.11.1943	Wound Badge in Black	01.05.1942	Kriegsoffizieranwärter
01.01.1944	Wound Badge in Silver	01.06.1942	Feldwebel
13.04.1944	Iron Cross 1st Class	01.03.1944	Leutnant der Reserve
04.08.1944	Luftwaffe Ground Assault Badge	01.03.1945	Oberleutnant der Reserve
16.08.1944	Tank Destruction Badge in Silver (2)	-----	-----
16.08.1944	German Cross in Gold	-----	-----
25.11.1944	Luftwaffe Close Combat Clasp in Bronze	-----	-----
03.04.1945	Luftwaffe Close Combat Clasp in Silver	-----	-----
03.04.1945	Wound Badge in Gold	-----	-----

HERBERT CHRISTOPH KARL BEYER

(04.08.1913 – 04.09.1966)   *Major*

(Author's Collection)

Knight's Cross: Awarded on 9th June 1944 as *Hauptmann* and Commander I Battalion, 4th *Fallschirmjäger* Regiment for his outstanding leadership in Monte Cassino.

Herbert Beyer was born on 4th August 1913, in Lübeck and joined the Navy in October 1931 and trained on the battleship Hessen until April 1934. After taking a submarine course he became a *Feldwebel* in November 1939 and an *Oberfeldwebel* in February 1940. He served with the 7th Luftwaffe Propaganda Company until October 1941, and was promoted to *Oberleutnant* in December 1940 before being transferred to the XI Air Corps. He trained as a paratrooper and after various postings he was appointed battalion commander in the 4th *Fallschirmjäger*

Regiment in February 1944. In March, he saw action at Monte Cassino where he was awarded the Knight's Cross. On 16th March 1944, troops of the 4th Indian Division attacked and captured Hill 193, and on the morning of 19th March, Beyer's battalion attacked Hill 193. The attack shattered the three battalions of the 5th Indian Brigade and Beyer prevented them from linking up with the Gurkas beyond Hill 435 and avoided the capture of Monte Cassino.

On 8th May 1945, he surrendered to Allied troops in Italy and was released later in the year. He was captured by Allied forces on 8th May 1945 and was released in August of that year. He died on 4th September 1966 in Bad Wiesee.

OTHER AWARDS		PROMOTIONS	
02.10.1936	Armed Forces Long Service Award 4th Class	01.10.1933	Obermatrose
00.00.1941	Parachutist Badge	01.10.1934	Unterwart
17.08.1943	Iron Cross 2nd Class	01.10.1935	Obergefreiter
21.01.1944	Iron Cross 1st Class	01.12.1937	Unteroffizier
-----	-----	01.11.1939	Feldwebel
-----	-----	01.02.1940	Oberfeldwebel
-----	-----	17.10.1940	Offiziers-Anwärter
-----	-----	11.12.1940	Oberleutnant der Reserve
-----	-----	01.12.1941	Oberleutnant (active)
-----	-----	14.07.1943	Hauptmann
-----	-----	01.06.1944	Major*

* *There is no official proof in the Federal Archives, only Beyer himself states that he was promoted to this rank – therefore remains unofficial.*

ERNST BLAUENSTEINER

(16.05.1911 – 18.08.1995)   *Oberst im Generalstab*

Knight's Cross: Awarded on 29th October 1944 as *Oberstleutnant.i.G* and Chief of the General Staff of the II *Fallschirmkorps* for actions in the Falaise Pocket. He was appointed one of the commanders' of the two groups responsible for the German breakout of the Falaise Pocket.

Blauensteiner with General Eugen Meindl. (Author's Collection)

General Meindl recognized the outstanding leadership and bravery of both Stephani and Blauensteiner, recommending them both immediately for the Knight's Cross. Major Stephani was awarded posthumously as he was killed during the breakout. Blauensteiner died on 18th August 1995, in Vienna, Austria. (Wehrkundearchiv)

Ernst Blauensteiner was born 16th May 1911, in Vienna-Hietzing, part of the Austro-Hungarian Empire and he joined the Austrian Army in September 1929. After basic training he joined the 6th Company of the 4th Infantry Regiment and in September 1930 he underwent officer training. In September 1933, he served as a Platoon Leader with the 3rd Infantry Regiment and in January 1934, he was commissioned as a *Leutnant* and served as a battalion commander with the 3rd Infantry Regiment. In 1935, he was assigned to the Reich Air Ministry.

In 1940, now with the rank of *Hauptmann* he took part in the Norwegian Campaign where he won the Iron Cross 1st and 2nd Classes. In June 1941, he was serving as Operations Officer of the Air Commander North and later with the 5th Air Fleet. In September 1942, he joined the staff of the II Parachute Corps and in February 1944, was appointed the corps' Chief of Staff with the rank of *Oberst*.

In August 1944, the Commander of the 7th Army, *SS-Oberst-Gruppenführer und Generaloberst der Waffen-SS* Paul Hausser ordered the breakout from the Falaise Pocket. He appointed *Generalleutnant* Eugen Meindl, Commanding General of the II Parachute Corps, in charge of the breakout. There were to be two main groups making a breakout, one was headed by *Major* Stephani and the other by *Oberstleutnant* Blauensteiner. Both groups succeeded in breaking out, something nobody thought possible – in fact over 90,000 troops escaped.

OTHER AWARDS		PROMOTIONS	
03.06.1935	Austrian Observers Badge	15.09.1930	Gefreiter
01.07.1937	Austrian Pilot's Badge	16.09.1931	Korporal
27.07.1937	Austrian Army Driving Instructors Badge	04.04.1933	Wachtmeister
28.09.1938	Luftwaffe Observers Badge	24.09.1933	Fähnrich
11.12.1939	Combined Pilots and Observers Badge	02.01.1934	Leutnant
12.04.1940	Iron Cross 2nd Class	30.12.1937	Oberleutnant
27.06.1940	Iron Cross 1st Class	01.04.1939	Hauptmann
23.08.1942	Finnish Freedom Cross 3rd Class	01.04.1942	Major
06.02.1944	Parachutist Badge	01.07.1942	Major im Generalstab
21.08.1944	Luftwaffe Ground Assault Badge	20.04.1943	Oberstleutnant im Generalstab
05.09.1944	German Cross in Gold	25.02.1945	Oberst im Generalstab

WOLFGANG HENNER PETER LEBRECHT GRAF VON BLÜCHER

(31.01.1917 – 21.05.1941)   *Oberleutnant der Reserve*

(Author's Collection)

Knight's Cross: Awarded on 24th May 1940 as *Leutnant der Reserve* and Platoon Leader, 2nd Company, 1st *Fallschirmjäger Regiment* for actions during the invasion of Holland. On 10th May, his platoon provided covering fire for the 3rd Company, which had jumped near Tweede Tool and then became involved in street fighting in Dordrecht. Blücher and his platoon took a strongly-manned nest of bunkers and for this he was awarded the Knight's Cross (and because he hadn't yet been awarded the Iron Cross 1st Class this was presented to him on the same day).

Wolfgang Henner Peter Lebrecht Graf von Blücher was born on 31st January 1917, in Altengottern, Mühlhausen and joined the 14th Cavalry Regiment as a volunteer in October 1934. After taking part in two military exercises he was promoted to *Leutnant* in April 1938. In February 1939, he was assigned to the 12th Anti-tank Battalion, and from there he volunteered for the Luftwaffe and requested to be assigned to the 132nd Fighter Wing. However the request was turned down and he remained with the 12th Anti-tank Battalion. In December 1939, he again applied to join the Luftwaffe and this time he was successful. He was assigned to the 3rd Company of the 1st *Fallschirmjäger Regiment* and in April 1941 he became a platoon leader with the 2nd Company.

After winning the Knight's Cross, he took part in the invasion of Crete, where on on 21st May 1941, along with his two brothers he was killed. The first to fall was Hans-Joachim, who was attempting to resupply his brother, Wolfgang, with ammunition when the latter and his platoon were surrounded by members of the British Black Watch. Hans-Joachim had grabbed a horse and had tried to gallop through the British lines but was shot in front of his brother. A little while later the same day the third brother nineteen-year-old Leberecht Graf von Blücher was reported killed but his body was never recovered. The three brothers were descendants of General von Blücher who had commanded the Prussians at Waterloo.

OTHER AWARDS		PROMOTIONS	
02.10.1939	Armed Forces Long Service Award 4th Class	12.10.1935	Gefreiter der Reserve
00.00.1939	Parachutist Badge	30.09.1936	Unteroffizier der Reserve
18.04.1940	Iron Cross 2nd Class	29.10.1936	Wachtmeister der Reserve
24.05.1940	Iron Cross 1st Class	20.04.1938	Leutnant der Reserve
-----	-----	31.07.1940	Oberleutnant der Reserve

RUDOLF BOEHLEIN

(04.01.1917 – 19.04.1945)   *Hauptmann*

(Author's Collection)

Knight's Cross: Awarded on 30th November 1944 as *Oberleutnant* and Company *Führer,* I Battalion, 4th *Fallschirmjäger Regiment* for his distinguished leadership during the Battle of Monte Cassino. His battalion had managed to close the gap in the German front between monastery hill and the city of Cassino. Boehlein led a series of attacks on the enemy and seriously damaged their supply lines and took a number of prisoners. He was recommended for the Knight's Cross by *Generalleutnant* Richard Heidrich and shortly after receiving the award he was promoted to *Hauptmann.*

Rudolf Boehlein was born on 4th January 1917 in Lubahn, Berent, West Prussia. He entered the Army in October 1936, after completing his training he was assigned to the 140th Mountain Infantry Regiment in November 1938. He saw action in Poland in 1939 where he won the Iron Cross 2nd Class. He later took part in the Western Campaign as an officer candidate with the 8th Company of the 140th Mountain Infantry Regiment. In August 1941 he transferred to the Luftwaffe and was appointed a Platoon Leader in the 9th Company of the 4th *Fallschirmjäger* Regiment. After seeing action in Russia he was deployed to Sicily in early 1943 where he took part in the defence at the Bottaceto Ditch.

In January 1944 he became acting commander of the 2nd Company and his unit moved to the fighting in Cassino. In November 1944, he was recommended for accelerated promotion to *Hauptmann,* his commander wrote: *"Oberleutnant Boehlein is above average in his general education and military knowledge … he is tough and possess a great amount of energy. He has excelled as a company leader."* On 1st January 1945, Boehlein was promoted to *Hauptmann.* He would later distinguish himself during the fighting at Monte Cassino where he was awarded the German Cross in Gold. He assumed command of the 2nd Battalion of the 4th *Fallschirmjäger Regiment* in March 1945. He was killed during the fierce fighting at La Futa-Paß, south of Bologna, Italy and is buried in the German Military Cemetery at Futa Pass (Block 45, Grave 130).

OTHER AWARDS		PROMOTIONS	
01.10.1939	Iron Cross 2nd Class	01.10.1937	Gefreiter (Heer)
01.10.1940	Armed Forces Long Service Award 4th Class	01.10.1938	Unteroffizier
00.12.1941	Parachutist Badge	16.08.1940	Feldwebel
04.01.1943	Iron Cross 1st Class	17.06.1941	Leutnant
24.02.1944	German Cross in Gold	00.08.1941	Leutnant (Luftwaffe)
00.07.1944	Wound Badge in Black	10.12.1943	Oberleutnant
-----	-----	01.01.1945	Hauptmann

RUDOLF BÖHMLER

(12.06.1914 – 24.11.1968)   *Oberst*

(Author's Collection)

Knight's Cross: Awarded as *Major* and Commander I Battalion, 5th *Fallschirmjäger Regiment* on 26th March 1944, for his leadership during the campaign in Monte Cassino. He led his battalion during the defence of the area around the monastery against attacks by the 4th Indian Division. The Indian division was pushed back and the monastery area remained in German hands.

Rudolf Böhmler was born on 12th June 1914 in Weilimdorf, Stuttgart in Baden-Württemberg. He joined the Reichswehr in April 1934, and initially served with the 13th Infantry Regiment and after he was commissioned as a *Leutnant* in 1936 and became Platoon Leader in the 55th Infantry Regiment. In 1938, he was assigned to the Paratrooper Infantry Company at Stendal and in August 1938 the unit became a battalion and in December he transferred along with his unit to the ranks of the Luftwaffe.

In January 1939, he transferred to the Luftwaffe, and shortly after being promoted to *Oberleutnant* he saw action during the Polish campaign where he won the Iron Cross 2nd Class. In October 1939, he became the acting commander of the 8th Company of the 1st *Fallschirmjäger* Regiment and in May 1940 he jumped into Moerdijk, Holland with his unit to seize a key railroad bridge over the Maas River leading to Rotterdam. His unit held the bridge for seven days until relieved by the advancing 9th Panzer Division and for this Böhmler was awarded the Iron Cross 1st Class.

Böhmler and his unit jumped into Crete at Heraklion on 20th May 1941 as part of the German airborne invasion. On 1st June, he became the acting commander of the 2nd Battalion of the 3rd *Fallschirmjäger Regiment*, a position he held until January 1942. From October to November 1941, his unit fought along the Neva River east of Leningrad. In February 1942, he assumed acting command of the 4th Battalion of the 3rd *Fallschirmjäger Regiment* and was made official commander in October 1942. From autumn 1942 to spring 1943, he saw action in the southern sector of the Eastern Front, before being transferred to Italy. During the third Cassino battle his battalion defended Cavalry Mountain, again very successfully, although Böhmler was wounded. Once recovered he again assumed command of his battalion and after winning the Knight's Cross he took part in several more combat actions at Cassino, including a defence on 12th May 1944 against the 5th Polish Division, during which he was once again wounded. In August he assumed acting command of the 4th *Fallschirmjäger Regiment*, which was made permanent in January 1945.

At the end of the war he commanded several ad hoc battle groups and he surrendered to Allied troops in early May 1945. He died in Stuttgart on 11th November 1968.

OTHER AWARDS		PROMOTIONS	
05.04.1939	Armed Forces Long Service Award 4th Class	01.04.1936	Leutnant
00.00.1939	Parachutist Badge	01.01.1939	Leutnant (Luftwaffe)
13.10.1939	Iron Cross 2nd Class	01.04.1939	Oberleutnant
23.05.1940	Iron Cross 1st Class	01.02.1942	Hauptmann
19.03.1942	German Cross in Gold	01.07.1943	Major
01.11.1942	Luftwaffe Ground Assault Badge	01.06.1944	Oberstleutnant
05.01.1943	Wound Badge in Black	30.01.1945	Oberst
20.05.1943	KRETA Cuff title	-----	-----

BRUNO OSWALD BRÄUER

(04.02.1893 – 20.05.1947) *General der Fallschirmtruppe*

Bruno Bräuer pictured on a Wolfgang Willich wartime propaganda postcard. (Author's Collection)

In May 1945, Bräuer was captured by British troops and held in a prison camp until early 1946, when he was handed over to Greek authorities who had demanded his extradition. Together with another former German commander of Greece, General Friedrich-Wilhelm Müller, Bräuer was charged with war crimes after the war for crimes committed in Greece. He stood trial in Athens and was accused of the deaths of 3,000 Cretans, massacres, deportation, pillage, wanton destruction, torture and ill treatment. He was convicted and sentenced to death on 9th December 1946. At 5:00am on 20th May 1947, he was executed by firing squad. Historian Antony Beevor describes him as "a truly unfortunate man" having been executed for crimes committed under another general. (Author's Collection)

Knight's Cross: Awarded on 24th May 1940 as *Oberst* and Commander 1st *Fallschirmjäger Regiment* for his leadership during the air assault on Crete. Upon landing in Crete his first objective was to capture and hold key bridges. The first one at Moerdijk was successfully captured but the second proved to be more difficult, and the Dutch defenders put up tough resistance. In the meantime Bräuer led an attack against the local airfield. His troops lured the defenders away from the airfield so German aircraft could land. He now took drastic action in order to secure the second bridge, he commandeered Dutch vehicles and after fierce fighting on both sides and some incredible feats of bravery especially by Bräuer himself the bridge was taken intact. For this a grateful Hitler personally presented Bräuer with his Knight's Cross.

Bruno Bräuer was born in Willmannsdorf, Jauer, on 4th February 1917 and began his military career as a cadet in April 1905, when he attended the military school at Treptow. In 1912 he transferred to the 155th Infantry Regiment and it was with this unit that he served throughout World War I. Accepted into the *Reichswehr* in 1919 he was commissioned and in January 1920 joined the State Police. From June 1935, he led the *Landespolizeigruppe "Hermann Göring,"* and in October was transferred to the Luftwaffe as part of the new *"Hermann Göring" Regiment* now with the rank of *Major*. Bräuer's command was selected to begin the first parachute training course in March 1936. In November 1938, he was transferred to the 1st *Fallschirmjäger Regiment* as a battalion commander. In September 1939, he saw action during the invasion of Poland and in May the following year he saw action during the airborne invasion of Holland – where he won the Knight's Cross.

When Crete was finally occupied, orders were issued on 31st May 1940 which stated: "*… the civilian population including women and children who have taken part in the fighting and have committed sabotage and killed or wounded German soldiers will be punished.*" Although Bräuer disagreed with these orders, he made no attempt to voice his opinion to his commanding officer.

In November 1942, Bräuer succeeded *General der Flieger* Alexander Andae as Commander of Fortress Crete. Bräuer proved to be a more humane commander. On 25th March 1943, Greek National Day, Bräuer ordered the release from prison of hundreds of Greek nationals. They included Constantinos Mitsotakis, later to become the Prime Minister of Greece.

OTHER AWARDS		PROMOTIONS	
14.10.1914	Iron Cross 2nd Class	01.12.1911	Gefreiter
01.04.1917	Iron Cross 1st Class	01.07.1912	Unteroffizier
00.00.1934	Cross of Honour for Frontline Combatants	01.10.1915	Sergeant
00.00.1936	Parachutist Badge	01.12.1916	Vizefeldwebel
02.10.1936	Armed Forces Long Service Award 4th to 1st Class	01.10.1917	Offizier-Stellvertreter
00.00.1938	Commemorative Medal of 13th March 1938	07.08.1919	Leutnant
20.10.1939	Bar to the Iron Cross 2nd Class	01.01.1920	Leutnant der Schutzpolizei
28.11.1939	Commemorative Medal of 1st October 1938	29.09.1923	Oberleutnant der Polizei
23.05.1940	Bar to the Iron Cross 1st Class	04.04.1928	Hauptmann der Polizei
31.03.1942	German Cross in Gold	01.06.1935	Major der Polizei
00.00.1942	Luftwaffe Ground Assault Badge	15.10.1935	Major (Luftwaffe)
00.00.1943	KRETA Cuff title	01.01.1938	Oberstleutnant
-----	-----	01.01.1939	Oberst
-----	-----	01.09.1941	Generalmajor
-----	-----	06.09.1942	Generalleutnant
-----	-----	01.06.1944	General der Fallschirmtruppe

MANFRED BÜTTNER

(15.02.1921 – 29.05.1992)

Fahnenjunker-Oberfeldwebel

Knight's Cross: Awarded on 29th April 1945 as *Fahnenjunker-Oberfeldwebel* and *Führer* 2nd Company, 26th *Fallschirmjäger Regiment* for his bravery during the heavy fighting near Greifenhagen on the Eastern Front. He led repeated attacks, against a vast superior enemy, for possession of Fortress Stettin, he led counterattack after counterattack to regain the main line of resistance. He was recommended for the Knight's Cross by *General der*

Büttner later served in the Bundeswehr rising to the rank of Hauptmann in July 1971. He died on 29th May 1992 in Plön. (Author's Collection)

(Author's Collection)

Fallschirmtruppe Bräuer, but it seems not officially ever presented with it. *There is no proof in any surviving records of Büttner being awarded the Knight's Cross. It seems that Büttner was recorded as a holder just because he was a serving member of the Bundeswehr and, "had characterized himself as a Knight's Cross recipient."*

Manfred Büttner was born on 15th February 1921, in Spittelndorf, Liegnitz he saw service in the Reich Labour Service before transferring to the army in August 1939. He joined the 100th Pioneer Battalion in Hindenburg, Upper Silesia and saw combat during the Polish campaign at the beginning of World War II. During the campaign in France he served as a radioman and radio squad leader in the 9th Training Wing and after completing a radio course he joined the parachute troops.

In Russia he served as a Platoon Leader in the 7th *Fallschirmjäger Regiment* and won the Iron Cross 1st Class. In October 1943, he served on the island of Elba with the 7th *Fallschirmjäger Regiment* as the regiments Signals Officer. In April 1944, Büttner was promoted to *Fahnenjunker-Oberfeldwebel* and was named as leader of the Battalion Signals Platoon of Battle Group 300. In January 1945 Büttner joined the I Battalion of the 26th *Fallschirmjäger* Regiment and later became special duties officer and commander of the 2nd Company. From March 1945, he saw heavy fighting against Soviet troops who were attempting to take the Oder crossings east of Stettin. He was captured by British troops in May 1945 and was released the next month.

OTHER AWARDS		PROMOTIONS	
24.02.1940	Marksmanship Badge	01.10.1940	Gefreiter
01.01.1942	War Service Cross 2nd Class + Swords	01.09.1941	Unteroffizier
14.07.1942	Parachutist Badge	20.10.1943	Feldwebel
11.02.1943	Iron Cross 2nd Class	20.04.1944	Fahnenjunker- Oberfeldwebel
25.02.1943	Iron Cross 1st Class	-----	-----
06.11.1943	Wound Badge in Black	-----	-----

GEORG LE COUTRE
(13.09.1921 – 08.01.2009)   *Leutnant*

Knight's Cross: Awarded on 7th February 1945 as *Leutnant* and *Führer* 10th Company, 6th *Fallschirmjäger Regiment* for actions during the Ardennes Offensive. He saw action on the Cotentin Peninsula before distinguishing himself several times during the last actions of the Ardennes Offensive. Courte was recommended for the Knight's Cross by the commander of the 1st Parachute

(Author's Collection)   (Author's Collection)

Army Weapons School, *Major* von Huetz. He was taken prisoner by the British on 16th February 1945, *Major* von Huetz received telex messages two days later telling him that *Leutnant* le Courte had been awarded the Knight's Cross.

George le Courte was born on 13th September 1921 in Memel and joined the 1st Replacement Cavalry Regiment in March 1940, and five months later he transferred to the *Fallschirmjäger*. He saw action during the invasion of Crete where he was awarded Iron Cross 2nd Class.

In December 1941, he was promoted to *Oberjäger* and in January 1942, he was made leader of a heavy machine-gun squad in the 4th Company of the 4th *Fallschirmjäger Regiment*. From April 1943 he was attached to the 9th Air Warfare School in Tschenstochau. In February 1944, he saw action in Italy where he was commissioned as a *Leutnant* and in June was awarded the German Cross in Gold. In July 1944, he transferred to the 6th *Fallschirmjäger Regiment* and became commander of the 9th Company. He saw action on the Cotentin Peninsula and in September was made commander of the 10th Company.

Le Courte was captured on 16th February 1945 and remained in captivity until 20th October 1946. He died on 8th January 2009, in Bonn.

OTHER AWARDS		PROMOTIONS	
12.12.1940	Parachutist Badge	01.04.1941	Gefreiter
04.05.1941	Iron Cross 2nd Class	31.12.1941	Oberjäger
26.06.1941	Iron Cross 1st Class	01.06.1943	Feldwebel
20.05.1943	KRETA Cuff title	20.04.1944	Leutnant
17.04.1944	Wound Badge in Black	-----	-----
28.05.1944	Wound Badge in Silver	-----	-----
14.06.1944	German Cross in Gold	-----	-----
05.11.1944	Wound Badge in Gold	-----	-----

EGON DELICA
(04.01.1915 – 26.04.1999) *Hauptmann*

(Author's Collection)

Knight's Cross: Awarded on 12th May 1940 as *Leutnant* and Deputy *Führer* of Assault Group *Granit*, Air-Landing Assault Battalion Koch for actions during the attack on the fort at Eben Emael, Belgium. On 10th May Delicia led his assault group against the enemy at Works 18 at the Belgian fort and pushed back the Belgian counterattack, the following day he linked up with the first soldiers of the 51st Army Pioneer Battalion. When the Knight's Cross was presented to him he was also informed that he had been promoted to *Oberleutnant*.

Egon Delica was born on 4th January 1915, in Stettin and after serving in the artillery as a gunner in April 1933, he transferred to the Luftwaffe and trained as an observer. During the Polish campaign he flew in a Heinkel He 111 as a deputy observer.

On 28th December 1939, he was promoted to *Leutnant* and transferred to the Parachute Assault Battalion in January 1940, and after his success in Belgium he saw further fighting on the western front. In April 1942, he saw action in Russia where he was wounded. In December, he became commander of II Group, 2nd Glider Wing, whose area of operations included the Crimea and the Taman Peninsula. He was wounded again in April 1943 and after he recovered he was appointed commander of the II battalion in the 19th *Fallschirmjäger Regiment*. He was captured by British forces near Kleve in February 1945 and remained in captivity until August 1947. He later joined the *Bundeswehr* where he became an *Oberstleutnant* in November 1966. He died on 26th April 1999 in Pullach, Munich.

OTHER AWARDS		PROMOTIONS	
01.04.1936	Armed Forces Long Service Award 4th Class	01.06.1934	Unteroffizier
16.09.1939	Iron Cross 2nd Class	01.04.1937	Unterfeldwebel
13.05.1940	Iron Cross 1st Class	01.04.1938	Feldwebel
00.10.1942	Eastern Front Medal	28.12.1939	Leutnant
00.06.1943	Wound Badge in Black	16.05.1940	Oberleutnant
21.11.1943	Parachutist Badge	01.07.1942	Hauptmann
26.11.1943	KRETA Cuff title	-----	-----
26.12.1943	German Cross in Gold	-----	-----

RUDOLF DONTH

(16.02.1920 – 19.06.2001)   *Oberleutnant*

Knight's Cross: Awarded on 14th January 1945 as *Feldwebel* and *Führer* 6th Company, 4th *Fallschirmjäger Regiment* for actions in Italy.

Rudolf Donth was born in Ober-Schreiberhau, Hirschberg on 16th February 1920 and joined the Luftwaffe on 1st October 1939, and after attending various course, including a parachutist-rifleman course in Wittstock. Once the course was completed he was assigned to the Headquarters Company of the 3rd *Fallschirmjäger Regiment*. From there he saw action during the invasion of Crete and won the Iron Cross 1st and 2nd Classes.

Rudolf Donth was captured by Allied forces in May 1945, and was released in April 1946. He entered the Bundeswehr in 1956, rising to the rank of Oberstleutnant before retiring in April 1977. Donth died on 19th June 2001, in Hahnenklee. (Author's Collection)

(Wehrkundearchiv)

From October 1942 until April 1943, he commanded the 2nd Company of the *Fallschirmjäger* Ski Regiment before joining the 6th Company of the 4th *Fallschirmjäger* Regiment which he remained with for the rest of the war. On 1st September 1944, Donth was appointed commander of the 6th Company. In October 1944, his company successfully defeated an enemy attack of ten tanks, a second attack followed this time with strong infantry support – this was also defeated. A third attack, made by twenty tanks and a battalion of infantry was eventually pushed back after a fierce bloody battle. Donth destroyed six tanks at close range, led a counterattack and freed a number of wounded comrades who had been captured by the enemy. The following month he led another counterattack against a hill east of Bologna where his troops took eighty-one prisoners. In December, near Monte Castellero his troops defeated a British battalion during a night attack, and for his bravery and leadership he was awarded the Knight's Cross.

OTHER AWARDS		PROMOTIONS	
15.11.1940	Parachutist Badge	01.11.1940	Gefreiter
12.06.1941	Iron Cross 2nd Class	01.10.1942	Oberjäger
22.06.1941	Iron Cross 1st Class	01.04.1944	Feldwebel
20.05.1943	KRETA Cuff title	01.09.1944	Leutnant
01.02.1944	Wound Badge in Black	20.04.1945	Oberleutnant
20.03.1944	Luftwaffe Ground Assault Badge	-----	-----
22.04.1944	Tank Destruction Badge in Silver	-----	-----
14.06.1944	German Cross in Gold	-----	-----

REINHARD KARL EGGER

(11.12.1905 – 10.06.1987)   *Oberstleutnant*

Knight's Cross: Awarded on 9th July 1941 as *Oberleutnant* and *Führer* 10th Company, 1st *Fallschirmjäger* Regiment in recognition of his brave actions near Heraklion, Crete where he took part in an eight day defensive battle with British troops.

(Wehrkundearchiv)   (Wehrkundearchiv)

Knight's Cross with Oakleaves: Awarded on 24th June 1944 to become the 510th recipient, as *Oberstleutnant* and *Führer* 4th *Fallschirmjäger* Regiment for his bravery and leadership during actions at Monet Cassino. He assumed command of the 4th Regiment after the wounding of *Oberst* Walther.

Reinhard Egger was born in Klagenfurt on 11th December 1905 and entered the 11th Alpine Light Infantry Regiment in April 1929, and by 1937 he had been promoted to the rank of *Wachtmeister*. He was transferred to the Military Academy at Wiener-Neustadt in September 1937 and in March the following year he joined the Luftwaffe and was assigned to the 10th Company of the 1st *Fallschirmjäger* Regiment.

After attending the 2nd Luftwaffe Officer Candidate School, Becker was assigned to various postings until October 1938, when he was transferred to the *General Göring's* Regiment airborne battalion. In January 1939, he was company leader in the 3rd Battalion of the 1st *Fallschirmjäger* Regiment, and later took part in the action against Rotterdam's airport. In October 1940, he became a company commander and saw action in Crete as part of Karl-Lothar Schulz's battalion. He played a key role in the fighting withdrawal up the Italian mainland. In July 1942, Becker became regimental adjutant of the 1st *Fallschirmjäger* Regiment and by the end of the year he was a battalion commander and undertook one of the last attempts to relieve the garrison of the fortress of Velikiye Luki under *Oberstleutnant* von Sass. He was wounded on the Eastern Front in January 1943, and while recovering from his wounds he was promoted to *Hauptmann*. In May he took command of the 5th Regiment of the 3rd *Fallschirmjäger* Division. He later saw action during the Ardennes Offensive and led his unit back through the West Wall in the final weeks of the war. He was captured by British troops on 31st July 1944, when his position was overrun. He died on 10th June 1987, in Seeboden, Austria.

OTHER AWARDS		PROMOTIONS	
21.11.1934	Military Service Award 2nd Class	03.11.1931	Gefreiter
23.01.1935	Training Award 1st Class	27.12.1932	Korporal
08.04.1936	Armed Forces Long Service Award 4th Class	20.01.1934	Scharfschützen

01.10.1939	Iron Cross 2nd Class		26.01.1935	Zugsführer
19.12.1939	Iron Cross 1st Class		02.01.1936	Wachtmeister
00.00.1940	Parachutist Badge		14.03.1938	Feldwebel
00.00.1943	KRETA Cuff title		01.09.1938	Oberfähnrich
24.02.1944	German Cross in Gold		01.04.1939	Leutnant
-----	-----		25.10.1940	Oberleutnant
-----	-----		01.10.1941	Hauptmann
-----	-----		01.04.1942	Major
-----	-----		01.04.1944	Oberstleutnant

DR. JOHANN ENGELHARDT
(11.12.1916 – 04.03.2001)   *Major*

(Wehrkundearchiv)

Knight's Cross: Awarded on 29th February 1944 as *Oberleutnant* and Commander 8th Company, 6th *Fallschirmjäger Regiment* for actions in Italy. On 29th January, immediately after the Allied landings near Anzio, Engelhardt saw action as part of the 4th *Fallschirmjäger* Regiment, and where he distinguished himself during battle and was recommended for the Knight's Cross.

Johann Engelhardt was born on 10th January 1916, in Plauen and entered Officer Candidate School in Berlin-Gatow, as a *Fahnenjunker* in April 1937. He was assigned to the 1st *Fallschirmjäger Regiment* in April 1938, and sent to Stendal Parachute School to take the parachutist-rifleman course.

Engelhardt was assigned to the Assault Battalion Koch and took part in the attack on Holland where he won the Iron Cross 1st and 2nd Classes. In September 1940, he took command of a platoon in the 13th Company of the 1st Glider Assault Regiment and in February 1942 was appointed adjutant of the IV Battalion. In July, he was made commander of the 8th Company of the 6th *Fallschirmjäger Regiment* and took part in the parachute operation against the Italian headquarters on Monte Rotondo under the command of *Major* Gericke. In June 1944, he was promoted to *Hauptmann* and named as commander of the II Battalion of the 11th *Fallschirmjäger Regiment*. He served with this unit in Italy until the end of the war. He died on 4th March 2001 in Erlangen.

OTHER AWARDS		PROMOTIONS	
15.05.1940	Iron Cross 2nd Class	01.04.1937	Fahnenjunker
17.05.1940	Iron Cross 1st Class	01.01.1939	Leutnant
00.00.1941	Parachutist Badge	01.08.1942	Oberleutnant
-----	-----	01.06.1944	Hauptmann
-----	-----	20.04.1945	Major

WOLFGANG ERDMANN

(13.11.1898 – 05.09.1946)   *Generalleutnant*

Erdmann saw action during the attack on Arnhem and was captured by British forces on 8th May 1945. He committed suicide whilst in captivity at the Prison Camp at Munster, known as Munster-lager on 5th September 1946. (Wehrkundearchiv)

Knight's Cross: Awarded on 8th February 1945 as *Generalleutnant* and Commander 7th *Fallschirmjäger* Division in recognition of his leadership and bravery during the heavy fighting in the Arnhem area. In August 1944, Erdmann had been appointed commander of Parachute Training Division "Erdmann," an emergency unit formed in Bitsch to help reinforce the army at Arnhem. It had been formed from the remnants of other units and from units attached to the parachute training schools in Germany. In October it was renamed the 7th *Fallschirmjäger Division* and operated in Hechtel, Arnhem and in the Venlo areas. He later took part in the fighting in Alsace and fought in the Hagenau Forest and near Seseheim.

Wolfgang Erdmann was born in Königsberg, East Prussia on 13th November 1898 and saw active service in the Artillery during World War I where he won the Iron Cross 1st and 2nd Classes. In July 1916, he was assigned to the 26th Foot Artillery Regiment and was commissioned in January 1917 as a *Leutnant*.

He remained in the army after the war and served first as an adjutant then as an ordnance officer. He was later allowed leave to finish his studies at the Berlin Technical College where he graduated with an engineering degree in 1924. Promoted to *Oberleutnant* in April 1925, he served for the next ten years as a battery officer in the 2nd Artillery Regiment. He transferred to the Luftwaffe in July 1937, and served as a General Staff officer in the Luftwaffe Organization Department. A year later he became Chief of Operations on the staff of Air Region Command XVII in Vienna. In March 1939, he was appointed commander of the newly formed 2nd Group of the 34th Bomber Wing *"General Wever."* Named as Chief of the 2nd Department in the Luftwaffe General Staff in January 1940, he was promoted to *Oberst* in November. In March 1943, after his promotion to *Generalmajor,* he took command of the 18th Luftwaffe Division covering the areas around Dunkirk and Calais, as part of the 82nd Army Corps. He succeeded *Generalleutnant* Wolfgang von Chamier-Glisczinski as Air Leader in Croatia in August and in May 1944 transferred to France where he joined the 1st *Fallschirm* Army as Chief of Staff, under the command of *Generaloberst* Kurt Student.

OTHER AWARDS		PROMOTIONS	
00.00.191_	Iron Cross 2nd Class	10.01.1916	Fahnenjunker
00.00.191_	Iron Cross 1st Class	08.11.1916	Fähnrich
00.00.1917	Wound Badge in Black	27.01.1917	Leutnant
00.00.1935	Cross of Honour for Frontline Combatants	01.04.1925	Oberleutnant
02.10.1936	Armed Forces Long Service Award 4th to 2nd Class	01.04.1933	Hauptmann
16.09.1939	Bar to the Iron Cross 2nd Class	01.08.1936	Major
14.06.1940	Bar to the Iron Cross 1st Class	14.10.1937	Major (Luftwaffe)

30.01.1943	War Service Cross 2nd Class + Swords	01.01.1939	Oberstleutnant im Generalstab
28.12.1943	German Cross in Gold	22.11.1940	Oberst im Generalstab
00.00.1945	Tank Destruction Badge in Silver (2)	01.03.1943	Generalmajor
-----	-----	01.07.1944	Generalleutnant

WERNER EWALD
(23.10.1914 – 05.10.1993)   *Major*

Knight's Cross: Awarded on 19th September 1944 as *Major* and Commander II Battalion, 2nd *Fallschirmjäger Regiment* for his leadership and bravery during the fierce fighting in Fortress Brest. In August 1944, Ewald took command of a battalion and was responsible for driving back a strong U.S. attack into the northwest part of the city. He continued to distinguish himself in the action until the surrender on 20th September 1944.

(Wehrkundearchiv)

(Wehrkundearchiv)

Werner Ewald was born 23rd October 1914, in Hamburg and joined the Army in April 1936 as an officer candidate. In July 1939, he joined the II Battalion of the 2nd *Fallschirmjäger Regiment* and took part in the Polish Campaign and later saw action in Holland. In May 1941, he saw action during the invasion of Crete, where he won the Iron Cross 1st Class. He was appointed a company commander in May 1941 and later took part in the invasion of Russia. In October he was promoted to *Hauptmann* and fought in the defensive battles in the southern sector of the Eastern Front under *Oberst* Kroh and was awarded the German Cross in Gold. Captured by Allied troops when Fortress Brest fell, he was released from captivity in May 1946. He later joined the *Bundswehr*, rising to the rank of *Oberst* in October 1967, and retired in 1973. He died in Bonn on 5th October 1993.

OTHER AWARDS		PROMOTIONS	
12.02.1940	Parachutist Badge	15.04.1936	Fahnenjunker
15.04.1940	Armed Forces Long Service Award 4th Class	00.00.1937	Fähnrich
25.05.1940	Iron Cross 2nd Class	01.01.1938	Leutnant
29.05.1941	Iron Cross 1st Class	01.06.1940	Oberleutnant
22.06.1942	General Assault Badge	01.10.1942	Hauptmann
14.07.1942	Eastern Front Medal	17.09.1944	Major
06.11.1942	Luftwaffe Ground Assault Badge	-----	-----
12.11.1942	AFRIKA Cuff title	-----	-----
29.03.1944	German Cross in Gold	-----	-----
26.06.1944	Wound Badge in Black	-----	-----

FERDINAND FOLTIN

(30.11.1916 – 18.05.2007)   *Major*

(Wehrkundearchiv)

Knight's Cross: Awarded on 9th June 1944 as *Hauptmann* and Commander II Battalion, 3rd *Fallschirmjäger Regiment* for actions during the fighting at Cassino.

Ferdinand Foltin was born on 30th November 1916, in Vienna and joined the Austrian Army as a volunteer in September 1936. In October 1937 he attended the Military Academy in Wiener-Neustadt and in April 1938 transferred to the German Army.

He served with the 107th Infantry Regiment and later joined the *Fallschirmjäger* and in August 1940 he took over a platoon of the 5th Company of the 3rd Fallschirmjäger Regiment. He was severely wounded during the invasion of Crete where he was awarded the Iron Cross 1st and 2nd Classes. After serving as ordnance officer with the 7th Air Division, in January 1944, he was appointed commander of the II Battalion, 3rd *Fallschirmjäger Regiment*. He was then transferred to Italy where he took part in the fighting at Monte Cassino. On the first day of the second battle of Cassino on 15th March 1944, the 7th Company of the 3rd *Fallschirmjäger Regiment* suffered heavy losses during an allied bombing raid, and was virtually destroyed. Foltin however had ordered his men out of the basement buildings they were resting in and led them to some caves outside the town where they sheltered from the air attack. The following day, armed with only one assault-gun, his men destroyed ten enemy tanks and later captured a large group of New Zealand troops who were defending the railway station. On the third day of the battle, his troops defended their high position from the enemy with hand-grenades, mortar fire and even large rocks, thrown down on the enemy positions. On the fifth day the German's managed to hold back a strong armoured allied force and Foltin's troops played a decisive role in holding the forces back, until reinforcements could arrive.

After winning the Knight's Cross in Cassino he was assigned to Headquarters of the 1st *Fallschirmjäger Army*. He surrendered to British forces on 8th May 1945 and was released five months later. He joined the Bundeswehr in September 1952, rising to the rank of Brigadier in 1969. Foltin died in Linz, Austria on 18th May 2007.

OTHER AWARDS		PROMOTIONS	
20.03.1940	West Wall Medal	01.09.1938	Fähnrich
08.08.1940	Parachutist Badge	01.01.1939	Leutnant
03.09.1940	Armed Forces Long Service Award 4th Class	01.08.1940	Oberleutnant
01.07.1941	Iron Cross 2nd Class	01.10.1943	Hauptmann
01.07.1941	Iron Cross 1st Class	01.06.1944	Major
01.08.1941	Wound Badge in Black	-----	-----
20.05.1943	KRETA Cuff title	-----	-----
16.12.1943	War Service Cross 2nd Class + Swords	-----	-----
05.10.1944	Luftwaffe Ground Assault Badge	-----	-----

HERBERT FRIES

(01.03.1925 – 06.01.2014)   *Oberfähnrich*

Knight's Cross: Awarded on 5th September 1944 as *Gefreiter* and attached to the 2nd Company, 1st *Fallschirm-Panzerjäger* Battalion for actions in Italy.

Fries named in the Official Armed Forces Communiqué of the 25th July 1944: "… Individual fighters distinguished themselves in the battle, one of them was Oberjäger Fries, a gunner in the armoured infantry company who destroyed seventeen enemy tanks within two day." (Author's Collection)

(Author's Collection)

Herbert Fries was born in Waldmühlen, Westerburg on 1st March 1925 and volunteered for the *Fallschirmjäger* in March 1943 and after three months service in the Reich Labour Service he arrived in Gardelegan. From there he was sent to Salzwedel for training on anti-tank guns and later to France for further training in tank tactics. In February 1944 he moved with the 2nd Company of the 1st *Fallschirm* Anti-tank Battalion to Piedimonte near Cassino. There he took command of a *Jagdpanzer IV* and saw heavy action during the third battle of Cassino. After the battle was over twenty paratroopers and three tank-destroyers held the village of Piedimonte, preventing a rapid advance by the enemy. In early 1944 he was commander of Panzer IV and saw action with his unit during the third battle of Cassino. After the battle was over twenty paratroops and three tank-destroyers held the village of Piedimonte, preventing the enemies advance and the possible encirclement of the 1st *Fallschirmjäger* Division. When the Allies attacked on 21st May, Fries knocked out seven Sherman tanks and prevented an enemy breakthrough. The second attempt on 22nd May, the enemy attacked once again and this time Fries destroyed six tanks and on the next day knocked out another seven.

He was captured by Allied troops in May 1945 and remained in captivity in Italy until July 1947. He died in the town of Rennerod-Emmerichenhain, Westerwald in the Rhineland-Palatinate on 6th January 2014.

OTHER AWARDS		PROMOTIONS	
22.05.1944	Iron Cross 2nd Class	22.05.1944	Gefreiter
22.05.1944	Iron Cross 1st Class	01.10.1944	Oberjäger
00.00.1944	Luftwaffe Ground Assault Badge	20.12.1944	Fähnrich
-----	-----	01.04.1945	Oberfähnrich
-----	-----	20.04.1945	Leutnant

ERNST FRÖMMING

(04.02.1911 – 18.08.1959) *Major*

(Wehrkundearchiv)

Knight's Cross: Awarded on 18th November 1944, as *Major* and Commander 1st *Fallschirm-Pioniere* Battalion, 1st *Fallschirmjäger Division* for his successful leadership during the fighting in Monte Cassino.

Ernst Frömming was born on 4th February 1911 in Rotenburg an der Wümme near Stade in Lower Saxony. He entered military service with the army in May 1930 and at first served with the 18th Infantry Regiment before being transferred to the engineers. He saw brief action on the Western Front with the 34th Pioneer Battalion, winning the Iron Cross 1st and 2nd Classes.

He transferred to the Luftwaffe on 24th March 1941 and joined the Parachute Engineer Battalion, jumping into Crete in May as part of the German airborne invasion of the island. He fought in Priosn Valley south of Kirtomados, the engineer's battle with the 8th Greek Regiment. In November 1941, he was promoted to *Oberleutnant* and in February 1942 he became a Platoon Leader in the Parachute Engineer Battalion, but one week later he was transferred to become the acting commander of the 13th Company of the 1st Parachute Training Regiment. He later took this unit to Russia. In March 1943, he saw action near Smolensk where he led an attack which recaptured a strongpoint near Massejnik. He was promoted to *Hauptmann* on 21st May 1943, and was transferred to Sicily where he led the 2nd Company. His battalion managed to build a bridge across the Savio River which enabled the 1st *Fallschirmjäger Division* to cross the river with its heavy weapons. His troops blew up roads and bridges – in fact Frömming's men destroyed 146 river crossings and laid more than 5,000 mines, stopping the pursuing enemy and enabling German forces to escape across the Strait of Messina. His unit went on to Monte Cassino where they helped to repel the 5th Indian Brigade from seizing Hill 236, and pushed back the 1st Battalion of the 4th Essex Regiment, which denied them from taking Hiull 435. Frömming won the German Cross in Gold in March 1944, and was promoted to *Major* in May. His bravery and leadership was further recognized when he was awarded the Knight's Cross in November 1944.

Frömming was taken prisoner by the Americans on 2nd May 1945 and was released five months later. He died on 18th August 1959 in Rotenberg an der Wümme. He is buried there at the local Cemetery (Block 2, Row 6, Grave 27).

OTHER AWARDS		PROMOTIONS	
01.05.1936	Armed Forces Long Service Award 4th Class	01.05.1932	Oberpionier
00.00.1940	Parachutist Badge	01.05.1934	Gefreiter
12.06.1940	Iron Cross 2nd Class	01.10.1935	Unteroffizier
12.11.1940	Iron Cross 1st Class	01.03.1937	Feldwebel
05.09.1942	Luftwaffe Ground Assault Badge	01.06.1938	Oberfeldwebel
07.12.1942	Luftwaffe Salver of Honour	01.07.1940	Kriegsoffizieranwärter
14.06.1944	German Cross in Gold	01.12.1941	Leutnant
-----	-----	01.12.1941	Oberleutnant
-----	-----	31.05.1943	Hauptmann
-----	-----	31.05.1944	Major

WILHELM FULDA

(21.05.1909 – 08.08.1977)   *Hauptmann*

Knight's Cross: Awarded as *Leutnant* and Platoon Leader in the 6th Company, 2nd *Fallschirmjäger Regiment* on 14th June 1941, for actions during the campaign in the Balkans. During the invasion of Greece he served as a glider pilot in the 1st Air Landing Wing, and during the attack on the Isthmus of Corinth he successfully landed a glider full of troops during heavy fighting with the enemy. During this

(Author's Collection)

(Wehrkundearchiv)

operation, he not only piloted a glider during a difficult landing at the bridge, but he also led all the gliders in the mission. Once landed Fula took command of a platoon during the attack. The German engineers captured the bridge, but the British exploded the demolition charges on the bridge by shooting at them. The Germans lost sixty-three soldiers and 174 were wounded; they captured 900 British, Australian and New Zealand troops and 1,450 Greek soldiers.

Wilhelm Fulda was born on 21st May 1909 in Antwerp, Belgium and he joined the German armed forces in November 1935 and after his basic training he attended a NCO course. From October 1939 he served as a pilot with the 52nd Pilot Training Regiment and later became a very skilful glider pilot. His first mission as a glider pilot was during the aerial assault on the Belgian fortress of Eben Emael where he won the Iron Cross 1st Class.

He later served as a training director and after his promotion to *Leutnant* in January 1941 he commanded a glider platoon and took part in the action at the Corinth Canal in Greece. During the invasion of Crete, he served as a glider pilot and upon landing he led his company during some of the bloodiest battles of the invasion, his troops suffered heavy losses but captured more than 2,300 Allied prisoners. For his leadership and bravery he was awarded the Knight's Cross. In November 1943, Fulda joined the German air defence where he was assigned to the 301st Fighter Wing, and was placed in command of the 2nd Group. In November 1944, he was a group commander in *Jagdgeschwader* 400, equipped with Messerschmitt Me 163 rocket-powered fighters. He was credited with shooting down one four-engine bomber. He died on 8th August 1977 in Hamburg-Wandsbeck.

OTHER AWARDS		PROMOTIONS	
01.11.1939	Armed Forces Long Service Award 4th Class	19.08.1937	Unteroffizier-Anwärter
12.05.1940	Iron Cross 2nd Class	14.10.1937	Gefreiter der Reserve
13.05.1940	Iron Cross 1st Class	01.01.1940	Unteroffizier der Reserve
00.00.1940	Glider Pilots Badge	01.05.1940	Feldwebel der Reserve
00.00.1942	NSFK Large Glider Pilots Badge	01.01.1941	Leutnant
-----	-----	01.02.1943	Oberleutnant
-----	-----	01.01.1944	Hauptmann

ROBERT GAST

(28.03.1920 – 00.11.2011)   *Leutnant*

(Wehrkundearchiv)

Knight's Cross: Awarded on 6th October 1944 as *Leutnant* and *Führer* 9th Company, 7th *Fallschirmjäger Regiment* for actions near Normandy, France. His company was involved in heavy fighting near Brest. The 7th *Fallschirmjäger Regiment* fought a tough defensive battle at the eastern end of the city. He led his troops brilliantly and was recommended for the Knight's Cross by his commanding officer, for his outstanding bravery in leading various offensive patrols. Unfortunately he was captured by American troops on 20th September, before the award could be presented. Whether or not he received the award later as a prisoner-of-war is unknown.

Robert Gast was born on 28th March 1920 in Kapsweyer in the Rhineland-Pflaz. He joined the Luftwaffe in January 1940 and served with the 2nd *Fallschirmjäger Regiment* before undergoing officer training.

He saw his first action in Russia in the autumn of 1941 where he won the Iron Cross 1st and 2nd Classes. In April 1943, he became a wartime officer candidate and entered the Luftwaffe ground warfare school in Mourmelon. He finally qualified as an officer in July 1944, and was made commander of the 9th Company of the 7th *Fallschirmjäger Regiment*. In July 1944, he was transferred to Normandy where he was part of the defenders of the Atlantic fortifications. His unit entered Brest, France in August 1944, as part of the 2nd *Fallschirmjäger Division*. The Allied assault on the city began on 29th August, when RAF heavy bombers struck Brest at night, and bombers from the U.S. 8th Air Force hit the fortress the next day. Then the U.S. 2nd, 8th and 29th Infantry Divisions began their assault. Hitler ordered Brest to be held to the last man. However the U.S. attack was relentless and Gast and his troops were forced to surrender on 18th September 1944. Gast remained in captivity until the end of 1945 when he returned to Germany. He died in November 2011.

OTHER AWARDS		PROMOTIONS	
17.03.1942	Iron Cross 2nd Class	01.01.1941	Gefreiter
00.00.1943	Luftwaffe Ground Assault Badge	01.01.1942	Obergefreiter
02.01.1943	Iron Cross 1st Class	01.04.1942	Unteroffizier
-----	-----	24.07.1943	Leutnant

ALFRED GENZ
(08.03.1916 – 23.04.2000)   *Major*

(Wehrkundearchiv)

Knight's Cross: Awarded on 14th June 1941 as *Oberleutnant* and Commander 1st Company, 1st *Fallschirmjäger Assault Regiment* for outstanding leadership qualities in Crete.

Alfred Genz was born on 8th March 1916 in Berlin and joined the Luftwaffe in April 1935, having had been one of the original members of the General Göring State Police Group. In January 1938, he started his training as a parachutist and in April was made a company commander in the 1st *Fallschirmjäger Regiment.*

He saw action in Poland and returned to Germany in early-1940 to prepare for the invasion of Crete. In May 1941, Genz led his company southwest of Chania on the Crete coast against a British anti-aircraft battery of four guns and about 180 men. His task had been made that much harder because he had lost almost 25% of his troops upon landing, most had drifted when the wind changed and some had landed in the wrong area completely. To add to his difficulties the enemy was much stronger than he had first thought. However his troops performed exceptionally and they stormed the British positions destroying the guns and capturing twelve enemy soldiers. He then managed to get through enemy lines by pretending to be a British unit. On 21st May, his troops engaged the enemy from their hill-top vantage point; there they kept the enemy pinned down until the arrival of the 1st Battalion of the 3rd *Fallschirmjäger Regiment.*

In recognition of his success in Crete, as well as being awarded the Knight's Cross he was mentioned in the Armed Forces Official Communiqué of 9th June 1941: *"In the battles in Crete parachute units under the command of Major Koch, Hauptmann Altmann and Oberleutnant Genz distinguished themselves through boldness and heroic courage."*

In April 1942, he was appointed to a staff position with the 5th *Fallschirmjäger Regiment,* with which he saw action in Tunisia. He later served in Student's special staff group and finally as an ordnance officer with the Commander-in-Chief of Parachute Troops. In December, he was appointed commander of the 12th *Fallschirmjäger Assault Regiment* and in April 1945 was promoted to *Major* and made commanding officer of the 29th *Fallschirmjäger Regiment.* He was captured by the Soviets at the end of the war and wasn't released until December 1949. He joined the Bundeswehr in April 1956 and retired as an *Oberst* in 1974. He lost both of his brothers during the war, Günther served in the 3rd *Fallschirmjäger Regiment* and Harald with the 2nd Assault Regiment – both brothers fell in Crete. He died on 23rd April 2000, in Schongau.

OTHER AWARDS		PROMOTIONS	
30.03.1938	Parachutist Badge	01.04.1935	Fahnenjunker der Landespolizei
01.04.1939	Armed Forces Long Service Award 4th Class	01.03.1938	Leutnant
15.05.1940	Iron Cross 2nd Class	01.04.1940	Oberleutnant
15.05.1940	Iron Cross 1st Class	01.03.1942	Hauptmann
27.08.1942	Luftwaffe Ground Assault Badge	01.04.1945	Major
00.00.1943	KRETA Cuff title	-----	-----

WALTER GERICKE

(23.12.1907 – 19.10.1991)   *Oberst*

(Author's Collection)

Gericke is seen here in a propaganda postcard by Wolfgang Willrich. (Author's Collection)

Gericke wearing his Knight's Cross with Oakleaves. He later joined the Bundeswehr, rising to the rank of Generalmajor in September 1963. He died on 19th October 1991, in Alsfeld, Hessen. (Author's Collection)

Knight's Cross: Awarded on 14th June 1941 as *Hauptmann* and Commander IV Battalion, 1st *Parachute* Assault Regiment in recognition of his leadership during the airborne invasion of Crete and especially of the success of his troops in seizing the airfield at Máleme.

Knight's Cross with Oakleaves: Awarded on 17th September 1944, as the 585th recipient as *Major* and Commander 11th *Fallschirmjäger Regiment* in recognition of his bravery and skill during the defensive combat in Italy, which included the defence of Futa Press. He was mentioned in the Armed Forces Daily Communiqué of 10th June 1944 for heroism and achievement in Italy.

Born on 23rd December 1907, in Bilderlahe near Gandersheim in Lower Saxony, Walter Gericke entered the police in 1929 and was later assigned to *Landespolzieigruppe "General Göring."* By September 1937, he had been transferred to the Luftwaffe where he assumed command of the 11th Company of the 4th Parachute Battalion. In April 1940, he won the Iron Cross 2nd Class, while seizing a key Danish bridge, during the invasion of Denmark. On 10th May, his troops fought at Dordrecht in an attempt to seize key bridges over the Maas River, for this he was awarded the Iron Cross 1st Class. He later became liaison officer to *Generalleutnant* Stumpff in Drontheim, Norway in support of the airborne transport effort to support German forces to the north at Narvik. In 1941, he took part in the invasion of Crete where he took temporary command of the regiment, when General Eugen Meindl was seriously wounded. Missing most of his heavy weapons, Gericke's battalion crossed the Tavronitis River and gained a foothold on Hill 107. His troops pinned down the enemy on the coastal road east of Máleme and on his own initiative launched an attack in the direction of Chania. The attack succeeded and opened the way for a German victory on the island, although the battalion lost 120 men.

On 9th September 1943, Gericke led an airborne attack on the Italian Supreme Headquarters at Monte Rotundo, after Italy changed sides in the war. The Germans captured 2,500 Italian soldiers and lost fifty-six paratroopers – their major target, Marshal Bagoglio was not found. On 1st July 1944, Gericke was promoted and appointed commander of the 1st Parachute Corps in Vienna, and in January 1945 took command of the newly formed 21st *Fallschirmjäger* Division in Holland. On 8th May, he surrendered his troops to the British at Wilhelmshaven and went into captivity, where he stayed until his release in 1946.

OTHER AWARDS		PROMOTIONS	
00.00.1936	Parachutist Badge	03.04.1929	Polizeianwärter
02.10.1936	Armed Forces Long Service Award 4th Class	01.04.1930	Polizei-Wachtmeister
00.00.1937	Reich Sports Badge in Silver	01.03.1932	Polizei-Oberwachtmeister
10.04.1940	Iron Cross 2nd Class	01.04.1933	Leutnant der Polizei
12.05.1940	Iron Cross 1st Class	31.08.1935	Oberleutnant der Polizei
00.05.1942	Luftwaffe Ground Assault Badge	01.03.1938	Hauptmann (Luftwaffe)
00.00.1943	KRETA Cuff title	01.08.1942	Major
12.12.1943	German Cross in Gold	01.07.1944	Oberstleutnant
-----	-----	30.01.1945	Oberst

ERNST GERMER

(15.12.1917 – 13.10.1990)   *Oberleutnant*

(Wehrkundearchiv)

Knight's Cross: Awarded on 29th October 1944 as *Fahnenjunker-Feldwebel* and *Führer* Bicycle Platoon in the Staff Company, 1st *Fallschirmjäger Regiment* for actions in Italy. He took participated in the Italian campaign from July 1943, seeing his first action during the bitter fighting in the Pesaro area. He led his Bicycle Platoon during the attack on the port and his men destroyed several tanks with anti-tank weapons and pushed back numerous enemy counterattacks. As a result positions which had been lost by the 1st *Fallschirmjäger Regiment* were recovered by the troops under Germer's command.

Ernst Germer was born on 15th December 1917 in Nienburg, Bernburg and after the parachutist-rifleman course in Stendal he saw action during the Polish campaign. He served in Norway in April 1940, and from May saw action during the battle for Narvik.

In May 1941, he fought during the campaign in Crete with the 3rd Company of the 1st *Fallschirmjäger Regiment*. In the autumn of 1941 he transferred to the northern sector of the Eastern Front and took part in fierce fighting at the Neva. Later, under the command of *Oberstleutnant* Karl Lothar Schulz, Germer saw action in offensive and reconnaissance patrols, which often had to be decided in close-quarters fighting. It was here that he won the German Cross in Gold, and was promoted to the rank of *Feldwebel*. From July 1943 until the end of the war, he saw action in Italy, fighting in the Pesaro area. He was captured by British troops in May 1945 and held as a prisoner of war until 1946. He died in Braunschweig-Stöckheim on 13th October 1990.

OTHER AWARDS		PROMOTIONS	
01.01.1940	Parachutist Badge	01.02.1940	Gefreiter
18.04.1940	Iron Cross 2nd Class	01.12.1940	Obergefreiter
24.06.1940	Iron Cross 1st Class	01.05.1941	Oberjäger
01.03.1941	Narvik Campaign Shield	01.03.1943	Feldwebel
01.11.1942	Luftwaffe Ground Assault Badge	01.07.1944	Fahnenjunker-Feldwebel
20.05.1943	KRETA Cuff title	01.09.1944	Fahnenjunker-Oberfeldwebel
24.06.1943	German Cross in Gold	01.10.1944	Leutnant
01.05.1944	Wound Badge in Silver	20.04.1945	Oberleutnant
08.11.1944	Wound Badge in Gold	-----	-----
18.04.1945	Luftwaffe Close Combat Clasp	-----	-----

SIEGFRIED JOSEF SIMPERT GERSTNER

(16.11.1916 – 11.01.2013)   *Major*

Siegfried Gerstner rejoined the German Bundeswehr after the war and retired as an Oberst on 31st March 1975. He died on 11th January 2013 in Deggendorf, at the age of ninety-six. (Wehrkundearchiv)

Knight's Cross: Awarded on 13th September 1944 as *Major* and Commander II Battalion, 7th *Fallschirmjäger Regiment* in recognition of his leadership during the heavy fighting in Brest. He led his battalion in Brittany near Landerneau where his troops destroyed the large bridge over the Elorne. He was later recommended for the Knight's Cross by General Ramcke for his leadership during the demolition work in the battle for Fortress Brest, denying the enemy entrance to the city.

Siegfried Gerstner was born on 16th November 1916 in Passau, Bavaria and joined the mountain infantry in December 1936. On 1st September 1938 he was promoted to *Leutnant* and transferred to the 82nd Mountain Engineer Battalion. He served with this unit during the Polish campaign and in the Norwegian campaign, winning the Iron Cross 1st and 2nd Classes. He transferred to the Luftwaffe on 1st August 1940 as an *Oberleutnant* and became a Platoon Leader in the 7th Parachute Engineer Battalion. In April 1941, he assumed command of the 4th Company, in the same battalion and saw action during the invasion of Crete. His company jumped into the western part of Prison Valley six miles southwest of Khania and they encountered heavy resistance from the 8th Greek Regiment. For his exploits and bravery he received the Luftwaffe Honour Goblet on 1st August 1941.

From September 1941, he saw action in Russia where he was wounded in October, during the fighting at the Neva. In January 1943, he was wounded once again and after recovering he was promoted to *Hauptmann* and made commander of the 2nd *Fallschirm-Pioniere Battalion*. He commanded this unit until 7th January 1944, when he was severely wounded in heavy fighting near Kirowograd and was evacuated to hospital. While recovering in hospital he was promoted to *Major* and took command of the 2nd Parachute Battalion in March 1944. During the battle for Brest in August and September, he fought with great skill and bravery and was awarded the Knight's Cross. On 19th September 1944, just six days later, Gerstner was taken prisoner by American troops.

OTHER AWARDS		PROMOTIONS	
01.02.1940	Iron Cross 2nd Class	01.09.1918	Leutnant (Heer)
01.06.1940	Iron Cross 1st Class	01.08.1940	Oberleutnant
00.00.1940	Parachutist Badge	19.10.1940	Leutnant (Luftwaffe)
01.08.1941	Luftwaffe Honour Goblet	19.10.1940	Oberleutnant
17.06.1942	German Cross in Gold	01.02.1943	Hauptmann
00.00.1942	Luftwaffe Ground Assault Badge	07.02.1944	Major
00.01.1943	Wound Badge in Black	-----	-----

HELMUT GUSTAV GÖRTZ

(07.08.1911 – 03.05.1979)   *Oberleutnant*

(Wehrkundearchiv)

Knight's Cross: Awarded on 29th May 1940 as *Feldwebel* and Platoon Leader in 3rd Company, 1st *Fallschirmjäger Regiment* for actions in Holland. He led his platoon during the bitter fighting near Dordrecht Station and in the Krispijn district of the city. When *Oberleutnant* von Brandis, Görtz's company commander was killed, Görtz took unofficial command and advanced the company and engaged the enemy – they halted the attack. Görtz held the bridge until the arrival of reinforcements from 2nd and 4th Company of the 1st *Fallschirmjäger Regiment*. It was this action that won him the Knight's Cross.

Helmut Görtz was born in Schleusenau, Bromberg on 7th August 1911 and entered the police in August 1933. Two years later he became a member of the *General Göring Regiment*. In August 1936, he attended a parachutist-rifleman course in Stendal and from there he was taken into the 1st Company of the 1st *Fallschirmjäger Regiment*. He took part in the Polish Campaign where he won the Iron Cross 2nd Class and during the fighting in Fortress Holland he won the Iron Cross 1st Class.

After success in Holland he saw action in Russia, taking part in the fighting in the Promklevo area of the Neva River. During the regiment's second tour of duty in Russia he saw action in the Promklevo area of the Orel bend. Görtz was present when the Russians tried to break through toward Baldusch in March 1943 and he later took part in the counterattack toward Aleshenka.

In July 1943, he transferred to Italy where he took part in the tough defensive fighting as a Platoon Leader in the 4th Company of the 1st *Fallschirmjäger Regiment*. In August 1944, he took command of a platoon and was awarded the German Cross in Gold. On 5th November 1944, he was promoted to *Leutnant* and within six months he had been promoted to *Oberleutnant*. The war ended for him in May 1945 when he was captured by Allied forces in Italy. Görtz died on 3rd May 1979 in Dinslaken, a town in the district of Wesel, in North Rhine-Westphalia, Germany.

Some sources state that Görtz was awarded the Oakleaves on 30th April 1945, but there is no evidence in any archive to substantiate this claim. Veit Scherzer in his book, *Die Ritterkreuzträger 1939-1945,* mentions nothing of the award.

OTHER AWARDS		PROMOTIONS	
14.12.1936	Parachutist Badge	16.08.1934	Wachtmeister der Landespolizei
21.08.1937	Armed Service Long Service Award 4th Class	02.09.1935	Oberwachtmeisteranwärter der Landespolizei
22.05.1939	Commemorative Medal of 13th March 1938	01.11.1935	Oberjäger
20.06.1939	Commemorative Medal of 1st October 1938 + Bar	01.11.1939	Feldwebel
18.04.1940	Iron Cross 2nd Class	01.08.1940	Oberfeldwebel
18.05.1940	Iron Cross 1st Class	26.10.1943	Kriegsoffizieranwärter
01.03.1941	Narvik Campaign Shield	12.10.1944	Oberfähnrich
04.02.1942	Wound Badge in Black	05.11.1944	Leutnant
01.10.1942	Luftwaffe Ground Assault Badge	01.05.1945	Oberleutnant
04.12.1942	Eastern Front Medal	-----	-----
18.11.1944	Wound Badge in Silver	-----	-----
05.12.1944	German Cross in Gold	-----	-----

FRANZ GRAßMEL
(08.01.1906 – 30.06.1985) *Oberstleutnant*

Graßmel was captured by Allied troops in May 1945 he remained a prisoner until mid-1946. He died at Stade an der Elbe, Lower Saxony on 30th June 1985. He is buried in the Cemetery in Geestberg (Section 11, Grave 97). (Author's Collection)

Knight's Cross: Awarded on 8th April 1944, as *Major* and Commander III Battalion, 4th *Fallschirmjäger Regiment* for actions during the second Battle of Cassino.

Knight's Cross with Oakleaves: The award of the Oakleaves came on 8th May 1945 as *Oberstleutnant* and Commander of the 20th *Fallschirmjäger Regiment. The award recommendation from the field has not survived. On 16th April 1946, the Commander-in-Chief Northwest sent the recommendation to the Luftwaffe High Command. However an approval of the award cannot be found in the Federal Archives. The Award Commission of the Award Association of the Knight's Cross considered the matter in 1974 and decided that Graßmel had been awarded the Oakleaves. The award they said had been approved by the "Dönitz Directive," which therefore makes the award illegal.*

Franz Graßmel was born on 8th January 1906 in Mochow, Lübben and entered the Brandenburg Police School in April 1928, and transferred to the army in August 1935. He served in various anti-tank battalions and took part in the Polish campaign in 1939 and the French campaign in 1940.

In June 1940, he attended the airborne school and from there joined the paratroopers. In July 1940 he commanded the 14th Anti-tank Company of the 1st *Fallschirmjäger* Regiment and then commanded a company during the Crete campaign where he was awarded the Iron Cross 1st Class. On 20th May 1941, Graßmel and his company were part of the massive airborne invasion of the island of Crete; his unit was part of the second assault wave, jumping into drop zones just outside the town of Heraklion. He fought with bravery and great leadership, personally leading two anti-tank guns against the western gate of the town and was awarded the Iron Cross 1st and 2nd Classes. In June 1942, he was named as the acting commander of the 3rd Battalion of the 4th *Fallschirmjäger* Regiment and in December was promoted to *Hauptmann*. Then from September to November 1941, he saw action in Russia as part of the 16th Army at Leningrad and then later near Rzev. Again Graßmel fought with great skill and bravery and was awarded the German Cross in Gold and was wounded twice in action.

In July 1943, he and his battalion jumped into Sicily as part of the attempt to stop the Allied invasion. His unit was tasked with the defence at Bottaceto Ditch and his battalion held out until August before being forced to withdraw to the Italian mainland. On 15th March 1944, 460 Allied bombers dropped 1,000 tons of bombs on Cassino and its German defenders and followed this attack with an eight hour artillery barrage. The constant barrage was not enough to dislodge the paratroopers, and after ninety-six hours of heavy ground combat, the Allies made an armoured thrust and attempted to turn the northern flank of the German positions through the mountains and seize the Albaneta Farm. Gräsmel and his regiment were there to stop the allied advance –

and they achieved it. The allies got bogged down by German anti-tank fire and the well-thought out use of anti-tank mines. As a result twenty-nine allied vehicles were destroyed, and Graßmel was awarded the Knight's Cross.

On 18th August, he became the acting commander of the 20th *Fallschirmjäger* Regiment, and as part of the 7th *Fallschirmjäger* Division he fought in Venlo and Overbeck, Holland, Weissenberg and Hagenau, France and later in Germany. He was again wounded on 10th February 1945, and his unit helped thousands of German soldiers and civilians escape westward away from the Soviets.

OTHER AWARDS		PROMOTIONS	
01.08.1939	Armed Forces Long Service Award 4th Class	01.10.1934	Polizei-Oberwachtmeister
10.06.1941	Iron Cross 2nd Class	01.08.1935	Hauptfeldwebel
10.06.1941	Iron Cross 1st Class	01.10.1938	Reserve- Offiziersanwärter
20.05.1942	KRETA Cuff title	10.04.1940	Leutnant
20.09.1942	Luftwaffe Ground Assault Badge	10.04.1940	Oberleutnant
18.12.1942	Wound Badge in Black	13.09.1940	Oberleutnant der Reserve
22.07.1943	German Cross in Gold	01.01.1941	Hauptmann der Reserve
10.02.1945	Wound Badge in Silver	21.02.1941	Hauptmann
-----	-----	12.07.1943	Major
-----	-----	12.03.1945	Oberstleutnant

KURT GRÖSCHKE

(17.07.1907 – 26.03.1996)   *Oberst*

Knight's Cross: Awarded as *Major* and Commander 2nd Battalion, 1st *Fallschirmjäger Regiment* on 9th June 1944, in recognition of his part in the prevention of an enemy break through northwest of Cassino, Italy.

Knight's Cross with Oakleaves: He became the 693rd recipient of the Oakleaves on 9th January 1945 as *Oberstleutnant* and Commander 15th *Fallschirmjäger Regiment* in recognition of his defence in the region of Harlange and Villers-la-Bonne-Eau during the Ardennes Offensive here he managed to hold back the US 26th Infantry Division.

In April 1945, Gröschke took command of the 5th Fallschirmjäger Division, and, almost four weeks later, surrendered to British troops. He was held in captivity until 26th February 1946. He died on 26th March 1996, in Odenthal, Westfalen. (Wehrkundearchiv)

(Wehrkundearchiv)

Kurt Gröschke was born on 17th July 1907 in Berlin-Charlottenburg and he joined the police in October 1927 as a cadet and then joined the *General Göring* State Police Group in April 1934. In July 1935, he was promoted to *Leutnant* and saw action during the invasion of Poland, Holland and Crete, and was decorated with the Iron Cross 1st Class for actions during the invasion of Holland in May 1940.

After the invasion of Crete his battalion fought in the northern sector of the Easter Front. In February 1942, he was appointed commander of the II Battalion of the 1st *Fallschirmjäger* Regiment. He was later involved in anti-partisan operations and saw heavy action in the Orel area where he won the German Cross in Gold. On 22nd January 1944, Gröschke was appointed acting commander of the 1st *Fallschirmjäger* Regiment. On 8th February his forces prevented the enemy from breaking through to the Cassino-Rome road.

OTHER AWARDS		PROMOTIONS	
00.00.1937	Parachutist Badge	11.10.1927	Polizeianwärter
23.08.1939	Armed Forces Long Service Award 4th Class	01.10.1928	Polizei-Wachtmeister
20.10.1939	Iron Cross 2nd Class	01.10.1932	Polizei-Oberwachtmeister
22.05.1940	Iron Cross 1st Class	22.06.1933	Polizei-Offiziersanwärter
00.00.1940	Narvik Campaign Shield	01.07.1935	Leutnant der Landespolizei
00.05.1943	KRETA Cuff title	01.10.1935	Leutnant (Luftwaffe)
21.06.1943	German Cross in Gold	01.10.1936	Oberleutnant
-----	-----	01.02.1940	Hauptmann
-----	-----	01.04.1942	Major
-----	-----	01.06.1944	Oberstleutnant
-----	-----	10.02.1945	Oberst

ANDREAS HAGL

(21.04.1911 – 29.04.1945)   *Hauptmann der Reserve*

(Wehrkundearchiv)

Knight's Cross: Awarded on 9th July 1941 as *Oberleutnant* and Platoon Leader in the 2nd Company of the 3rd *Fallschirmjäger Regiment* for actions during the invasion of Crete.

Andreas Hagl was born on 21st April 1911 in Farchant, Garmisch in Bavaria and entered the army in October 1931, with the 19th Infantry Regiment. In April 1937, he joined the Luftwaffe and volunteered for the paratroopers, joining the 2nd Battalion of the 1st *Fallschirmjäger Regiment* and saw action in Polish campaign. In 1940, Hagl fought in the campaign in Holland, helping to seize the key railroad bridge over the Maas River at Moerdijk as a platoon leader. He was wounded on 22nd May 1940 and in July he won the Iron Cross 1st Class.

On 1st November 1940, he was commissioned as a *Leutnant* and became Platoon Leader in the 2nd Company of the 3rd *Fallschirmjäger Regiment* and saw action during the airborne invasion of Crete. His unit jumped into Prison valley and began a difficult fight against the 10th New Zealand Brigade southwest of Khaniá. The 1st Battalion attempted to make contact with the 3rd Battalion and used Hagl's platoon to spearhead the effort. On 26th May, Hagl took command of the entire 2nd Company and that same day he was seriously wounded in the right thigh by a hand grenade, but he continued to lead the company. His bravery and efforts won him the Knight's Cross.

After the campaign in Crete he was deployed to Russia where he was once again wounded on 8th October 1941. He spent quiet sometime in a hospital and while recovering he was assigned to rear area postings, including time attached to the 1st Supplementary *Fallschirmjäger Regiment* in Braunschweig. In May 1944, he became supply officer in the 1st *Fallschirmjäger Division* in Italy.

There are other reports that state Hagl was killed in action on 28th July 1944. However other sources such as the German military cemeteries and the author Veit Scherzer state that Hagl died on 29th April 1945. What is certain is that he is buried at the German Military Cemetery at Costermano, Italy (Section 2, Grave 554). There are other sources that say that Hagl was murdered by Italian partisans near San Vito di Leguzzano, Italy.

OTHER AWARDS		PROMOTIONS	
02.10.1936	Armed Forces Long Service Award 4th Class	01.10.1933	Oberschütze
00.00.1937	Parachutist Badge	01.10.1934	Unteroffizier
13.10.1939	Iron Cross 2nd Class	01.10.1937	Feldwebel
00.10.1939	Commemorative Medal of 1st October 1938 + Bar	01.12.1938	Oberfeldwebel
22.05.1940	Wound Badge in Black	16.08.1940	Offiziersanwärter
05.07.1941	Wound Badge in Silver	01.11.1940	Leutnant
09.07.1941	Iron Cross 1st Class	16.01.1941	Oberleutnant der Reserve
20.05.1943	Kreta Cuff title	01.05.1943	Hauptmann der Reserve

REINO HAMER

(29.08.1918 – 24.07.1992)   *Major*

(Wehrkundearchiv)

Knight's Cross: Awarded on 5th September 1944 as *Hauptmann* and Commander 1st *Fallschirmjäger* Regiment for actions in France. In June 1944, he took command of the newly-formed 1st Battalion of the 7th *Fallschirmjäger* Regiment in Brest, France, where he led his battalion in a counterattack which eliminated an enemy penetration. However, within fourteen days of receiving his Knight's Cross he was captured by American forces at Brest and remained a prisoner of the Allies until 20th March 1946.

Reino Hamer was born on 29th August 1916 in Rastede near Oldenburg. He joined the Luftwaffe in December 1936, and served with the anti-aircraft units. He was commissioned as *Leutnant* in March 1939 and served as a battery commander in the 32nd Anti-Aircraft Regiment during the campaign in Norway. In November, he became a company commander in the battalion and saw action in Leningrad before taking command of an anti-tank company of the 100th Luftwaffe Field Battalion on the southern sector of the Eastern Front in December 1942.

Hamer was promoted to *Hauptmann* on 1st October 1943, and returned to the Eastern Front less than two months later and fought in several defensive battles along the Dnepr, Bug and Dniester Rivers. While still in Russia he became commander of the 1st Battalion of the 6th *Fallschirmjäger* Regiment in March 1944. He later assumed command of a battle group composed of the remnants of the regiment. In May he took command of the newly-formed 1st Battalion of the 7th *Fallschirmjäger* Regiment and now found himself deployed to Brest, France where he was awarded the German Cross in Gold for his leadership, and was promoted to *Major* in August. He continued to lead his men with great distinction and was awarded the Knight's Cross in September. Hamer was taken prisoner by the Americans when Brest fell on 19th September. After the war he joined the German army in 1956, and became an *Oberst* and retired in 1977. He died on 24th July 1992 in Ubstadt near Bruchsal in Baden.

OTHER AWARDS		PROMOTIONS	
01.12.1940	Armed Forces Long Service Award 4th Class	01.06.1937	Fahnenjunker-Unteroffizier
00.00.1941	Parachutist Badge	01.12.1937	Fähnrich
01.12.1941	Iron Cross 2nd Class	01.10.1938	Oberfähnrich
00.00.1942	Eastern Front Medal	01.03.1939	Leutnant
00.00.1942	Luftwaffe Ground Assault Badge	01.03.1941	Oberleutnant
01.02.1943	Iron Cross 1st Class	01.10.1943	Hauptmann
12.07.1944	German Cross in Gold	01.08.1944	Major
00.00.194_	Wound Badge in Silver	-----	-----

FRIEDRICH HAUBER

(01.03.1916 – 04.10.1944) *Hauptmann*

(Wehrkundearchiv)

Knight's Cross: Awarded on 5th September 1944 as *Hauptmann* and Commander II Battalion, 12th *Fallschirmjäger* Assault Regiment for actions in Italy. As part of Battle Group *Gericke,* he saw action during the encirclement of the enemy in the Anazio-Nettuno Pocket. In early-September he was involved in the heavy fighting against a vastly superior enemy and he distinguished himself during the fighting. A few days after receiving the Knight's Cross, Hauber was mentioned in the Armed Forces Communiqué of 24th September.

Friedrich Hauber was born on 1st March 1916 in Feuerbach, Stuttgart and joined the 9th Anti-Aircraft Regiment in April 1936 and two years later was transferred to the 1st Special Purpose Bomber Group. On 1st January 1938, he went to the large military flying school in Fassberg where he spent six months training to be a pilot. He was transferred, in January 1939, to the Parachute Assault Regiment and saw action during the invasion of Holland. During the winter of 1941-1942, he fought on the Neva where he was awarded the Iron Cross 1st Class.

In December 1943, he was named commanding officer of the II Battalion of the 12th Parachute Assault Regiment. In mid-1944, he transferred to Italy and was attached to Battle Group Gericke and saw heavy action. He went onto see further action in the approaches to Bologna and in the Po Plain. His battalion was encircled by the enemy, but was later freed by mortar fire. Hauber took some leave and on the way to the assembly point the driver of his car failed to see a closed railway barrier in the darkness and collided with it. Hauptmann Hauber was killed instantly. He rests today in the military cemetery in Costermano, Italy: Block 12, Grave 864.

OTHER AWARDS		PROMOTIONS		
00.00.1938	Parachutist Badge	24.02.1938	Leutnant	
06.04.1940	Armed Forces Long Service Award 4th Class	22.06.1940	Oberleutnant	
10.12.1941	Iron Cross 2nd Class	24.08.1942	Hauptmann	
05.01.1942	Iron Cross 1st Class	-----	-----	
00.09.1942	Eastern Front Medal	-----	-----	
00.00.1943	Luftwaffe Ground Assault Badge	-----	-----	
01.01.1945	German Cross in Gold	-----	-----	

RICHARD "ARNO" HEIDRICH

(28.07.1896 – 22.12.1947)   *General der Fallschirmtruppe*

(Author's Collection)

Knight's Cross: Awarded on 14th June 1941 as *Oberst* and Commander 3rd *Fallschirmjäger* Regiment, 7th Air Division for his part in the airborne invasion of Crete. At first the landing by troops under his command didn't go well as he found his command was scattered over a large area. His troops suffered heavy losses and were surrounded by New Zealand and Greek forces. He was rescued by German mountain troops under the command of *Oberst* Willibald Utz on the night of 24th-25th May, with Heidrich's command continuing its advance on Canea. Heidrich was presented with his Knight's Cross by Hitler at *Führer* Headquarters Wolfs Lair, Rastenburg on 18th July 1941.

Knight's Cross with Oakleaves: On 5th February 1944, Heidrich became the 382nd recipient of the Oakleaves as *Generalleutnant* and Commander 1st *Fallschirmjäger* Division, XIV Army Corps for actions in Italy and North Africa. For seven days his division fought against the British 8th Army in Africa where he inflicted great losses on British General Montgomery. When he was presented with the Oakleaves Heidrich said, *"every man in my division has earned this award."*

Knight's Cross with Oakleaves and Swords: Awarded on 25th March 1944, as *Generalleutnant,* becoming the 55th recipient as the Commanding General of the 1st *Fallschirmjäger* Division, XIV Army Corps for actions during the heavy fighting near Monte Cassino. Heidrich continued to see heavy action with his division and was mentioned in the Official Wehrmacht Daily Communiqué of the 19th June 1944, when he was thanked for his tough defence around the Monte Cassino area. He was presented with his Swords by Hitler on 31st August 1944 at Rastenburg.

Richard Heidrich was born on 27th July 1896, in Lewalde, Saxony and volunteered for active service at the beginning of World War I. He served on the Western Front with the 101st Reserve Infantry Regiment. He went on to serve as a Platoon Leader and won the Iron Cross 1st and 2nd Classes. After the war he was taken into the Reichswehr and served as a Platoon Leader in a number of different regiments before becoming a staff officer in August 1924. In February 1931, after being promoted to *Hauptmann* he took over as Company Commander in the 10th Infantry Regiment. He was appointed a tactics instructor at the Infantry School in Dresden in September 1934; he later served at the War Schools at Potsdam and Munich between October 1935 and October 1937. In June 1938 Heidrich commanded a parachute battalion that he had formed while an instructor in Munich. In January 1939, he was transferred to the Luftwaffe with the rank of *Oberstleutnant* and appointed commander of the 1st *Fallschirmjäger* Regiment. In February he was appointed Operations Officer with the 7th Air Division, under the command of *Generalmajor* Kurt Student, before being assigned to the staff of Hermann Göring in June. On 1st October 1939, he was transferred back to the army and served with 10th Infantry Replacement Battalion in Dresden, here he trained new recruits.

In February 1940, he commanded the 514th Infantry Regiment, part of the 194th Infantry Division which stayed in reserve during most of the French Campaign. He hated this time and wanted to get into the war. In April, he was promoted to *Oberst* and towards the end of May he finally saw some action. In June he transferred back to the Luftwaffe and was appointed commander of the 3rd *Fallschirmjäger* Regiment. For the planned invasion of England (Operation Sealion), his division was assigned drop zones in the areas of Lyming, Sellinge and Hythe as part of *Generaloberst* Busch's 16th Army, and was tasked with the capture of the high ground around Folkestone. When the invasion was called off, after months of training, the 7th Air Division was assigned to Greece. In May 1941, *General der Flieger* Student's 11th Air Corps started the invasion of Crete with a large air drop from gliders; Heidrich's regiment dropped southwest of Canea. The landing didn't go well and his command was scattered over a large area, by the end of the day his troops had suffered heavy losses and had been surrounded by New Zealand and Greek forces. He was rescued by German mountain troops under the command of *Oberst* Willibald Utz on the night of 24th-25th May. Heidrich then continued the advance, and his initial landing and defence against the strong Allied opposition earned him the Knight's Cross. By June the last British troops who had not been evacuated surrendered to the German forces.

Generalmajor Richard Heidrich reviews troops of the Fallschirmjäger together with General der Fallschirmtruppe Kurt Student. (Author's Collection)

In September 1941, the 7th Air Division was transferred to Russia, along with Heidrich's regiment, where it saw heavy combat near Leningrad until January 1942 when it was withdrawn from Russia. On 1st August Heidrich was given temporary command of the 7th Air Division and promoted to *Generalmajor*. He returned to Russia in October, in the central sector of the front, seeing action near Smolensk, Rzhev and Orel until its withdrawal to France in early-1943. On 1st May, the 7th Air Division was re-designated the 1st *Fallschirmjäger* Division while undergoing refitting in the south of France. By mid-July 1943, Heidrich now with the rank of *Generalleutnant* led his troops into Sicily to help the German forces there following the Allied invasion. However, after heavy combat the division was evacuated to the mainland, and when the British landed at

Taranto on 9th September Heidrich realising his command was outnumbered and in need of reinforcements decided to withdraw his division northwards beyond Foggia. He continued to lead his division along the Adriatic coast until early February 1944 when it was transferred to the critical Monte Cassino sector. Over the next few months the Allies suffered heavy casualties while trying to displace the German forces in the mountains defences. Heidrich was awarded the Knight's Cross with Oakleaves in February for his leadership and the part his troops played in the prevention of a British breakthrough. The Battle for Cassino went on and on, Heidrich continued to prove his worth as a divisional commander, he was mentioned in the Official German Communiqué of 25th March 1944 on the same day he was awarded the Knight's Cross with Oakleaves and Swords.

In May 1944, the Allies finally won the battle at Monte Cassino and captured Rome in June, and only then did the Germans start to withdraw. Heidrich was transferred to the Gothic Line defences along the Adriatic Coast and when the Allies broke through these defences his command withdrew to Imola. In October, he was promoted to *General der Fallschirmtruppe* and a month later was appointed Commanding General of the 1st Parachute Corps in Italy, succeeding *General der Fallschirmtruppe* Alfred Schlemm. In April 1945, the Allies launched what would be their final offensive in Italy. By the end of the month the 10th Army, under the command *of General der Panzertruppe* Traugott Heer, which included the 1st *Fallschirmjäger* Corps, had been pushed back by the British 8th Army to the Italian-Yugoslav border.

By the beginning of May, the end for Germany was in sight and on 3rd May Heidrich surrendered to the Americans. He was later handed over to the British. He spent time in various prison camps including the famous Long Cage and Island Farm Special Camp. On 16th January 1947 he was transferred to hospital where he died on 22nd December in Hamburg-Bergedorf, completely exhausted by nearly six years of fighting.

OTHER AWARDS		PROMOTIONS	
00.00.191_	Iron Cross 2nd Class	18.08.1914	Kriegsfreiwilliger
00.00.191_	Iron Cross 1st Class	17.11.1914	Gefreiter
00.00.191_	Knight's Cross of the Royal Saxony Albert Order 2nd Class + Swords	18.05.1915	Unteroffizier
00.00.191_	Knight's Cross of the Royal Saxony Service Order 2nd Class + Swords	14.07.1915	Fähnrich
00.00.1917	Wound Badge in Black	20.08.1915	Leutnant
00.00.1935	Cross of Honour for Frontline Combatants	31.07.1925	Oberleutnant
02.10.1936	Armed Forces Long Service Award 4th to 1st Class	01.02.1931	Hauptmann
20.06.1939	Commemorative Medal of 1st October 1938 + Bar	18.01.1936	Major
25.05.1941	Bar to the Iron Cross 2nd Class	23.12.1938	Major (Luftwaffe)
25.05.1941	Bar to the Iron Cross 1st Class	01.01.1939	Oberstleutnant
31.03.1942	German Cross in Gold	20.04.1940	Oberst
00.00.1943	KRETA Cuff title	04.08.1942	Generalmajor
12.12.1943	Parachutist Badge	01.07.1943	Generalleutnant
-----	-----	31.10.1944	General der Fallschirmtruppe

SEBASTIAN LUDWIG HEILMANN

(09.08.1903 – 26.10.1959) *Generalmajor*

(Author's Collection)

Knight's Cross: Awarded on 14th June 1941 as *Major* and Commander III Battalion, 3rd *Fallschirmjäger* Regiment for actions in Crete. During the assault on Crete his parachute battalion suffered heavy losses and only one company landed on target, the other three were scattered around – one landed in a reservoir. However Heilmann showed great leadership qualities and he succeeded in rallying his troops who went on to play a major role in the German success on the island.

Knight's Cross with Oakleaves: For actions at Monte Cassino as *Oberst* and Commander III Battalion, 3rd *Fallschirmjäger* Regiment he became the 412th recipient of the Oakleaves on 2nd March 1944. He led his battalion during the heavy fighting near Francoforte and Centuripe near Regalbuto, Bronte and Maletto, and was awarded it for his great skills in leadership. In January his regiment again saw heavy action in Sicily and Italy as well as the tough defensive fighting in Monte Cassino.

Knight's Cross with Oakleaves and Swords: He became the 67th recipient of the Swords on 15th May 1944, as an *Oberst*, while still commanding the 3rd Battalion, 3rd *Fallschirmjäger* Regiment for continued actions at Monte Cassino. During the second major battle Heilmann led his troops with great skill against a tough enemy, he used every resource he had at his disposal and managed to support the German troops with accurate mortar and artillery fire. The British commander in Italy, General Alexander said of Heilmanns' troops, *"… I doubt if there is another force in the world that could fight with such ferocity as these troops."* Heilmann was finally presented with his Swords by Hitler on 31st August 1944, during the same ceremony as *Generalleutnant* Richard Heidrich.

Ludwig Heilmann became one of the most famous German parachute commanders of World War II, and one of the most decorated. He was born on 9th August 1903 in Würzburg and joined the Reichswehr at the age of seventeen spending the next twelve years as an enlisted man. He was commissioned in July 1934 and appointed commander of the 5th Company of the 20th Infantry Regiment. He saw action during the invasion of Poland where he won the Iron Cross 2nd Class and was awarded the Iron Cross 1st Class during the French Campaign.

In November, he was appointed commander of the 5th Fallschirmjäger Division and led them during the Ardennes Offensive where his troops suffered heavy losses while fighting on the German southern flank. In December, he was promoted to Generalmajor and in March 1945 he was captured by U.S. troops. He spent time in various prison camps, being transferred in May 1946 to the London Cage prison camp, and was described by the British as an ardent Nazi. Heilmann was released in August 1947 and returned to Germany. He died on 26th October 1959, in Kempten, Allgäu. (Author's Collection)

In June 1940, he was sent on a Parachute-rifleman's course in Wittstock, and a few weeks later he took over as commander of the 3rd Battalion of the 423rd Infantry Regiment. He transferred to the Luftwaffe in August 1940 with the rank of *Major* and was appointed commander of the 3rd Battalion of the 3rd *Fallschirmjäger* Regiment. In May 1941, he took part in the first assault on Crete and his command suffered heavy casualties and only one company managed to land on target, while the others were scattered with one company landing in a reservoir. But his troops fought with great bravery and played a vital role in the German victory. As a result Heilmann was awarded the Knight's Cross on 14th June 1941 for his part in the victory.

In the autumn of 1941 Heilmann and his troops were sent to Russia where they fought as infantry. They fought with much bravery and took part in the defence of the blood-soaked Vyborgskaya Bridgehead. In April 1942, Heilmann was promoted to *Oberstleutnant* and in November was appointed commander of the 3rd *Fallschirmjäger* Regiment. After the Allies landed in Sicily his regiment parachuted into the Catania Plain to reinforce the German troops there, who were part of the elite Hermann Göring Panzer Division. His command fought near Francoforte and Centuripe near Regalbuto, Bronte and Maletto.

In January 1944, Helmann's regiment continued to see action in Sicily and on the mainland during the tough defensive battles at Monte Cassino. On 2nd March, he became the 412th recipient of the Knight's Cross with Oakleaves. At Cassino his regiment was considered the anchor of the Cassino defence, and using every resource at his disposal, he managed to support his Battalion commanders with accurate mortar and artillery fire. His leadership and bravery was once again recognized when he was awarded the Knight's Cross with Oakleaves and Swords on 15th May 1944, to become the 67th recipient.

OTHER AWARDS		PROMOTIONS	
02.10.1936	Armed Forces Long Service Award 4th to 3rd Class	01.11.1924	Oberschütze
02.10.1939	Armed Forces Long Service Award 2nd Class	01.12.1924	Gefreiter
02.10.1939	Iron Cross 2nd Class	10.12.1924	Unteroffizier-Anwärter
00.00.1940	Parachutist Badge	01.05.1925	Unteroffizier
14.06.1941	Iron Cross 1st Class	01.10.1927	Unterfeldwebel
00.00.194_	Wound Badge in Black	01.07.1929	Feldwebel
26.02.1942	German Cross in Gold	01.07.1934	Leutnant
00.00.1942	Luftwaffe Ground Assault Badge	02.02.1935	Oberleutnant
20.05.1943	KRETA Cuff title	01.12.1935	Hauptmann
-----	-----	25.10.1940	Hauptmann (Luftwaffe)
-----	-----	27.10.1940	Major
-----	-----	20.04.1942	Oberstleutnant
-----	-----	01.12.1943	Oberst
-----	-----	03.01.1945	Generalmajor

ERICH HELLMANN
(13.02.1916 – 24.01.1998)   *Oberleutnant*

(Author's Collection)

Knight's Cross: Awarded on 30th September 1944 as *Leutnant* and *Führer* 1st Company, 3rd *Fallschirmjäger* Regiment in recognition of his outstanding leadership in Italy.

Erich Hellmann was born on 13th February 1916 in Zollerndorf near Eckersberg in Johannisburg, Germany. He joined the 1st Anti-Aircraft Regiment on 17th March 1938 and saw little action until his transfer to the 3rd *Fallschirmjäger* Regiment in November 1943. He saw action in Russia, as company commander and was promoted to *Leutnant* in recognition of his bravery and leadership during the numerous reconnaissance and combat patrols he led, in raids and defensive actions and was awarded the German Cross in Gold.

During the fighting at Cassino, Hellmann served in the 1st *Fallschirmjäger* Division which was deployed to help with the defence. He served as part of Battle Group Schulz and defended the high area around the monastery to Hill 593, Calvary Mountain. After February 18th, the Schulz Regiment was located between the 4th *Fallschirmjäger* Regiment and the sector held by the 5th Mountain Infantry Division. At the start of the Third Battle of Cassino the 1st *Fallschirmjäger* Regiment was kept in reserve but later had to be deployed south of the Via Casilina to guard the division's flank. The men of the 1st *Fallschirmjäger* Division fought a defensive battle between Aquino and Monet Cassino against the British 6th Armoured Division and the 3rd Battalion of the Grenadier Guards until 24th May 1944. During this time Hellmann and his company took part in the bitter defensive fighting and covered the retreat by LI Mountain Corps. Hellmann's leadership, courage and decisiveness stood out and he was recommended for the Knight's Cross.

He was promoted to *Oberleutnant* on 1st January 1945 and was taken prisoner by the British at the end of the war while in Italy. He died on 24th January 1998 in Dortmund, Germany.

OTHER AWARDS		PROMOTIONS	
00.00.1943	Luftwaffe Ground Assault Badge	00.00.1943	Oberfeldwebel
17.03.1943	Iron Cross 2nd Class	01.11.1943	Leutnant
12.07.1943	German Cross in Gold	01.01.1945	Oberleutnant
18.01.1944	Iron Cross 1st Class	-----	-----
00.00.194_	Wound Badge in Silver	-----	-----

HARRY HERRMANN

(27.05.1909 – 12.03.1995) *Oberst*

(Wehrkundearchiv)

Knight's Cross: Awarded on 9th July 1941 as *Oberleutnant* and Commander 5th Company, 1st *Fallschirmjäger* Regiment for actions during the invasion of Crete. Upon landing in Crete he was temporarily blinded and despite this he managed to guide his company to their objective, the airfield which they quickly secured.

Harry Herrmann was born in Berlin on 27th May 1909 and joined the Berlin police in April 1930 and three years later he transferred to the 1st Company of the Police Battalion Wecke. When his unit became part of the Luftwaffe in January 1934, Herrmann became a member of 1st Company of the *General Göring* State Police Group. By October 1937 he had become an adjutant of the I Battalion of the *General Göring* Regiment and had been promoted to *Oberleutnant*. In January 1939, he became adjutant of the 1st *Fallschirmjäger* Regiment and in August was appointed Ordnance Officer at the headquarters of the 7th Air Division.

His first action of World War II was the airborne invasion of Holland, where he won the Iron Cross 1st and 2nd Classes. He then took part in the airborne invasion of Crete. Herrmann parachuted into Crete with his company and upon landing was wounded in the head while hanging beneath his parachute and was temporarily blinded. His company had landed near its objective and his senior NCO *Hauptfeldwebel* Alfred Kurth took temporary command of the company. Herrmann although severely handicapped by his blindness was guided to the company's objective and when Kurth was killed Herrmann took command once again. With his sight slowly returning Herrmann was an inspiration to his men and his company reached their target of the airfield which they quickly secured. For this he was awarded the Knight's Cross.

After his success in Crete he was transferred to the XI Air Corps as Operations Officer and later led the Parachute Instruction Regiment in action near Anzio-Nettuno. In January 1945, he was made Commander of Parachute Panzer Brigade "*Herrmann*" and from 19th April until the end of the war he was temporary commander of the 9th *Fallschirmjäger* Division. He was captured by Soviet forces on 2nd May 1945 and held in captivity until the October 1955. He joined the Bundeswehr in May 1957 and retired as an *Oberst* in September 1967. He died on 12th March 1995 in Altenstadt, Schongau.

OTHER AWARDS		PROMOTIONS	
00.00.1937	Parachutist Badge	03.04.1929	Polizeianwärter
02.10.1939	Armed Forces Long Service Award 4th Class	01.04.1930	Gefreiter der Schutzpolizei
00.11.1939	Commemorative Medal of 1st October 1938 + Bar	00.00.1931	Obergefreiter der Schutzpolizei
22.05.1940	Iron Cross 2nd Class	01.10.1935	Leutnant (Luftwaffe)
22.05.1940	Iron Cross 1st Class	01.01.1938	Oberleutnant
00.00.1942	Wound Badge in Black	25.07.1941	Hauptmann
00.00.194_	Luftwaffe Marksman Lanyard	01.04.1942	Major
00.00.1943	KRETA Cuff title	01.08.1944	Oberstleutnant
-----	-----	01.04.1945	Oberst

MAX HERZBACH

(17.01.1914 – 02.05.2002)   *Major*

(Wehrkundearchiv)

Knight's Cross: Awarded on 13th September 1944 as *Hauptmann* and Commander 7th Company, 7th *Fallschirmjäger* Regiment for his leadership and skill during the fierce fighting while defending Fortress Brest.

Max Herzbach was born on 17th January 1914 in Drewitz, Tltow and joined the 9th Prussian Infantry Regiment "Potsdam" in November 1932. Six years later he transferred to the army's parachute-rifle battalion and in October was transferred to the 5th Company of the 1st *Fallschirmjäger* Regiment.

He saw action during the Polish Campaign and in Holland. In February 1942, he joined the 6th Company of the 2nd *Fallschirmjäger* Regiment as a Platoon Leader, and was wounded after heavy fighting in Crete in May. Under the command of *Oberst* Sturm he jumped at the Corinth Canal and on 25th June 1941 he won the Iron Cross 1st Class. Exactly a month earlier he had been wounded after the heavy fighting in Crete and did not return to his until October 1942. He then became a Platoon Leader in the 8th Company of the 2nd *Fallschirmjäger* Regiment and was promoted to *Oberleutnant* in November. His regiment now fought as part of the 2nd *Fallschirmjäger* Division under *Generalleutnant* Ramcke in Russia between Kiev and Kirovograd. Herzbach was appointed commander of the 10th Company of the 2nd *Fallschirmjäger* Regiment in July 1943 and a year later he received early promotion to *Hauptmann* for bravery. Herzbach was then transferred to Normandy where he led his company during the heavy fighting and during the approaches to Brest and in the fortress itself. The Americans were pushed back near Huelgoat, losing thirty-two tanks. However, during the course of the fighting the II Battalion of the 7th *Fallschirmjäger* Regiment was overrun by the enemy but were freed in a daring raid by *Leutnant* Erich Lepkowski. Herzbach led his company with great skill and defended Fortress Brest with great determination – so much so that he was seriously wounded during the fighting. Less than a week after the award of the Knight's Cross, Herzbach was captured by the Americans; he remained in captivity until March 1946. He died in Cologne on 2nd May 2002 at the age of eighty-eight.

OTHER AWARDS		PROMOTIONS	
02.10.1936	Armed Forces Long Service Award 4th Class	00.00.1933	Gefreiter
30.06.1938	Parachutist Badge	00.00.1935	Unteroffizier
30.04.1941	Iron Cross 2nd Class	00.00.1936	Feldwebel
25.06.1941	Iron Cross 1st Class	00.00.1938	Oberfeldwebel
01.03.1942	KRETA Cuff title	01.08.1942	Leutnant
01.04.1943	Luftwaffe Ground Assault Badge	01.11.1942	Oberleutnant
23.07.1944	German Cross in Gold	01.11.1943	Hauptmann
15.08.1944	Wound Badge in Silver	01.09.1944	Major

DR. JUR. FRIEDRICH-AUGUST FREIHERR VON DER HEYDTE

(30.03.1907 – 07.07.1994)   **Oberstleutnant**

(Author's Collection)

Knight's Cross: Awarded on 9th July 1941 as *Hauptmann* and Commander 1st Battalion, 3rd *Fallschirmjäger* Regiment, in recognition of his leadership and in being the first battalion to enter Canea during the invasion of Crete.

Knight's Cross with Oakleaves: He became the 617th recipient of the Oakleaves on 30th September 1944 as *Oberstleutnant* and Commander 6th *Fallschirmjäger* Regiment for his success during the fighting near Normandy and for his achievements at Carentan, Coutances and Falaise where his regiment destroyed 250 Allied tanks.

Friedrich-August von der Heydte was born in Munich on 30th March 1907, in a noble family and was a cousin of Claus von Stauffenberg, the officer who planted the bomb at Hitler's headquarters on 20th July 1944. His father enjoyed a successful career with the Royal Bavarian Army and served with distinction in World War I. His mother emigrated from France and the family were stout Roman Catholic. Friedrich attended a Munich Catholic School and achieved excellent grades. After his schooling he joined the *Reichswehr* and after an unsuccessful application to join the cavalry he was posted to the 19th Infantry Regiment in April 1925.

In 1927, he was released from military service to attend Innsbruck University where he studied law and economics. During this time he became a private tutor to help to pay for his university fees, his family, although of noble status were in financial difficulties. After he graduated he travelled to Berlin and a year later he secured a posting to a diplomatic school in Vienna. In 1933, he entered the Nazi Party and joined the SA. In early-1935, he re-joined the *Reichswehr* and transferred to the 15th Cavalry Regiment and the following year he was commissioned as a *Leutnant*. He again secured his temporary release from military service and travelled to the Netherlands where he continued his education at The Hague.

In April 1937, he assumed command of the 2nd Company of the 6th Anti-tank Battalion with the rank of *Oberleutnant*. He didn't see action during the Polish Campaign but he served as an Ordnance Officer with the 246th Infantry Division during the Western Campaign. In May 1940, he was promoted to *Hauptmann* and at the same time he transferred to the Luftwaffe and underwent training as a paratrooper. He joined the 3rd *Fallschirmjäger* Regiment where he became a company commander. In May 1941, he took part in the airborne invasion of Crete while commanding the 1st Battalion of the 3rd *Fallschirmjäger* Regiment. It was here that he proved himself a capable commander and was awarded the Knight's Cross. In July 1942, he was promoted to *Major* and transferred to North Africa as commander of the elite Parachute Training Battalion. It was an integral part of Parachute Brigade Ramcke, and he remained with this unit until February 1943 when he and his officers were transferred to France to form the nucleus of the new 2nd *Fallschirmjäger* Division. Here Heydte became the Operations Officer serving once again under General Ramcke.

After the fall of Sicily during the summer of 1943, the Germans grew more and more suspicious of an Italian defection to the Allies. To counter this, the 2nd *Fallschirmjäger* Division was transferred to Rome. On 8th September, Italy decided to break its alliance with Nazi Germany and join the Allies. The Germans then started to disarm and disband all units of the Royal Italian Army, Navy and Air Force. The 2nd *Fallschirmjäger* Division was given orders to capture key positions in Rome. By 11th September the whole of Rome was under German control. The following day, Heydte was sent on a mission that required him to fly out of Rome, but unfortunately the aircraft crashed and Heydte was seriously wounded. In January 1944, once he had recovered from his wounds he was given command of the newly formed 6th *Fallschirmjäger* Regiment. The unit was formed from veteran paratroopers and Luftwaffe personnel and the average age was seventeen and it had a combined strength of 3,457 men and by June this had risen to over 4,500 men.

In 1951, von der Heydte became professor of constitutional and international law at the University of Mainz. He was also a judge at the Administrative Court at Rhineland-Palatinate. From 1953 to 1954, he was a visiting professor at the University of Saarland. He later headed the Institute for Military Law and Political Science at the University of Würzburg. From 1956 to 1971, he was an associate and a member of the Institute de Droit International. Parallel to his academic career, von der Heydte also continued with a post-war military career in the Bundeswehr and ended his career with the rank of Brigadegeneral der Reserve. He died in Aham, Landshut on 7th July 1994, after a long illness. (Wehrkundearchiv)

By the time of D-Day when the Allies launched their invasion of Europe, the 6th Paratroop Regiment had been detached as a third regiment to the newly formed 91st Air Landing Infantry Division and had been deployed in the Carentan area of the Cotentin Peninsula. About 500 U.S. paratroopers dropped southwest of Carentan, and Heydte's troops were there to meet them, the fighting went on all night. On 7th June, after fighting a combined assault of U.S. paratroopers and tanks most of the day, the battalion was destroyed. About 300 men surrendered. Only twenty-five reached Carentan. The 2nd Battalion found Saint-Mère-Eglise held by the U.S. 507th Infantry Regiment, and Heydte could see the vast Allied invasion armada just a few miles away. After heavy fighting the 2nd and 3rd battalions were withdrawn into Carentan. Heydte was told by *Generalfeldmarschall* Rommel to hold Carentan to the last man as it was the critical junction between Utah Beach and Omaha Beach. On 10th June, U.S. troops entered the outskirts of Carentan, and by the morning of the following day they were fighting house to house. On 12th June, the Germans tried to retake the town but this failed. Heydte's regiment was involved in the intense fighting and defended every inch of ground to the last man. On 22nd June, Heydte's 6th *Fallschirmjäger* Regiment was mentioned in the Official Armed Forces Communiqué of the day. On 6th August the 6th *Fallschirmjäger* Regiment participated in Operation Lüttich, the disastrous Mortain counterattack which attempted to cut off the Allies advance. The German 7th Army was subsequently encircled at Falaise Pocket, which was the final battle of the Normandy Campaign.

In September 1944, Heydte's unit was involved in defending the German lines in the Netherlands against the Allied forces attacking during Operation Market Garden. Heydte later saw action during the Ardennes Offensive in December, when he led a battle group of some 1,200 men. His unit was tasked with dropping at night onto a strategic road junction north of Malmédy and to hold it for twenty-four hours until relieved by the 12th SS-Panzer Division. However, things didn't go to plan. Heydte's men missed the drop zone and only around 125 men made it to the correct landing site, with no heavy weapons. Eventually, 300 men were gathered from the surrounding woods, but without sufficient forces, the task of capturing the crossroads to delay the American advance was abandoned. However because of the dispersal of the drop, the Americans thought that a whole division had landed and this caused them to secure the rear instead of facing the main German thrust at the front. For his leadership during this time Heydte was awarded the Knight's Cross with Oakleaves, and became the 617th recipient on 30th September 1944. By this time his forces were cut-off and without supplies he ordered them to breakout through the Allied lines and attempt to reach the German front.

On 21st December 1944, Heydte reached Monschau with a broken arm and sent a message to the Allies that he wanted to surrender. On 24th December he surrendered to US troops along with his men and was taken into captivity. He was held in England until 12th July 1947.

OTHER AWARDS		PROMOTIONS	
02.10.1936	Armed Forces Long Service Award 4th Class	01.04.1925	Offiziersanwärter
01.04.1937	Armed Forces Long Service Award 3rd Class	30.09.1926	Fahnenjunker-Unteroffizier
27.09.1939	Iron Cross 2nd Class	01.08.1936	Leutnant
26.09.1940	Iron Cross 1st Class	01.10.1936	Oberleutnant
00.09.1940	Parachutist Badge	01.10.1938	Hauptmann
26.02.1942	German Cross in Gold	01.08.1941	Major
00.08.1942	Eastern Front Medal	01.08.1944	Oberstleutnant
00.00.1942	KRETA Cuff title	-----	-----
00.00.1943	AFRIKA Cuff title	-----	-----

EDUARD GEORG HÜBNER

(16.04.1914 – 01.10.1996) *Hauptmann*

Knight's Cross: Awarded on 17th March 1945 as *Hauptmann* and Commander of an Assault Battalion of the 1st *Fallschirm* Army for his actions on the Western Front. During the heavy defensive fighting in the Wesel-Xanten area his Assault Battalion prevented an enemy breakthrough and the premature loss of the bridgehead. Hübner's actions allowed the German forces to withdraw east across the Rhine.

Hübner joined the Bundeswehr in September 1957, and rose to the rank of Major in August 1958. He retired from duty in September 1968, and died in Altenstadt on 1st October 1996. (Wehrkundearchiv)

(Wehrkundearchiv)

Georg Hüber was born on 16th April 1914 in Hinzweiler, Kusel and joined the 7th Bavarian Motor Transport Battalion on 1st October 1934, and after attending officer school he was assigned to the 5th Anti-aircraft Regiment in Munich. In April 1938, he was transferred to the General Göring Airborne Battalion and later took part in the march into the Sudentland. He transferred to the parachute troops in February 1940 and after his training he was appointed a Platoon Leader in the 1st Company of the 1st *Fallschirmjäger* Regiment in Stendal. He saw action in Poland and at Narvik and won the Iron Cross 1st Class in Crete. Wounded while serving in Russia in November 1941, he was assigned to the 16th Company of the 1st *Fallschirmjäger* Regiment in December and later became adjutant of the 1st Battalion of the 4th *Fallschirmjäger* Regiment. In July 194, he became commander of the 11th Company and in November was promoted to Oberleutnant. He then served a second tour on the Russian Front in the area around Smolensk. In Sicily he won the German Cross in Gold and participated in the battles from Reggio to Cassino. He was captured by British troops on 8th May 1945 and remained a prisoner until 31st July 1947

OTHER AWARDS		PROMOTIONS	
01.10.1939	Armed Forces Long Service Award 4th Class	01.04.1935	Fahnenjunker
00.03.1940	Parachutist Badge	20.04.1937	Leutnant
29.05.1941	Iron Cross 2nd Class	01.11.1942	Oberleutnant
30.06.1941	Iron Cross 1st Class	10.05.1944	Hauptmann
14.08.1941	Narvik Campaign Shield	-----	-----
15.12.1941	Wound Badge in Black	-----	-----
22.07.1942	Eastern Front Medal	-----	-----
20.09.1942	Luftwaffe Ground Assault Badge	-----	-----
20.05.1943	KRETA Cuff title	-----	-----
21.06.1943	German Cross in Gold	-----	-----
20.04.1945	Army Close Combat Clasp in Bronze	-----	-----

DR. ROLF KARL ERNST JÄGER

(01.11.1912 – 06.01.1984)   *Oberstabsarzt*

Knight's Cross: Awarded as *Oberarzt* and Troop doctor in the Air-Landing Assault Battalion *Koch* on 15th May 1940, in recognition of his bravery and skill during the attack of Belgium and France

Rolf Jäger was born on 1st November 1912 in Klein Kunterstein near Graudenz and joined the 6th Prussian First-aid Battalion of the 6th Infantry Division in September 1934. After attending the Berlin Military Medical Academy in

Rolf Jäger wearing his white summer uniform. (Wehrkundearchiv)

(Wehrkundearchiv)

November/December he transferred to the Luftwaffe a year later. He served at the Berlin-Gatow School of Air Warfare from February until March 1936. In January 1937 he joined the 6th Air District First-aid Battalion in Münster.

In February 1940, he transferred to the Air-Landing Assault Battalion Koch and saw action in France and Belgium, where he took part in the airborne assault on the Albert Canal bridges. Immediately after landing with the battalion he set about treating those paratroopers who had been injured upon landing or wounded in the air. Jäger and his medical team successfully recovered the bodies of seven men who had been killed and treated twenty-four wounded, under extremely heavy fire and at great personal risk. During the airborne attack on Crete he served as a battalion medical officer and continued to save lives in Russia and in Italy, where he was director of Tarvis Military Hospital. He was taken prisoner by the British on 8th May 1945 and was released in January 1947.

OTHER AWARDS		PROMOTIONS	
00.00.193_	Parachutist Badge	01.10.1935	Fahnenjunker-Gefreiter
15.09.1939	Armed Forces Long Service Award 4th Class	01.11.1935	Fahnenjunker-Unteroffizier
12.05.1940	Iron Cross 2nd Class	01.08.1936	Fähnrich
13.05.1940	Iron Cross 1st Class	05.01.1938	Unterarzt
00.00.194_	NSFK Large Glider Pilots Badge	16.02.1939	Assistenzarzt
-----	-----	30.09.1939	Oberarzt
-----	-----	20.05.1940	Stabsarzt
-----	-----	24.08.1942	Oberstabsarzt

SIEGFRIED JAMROWSKI

(01.11.1917 – 03.09.2012)   *Major*

(Wehrkundearchiv)

Knight's Cross: Awarded on 9th June 1944 as *Oberleutnant* and Commander 6th Company, 3rd *Fallschirmjäger* Regiment for actions in Cassino.

Siegfried Jamrowski was born in Angerapp on 1st November 1917 and joined the I (Light Infantry) Battalion of the 2nd Infantry Regiment in East Prussia in October 1936, before leaving military service, with the rank of *Feldwebel* in 1938 to study forestry.

He was called up at the beginning of the war in September 1939 and was attached to the 2nd Infantry Regiment and served at the infantry school in Döberitz. He was later employed as an infantry instructor, before joining the parachute troops in June 1940. In September, he was appointed Platoon Leader in the 8th Company of the 3rd *Fallschirmjäger* Regiment. He later fought in Russia and in December 1941 he received the Iron Cross 1st Class. In February 1942, he was battalion adjutant of the IV Battalion of the 3rd *Fallschirmjäger* Regiment and then saw action in Monte Cassino. In February 1944, Jamrowski led his company during the bloody battles in Cassino where he relieved the 211th Grenadier Regiment. He led the 6th and 8th Companies of the 3rd *Fallschirmjäger* Regiment simultaneously and while leading the 6th Company he was trapped in the city during an allied bombardment, that last four hours. When the bombardment was over his company had miraculously suffered no losses and they attacked the New Zealanders and held their sector of the city. As a result of this success Jamrowski and his battalion commander, *Major* Froltin was awarded the Knight's Cross. In January 1945, he was made commander of the 3rd Battalion of the 3rd *Fallschirmjäger* Regiment and led this until he was captured on 2nd May 1945.

He remained in British captivity until April 1946. Jamrowski died on 3rd September 2012 in Nepphen, Germany he was ninety-four.

OTHER AWARDS		PROMOTIONS	
25.09.1937	West Wall Medal	01.10.1936	Jäger
01.04.1940	Armed Forces Long Service Award 4th Class	01.10.1937	Gefreiter
25.07.1940	Parachutist Badge	01.06.1938	Oberjäger
31.10.1941	Iron Cross 2nd Class	25.10.1938	Feldwebel der Reserve
01.10.1942	Luftwaffe Ground Assault Badge	01.02.1940	Leutnant
25.12.1942	Iron Cross 1st Class	01.04.1942	Oberleutnant
29.03.1944	German Cross in Gold	01.05.1944	Hauptmann
22.04.1944	Wound Badge in Black	28.03.1945	Major

WILHELM KEMPKE

(15.11.1920 – 19.12.1944) *Oberleutnant*

Left to right: Oberstleutnant Hans Kroh, Feldwebel Wilhelm Kempke and Feldwebel Erich Schüster seen here together shortly after being presented with the Knight's Cross by Reichsmarschall Göring. (Author's Collection)

Knight's Cross: Awarded on 21st August 1941 as *Feldwebel* and Section Leader in the 1st Company, 1st Air Landing Assault Regiment for actions in Crete. During the invasion of Crete Kempke the 1st Company was given the responsibility of eliminating a heavy anti-aircraft battery south of Chania. When *Oberleutnant* Kellner, the platoon leader was killed, Kempke assumed command of the platoon and captured the battery. He was presented with his Knight's Cross from personally from Göring.

Wilhelm Kempke was born on 15th November 1920 in Lalendorf, Güstrow and joined the Luftwaffe as a volunteer in July 1938. He was assigned to the 1st *Fallschirmjäger* Regiment and became a member of the Koch Parachute Assault Battalion and took part in the attack on Eben Emael, where he won the Iron Cross 1st Class. He took part in the invasion of Crete and fought as a member of the Koch Battalion's 1st Company commanded by *Oberleutnant* Genz. When the company commander was killed Kempke took over and his bravery and leadership was awarded with the Knight's Cross and promotion to the rank of *Oberfeldwebel*. He later saw action in Russia where he was promoted to *Leutnant* in August 1942 and a year later to the rank of *Oberleutnant*.

In March 1943, he joined KG 200, a special unit which was to investigate the use of gliders against enemy warships. In November, he became leader of the technical section of the II./KG 200. This was a new unit formed to investigate the use of Go 242W* gliders against enemy warships.

He was killed in an aircraft crash on 2nd December 1944, while flying over Germany. He now lies in the Military Cemetery in Güstrow-Rostock, Block III, Row 4, Grave 28.

Note: The Go 242 gliders were towed into the air by Heinkel He 111s or Junker Ju 52s, and were occasionally fitted with RATO (Rocket Assisted Takeoff) equipment. Most saw service in the Mediterranean, North Africa and Aegean. A few of the glider variants were constructed with a flying boat-style hull allowing water landings. It was proposed that some carry a small catamaran assault boat with 2,600 pound explosive charge suspended between its hulls. The proposed mission profile was for the pilot to land near an enemy ship and transfer to the assault boat, setting off at high speed for the enemy ship and locking the controls before bailing out.

OTHER AWARDS		PROMOTIONS	
02.12.1939	Parachutist Badge	17.08.1940	Feldwebel
17.05.1940	Iron Cross 2nd Class	27.07.1941	Oberfeldwebel
25.05.1940	Iron Cross 1st Class	01.08.1942	Leutnant
00.00.1940	Wound Badge in Black	01.08.1943	Oberleutnant
01.08.1942	Eastern Front Medal	-----	-----
30.05.1943	KRETA Cuff title	-----	-----

HORST KERFIN

(21.03.1913 – 22.01.1943)   *Hauptmann*

(Author's Collection)

Knight's Cross: Awarded on 24th May 1940 as *Oberleutnant* and Platoon Leader in the 11th Company, 1st *Fallschirmjäger* Regiment for actions in Holland.

Horst Kerfin was born on 21st March 1913 in Insterburg and joined the Reichswehr's 12th Infantry Regiment in March 1932, and three years later he transferred to the Luftwaffe. In April 1938, he joined the General *Göring* Airborne Battalion which later became the 3rd *Fallschirmjäger* Regiment. He saw action in Poland as a Feldwebel where he was awarded the Iron Cross 2nd Class, and was promoted to *Oberleutnant*, skipping the rank of *Leutnant*.

During the invasion of Holland, as part of the 1st *Fallschirmjäger* Regiment, he was given a special mission in the battalion's assault on Rotterdam's Waalhaven airport on 10th May 1940. He led his platoon during the attack through the village of Feyenoord and commandeered a streetcar. His men then took the streetcar to their objective where they silenced the anti-aircraft guns, advanced across the Willems Bridge and established a bridgehead until other German troops arrived. For this act Kerfin was awarded the Knight's Cross. Kerfin who had been promoted to *Hauptmann* in August 1941, would later make a name for himself during the fighting in Russia, where he was killed in the fighting near Alexeyevka, Orel on 22nd January 1943.

OTHER AWARDS		PROMOTIONS	
00.04.1936	Armed Forces Long Service Award 4th Class	01.10.1934	Unteroffizier
00.00.1937	Parachutist Badge	01.06.1938	Feldwebel
29.10.1939	Iron Cross 2nd Class	28.12.1939	Oberleutnant
16.05.1940	Iron Cross 1st Class	01.08.1941	Hauptmann
00.09.1942	Eastern Front Medal	-----	-----

HELLMUT KERUTT

(19.08.1916 – 02.09.2000)   *Major*

Knight's Cross: Awarded on 2nd February 1945 as *Major* and Commander *Fallschirmjäger* Battalion *Kerutt* in recognition of his bravery and leadership during the fighting in Holland. In September 1944, his battalion was responsible for pushing back the enemy advance from south of the Meuse. On 17th September, the enemy armoured units broke through the German lines and were pushed back by Kerutt's battalion in some of the bloodiest fighting of the campaign. In October, Kerutt led his battalion during the defensive fighting in the Verbraij area where he was seriously wounded while leading a successful counterattack.

After the war Hellmut Kerutt joined the Bundeswehr, serving from 1966 until 1974 as Deputy Commander of the Air-Landing School in Schongau. He died on 2nd September 2000 in Bornheim. (Wehrkundearchiv)

(Wehrkundearchiv)

Hellmut Kerutt was born on 19th August 1916 in Johannisburg, East Prussia and joined the 7th Anti-aircraft Regiment in April 1936 and in June 1937 he attended the Luftwaffe Officer Candidate School in Wildpark-Werder. In January 1938, he was commissioned as a Leutnant and was appointed Battery Communications Officer in the 84th Light Anti-aircraft Battalion in Bonn in February 1939.

When World War II began he was posted to the 841st Light Anti-aircraft Battalion as adjutant. On 28th July 1940, he attended the Braunschweig Parachute School for parachutist-rifleman training and on 15th August became adjutant of the 7th Parachute Anti-aircraft Battalion. He later led a platoon of the 2nd Battery of the 7th Parachute Anti-aircraft Battalion, and in April 1941, was made company commander. He saw action in Crete where he was wounded and awarded the Iron Cross 1st and 2nd Classes. In December 1942, he was wounded again in Russia and transferred to the Parachute Reserve Regiment. He returned to Russia to command a company of the 100th Luftwaffe Field Battalion and while serving in Russia he was awarded the German Cross in Gold. After recovering from his wound he received in Holland he was attached to the Parachute Officers School in Berlin from March 1945 until the end of the war.

OTHER AWARDS		PROMOTIONS	
00.00.1937	Reich Sports Badge in Bronze	01.01.1938	Leutnant
06.01.1940	Armed Forces Long Service Award 4th Class	01.07.1941	Oberleutnant
14.08.1940	Parachutist Badge	19.09.1942	Hauptmann
15.06.1941	Iron Cross 2nd Class	01.03.1944	Major
26.06.1941	Iron Cross 1st Class	-----	-----
16.07.1941	Wound Badge in Black	-----	-----

15.12.1941	Wound Badge in Silver	-----	-----
00.09.1942	Eastern Front Medal	-----	-----
18.10.1942	Luftwaffe Salver of Honour	-----	-----
12.11.1942	KRETA Cuff title	-----	-----
00.00.1942	Luftwaffe Ground Assault Badge	-----	-----
14.11.1943	German Cross in Gold	-----	-----

KARL KOCH
(16.11.1919 – 29.07.1944) *Oberfeldwebel*

Knight's Cross: Posthumously awarded on 24th October 1944 as *Oberfeldwebel* and *Führer* of an Assault Platoon in the III Battalion, 15th *Fallschirmjäger* Regiment for actions in France. In July 1944, the 5th *Fallschirmjäger* Division transferred to the defensive front on the Cotentin Peninsula. Koch's Assault Platoon played a major role in the German defensive effort, leading his troops as it eliminated enemy penetrations and closed gaps in the front. On 26th July during an assault on the enemy Koch was killed.

Karl Koch was born on 16th November 1919 in Battenfeld, Bierdenkopf and joined the 11th Infantry Regiment as a volunteer in October 1938. He took part in the Polish campaign attached to the Regiment's 6th Company and later he saw action in the Western campaign where he won the Iron Cross 1st and 2nd Classes.

On 1st April 1942, Koch joined the parachute troops and was assigned to the 16th Company of the 1st *Fallschirmjäger* Regiment in Stendal. In November, he was promoted to Feldwebel and became a Platoon Leader in the III Battalion of the 1st *Fallschirmjäger* Regiment seeing action on the Eastern Front near Smolensk and Orel in the winter of 1942-1943. There he won the German Cross in Gold after leading numerous reconnaissance and combat patrols. In December 1943, he was promoted to *Oberfeldwebel* for his leadership and bravery. He later saw action in Italy where again he performed well as an assault platoon leader in the 3rd Battalion of the 15th *Fallschirmjäger* Regiment before being transferred with his company to France where he would fight his last battle.

OTHER AWARDS		PROMOTIONS	
25.06.1940	Iron Cross 2nd Class	01.04.1940	Gefreiter
17.09.1941	Iron Cross 1st Class	01.11.1940	Obergefreiter
00.09.1942	Eastern Front Medal	01.11.1941	Oberjäger
12.07.1943	German Cross in Gold	01.11.1942	Feldwebel
-----	-----	15.12.1943	Oberfeldwebel

WALTHER KOCH

(10.09.1910 – 27.10.1943)   *Oberstleutnant*

Knight's Cross: Awarded on 10th May 1940 as *Hauptmann* and Commander Air-Landing Assault Battalion *Koch* in recognition for his bravery and leadership during the attack on the Belgium Fortress of Eben Emael. Koch played a leading role in the planning of the assault on the fortress, and his battalion also captured the four bridges over the Albert Canal, successfully carried out all the tasks assigned to it. As a result ten officers and men received the Knight's Cross for this daring action – including Koch.

The capture of the Fortress Eben Emael from the air will always be connected with Walter Koch. His superiors described him as a passionate officer, clever, energetic, and one of the most daring officer's of the German parachute troops. (Author's Collection)

(Wehrkundearchiv)

Walter Koch was born on 10th September 1910 in Bonn and transferred to the Luftwaffe from the police in August 1935 and served as a company officer in the *General Göring* Regiment. On 1st September 1937, after his training, he became a member of the IV *Fallschirmjäger* Battalion of the 1st Fallschirmjäger Regiment and the following year took over as a Company Commander.

He first saw action during the famous attack on the Fortress Eben Emael, on 10th May 1940. On 20th May, the Koch Assault Battalion, now designated the I Battalion of the 1st Parachute Assault Regiment, went into Crete. On the first day of the invasion, he suffered a serious head wound and was hospitalized. In March 1942, he was named commander of the 5th *Fallschirmjäger* Regiment and fought in Tunisia. In January 1943, his regiment became part of the Hermann Göring Panzer Division. In August 1943, he became a Reserve Officer and transferred to the Office of the Reich Minister of Aviation and Commander-in-Chief of the Luftwaffe.

Walther Koch had publicly denounced Hitler's infamous Commando Order, which ordered that all captured British commandos were to be executed. While in Africa, Koch's troops encountered the British 2nd Parachute Battalion under the command of Lieutenant-Colonel John Frost at Depienne Airfield. Frost had left a number of injured men under the protection of a single platoon behind at the airfield while he and his forces marched on. On their discovery, the British paratroopers were soon captured by Koch's men and made prisoners of war. The German commander than ordered his medics to treat the wounded. Before leaving, he ensured that the prisoners were give food and water, and even cigarettes. However, Koch returned just in time to stop the machine gunning of the captured British soldiers. After a heated debate with another German officer about the Commando Order, Koch managed to obtain adequate treatment for the allied prisoners who were transferred to a POW camp. Shortly after this episode Koch was wounded in the head. He was sent back to Germany to recover and placed on the reserves. While convalescing he was involved in a car accident, he died in a Berlin hospital from these injuries on 27th October 1943. However, many in his regiment believed that it wasn't an accident that killed him, they said that he had been killed by members of the SD (SS Security Services) because of his outspoken criticism of the Commando Order.

OTHER AWARDS		PROMOTIONS	
00.10.1936	Parachutist Badge	01.01.1935	Leutnant der Landespolizei
00.00.193_	Pilots Badge	01.09.1935	Oberleutnant der Landespolizei
01.10.1939	Armed Forces Long Service Award 4th Class	20.04.1938	Hauptmann (Luftwaffe)
12.05.1940	Iron Cross 2nd Class	16.05.1940	Major
12.05.1940	Iron Cross 1st Class	20.04.1942	Oberstleutnant
00.06.1941	Wound Badge in Silver	-----	-----
00.00.1942	Luftwaffe Ground Assault Badge	-----	-----
00.00.1942	Eastern Front Medal	-----	-----
31.03.1942	German Cross in Gold	-----	-----
00.00.1943	KRETA Cuff title	-----	-----
00.00.1943	AFRIKA Cuff title	-----	-----

WILLI KOCH
(01.12.1916 – 25.02.1996)   *Hauptmann*

(Wehrkundearchiv)

Knight's Cross: Awarded on 9th June 1944 as *Oberfeldwebel* and Platoon Leader in the 3rd Company, 1st *Fallschirmjäger* Regiment for actions in Italy. He served as part of a Battle Group commanded by *Oberst* Karl-Lothar Schulz during the fighting at Monte Cassino. He led his Platoon during some of the bloodiest battles of the campaign and played a major role in repulsing an enemy assault between the abbey and Hill 593.

Willi Koch was born on 1st December 1916 in Breslau and joined the 1st *Fallschirmjäger* Regiment "General Göring" in November 1936. In April 1938, he was attached to the 1st Company of the 1st *Fallschirmjäger* Regiment in Stendal and after completing an NCO course he transferred the 3rd Company.

He took part in the invasion of Poland and saw action in Norway, where he was dropped by parachute to relieve the German forces fighting near Narvik. Koch later saw action in Fortress Holland where he won both classes of the Iron Cross. He was appointed Platoon Leader of the 3rd Company in May 1941 and saw action in Crete and then in Russia. He was then transferred to Italy to the area near Monte Cassino where he and his troops were engaged in bitter fighting with British Gurkha troops and a battalion of the Sussex Light Infantry in brush-covered terrain where visibility was limited to just thirty feet. If his troops had not held their position and the enemy had been allowed to breakthrough then it would have been virtually impossible to hold the Cassino front.

After receiving the Knight's Cross at Monte Cassino, he was promoted to *Leutnant*, followed by his promotion to *Oberleutnant* in October 1944. He died on 25th February 1996 in Wuppertal.

OTHER AWARDS		PROMOTIONS		
23.01.1938	Parachutist Badge	01.10.1937	Gefreiter	
01.04.1939	Commemorative Medal of 13th March 1938	01.12.1938	Oberjäger	
01.04.1939	Commemorative Medal of 1st October 1938 + Bar	01.06.1940	Feldwebel	
25.05.1940	Iron Cross 2nd Class	01.01.1943	Oberfeldwebel	
25.05.1940	Iron Cross 1st Class	01.06.1944	Leutnant	
01.11.1940	Armed Forces Long Service Award 4th Class	01.10.1944	Oberleutnant	
01.03.1941	Narvik Campaign Shield	01.05.1945	Hauptmann	
01.10.1942	Luftwaffe Ground Assault Badge	-----		-----
00.11.1942	Eastern Front Medal	-----		-----
18.04.1945	Luftwaffe Close Combat Clasp in Bronze	-----		-----

RUDOLF JOHANN KRATZERT

(25.04.1898 – 16.01.1996)   *Major z.V*

(Wehrkundearchiv)

Knight's Cross: Awarded on 9th June 1944 as *Major z.V.*, and Commander III Battalion, 3rd *Fallschirmjäger* Regiment for actions in Italy. While leading his battalion near Eboli and Potenza Kratzert's troops repulsed heavy armoured attacks against his positions near Montecilfone and Palato in mid-October 1943. During the battles in Cassino he held his position on Hill 593, against a strong assault by an Indian unit almost ten times larger than his own unit. On 10th February 1944, his battalion took part in a surprise attack on Cavalry Mountain, and after more than two-hours of fierce fighting the mountain was taken and Kratzert was awarded the Knight's Cross.

Rudolf Kratzert was born on 25th April 1898 in Karlsburg part of Austro-Hungary, he joined entered the Imperial Austrian Army in January 1916 and attended the Breitensee-Vienna Infantry Cadet School as a *Leutnant*. From August 1917, he served in the 57th Infantry Regiment as a Platoon Leader and ended the war was deputy company commander. He joined the postal service in April 1920 and rose to the position of senior postal inspector.

On 30th April 1940, he was called up and placed at the disposal of the Luftwaffe. He attended a Luftwaffe officers course in Kamenz, Saxony and in June became company commander at Aibling airfield in Upper Bavaria. He was promoted to *Oberleutnant* in December 1941 and in June was transferred to the Luftwaffe reserves. In March 1942, he was attached at his own request to the 3rd *Fallschirmjäger* Regiment, and in June was made commander of the 11th Company and in February he took command of the III Battalion of the 3rd *Fallschirmjäger* Regiment. In October, he fought near Strynkovo and fought against partisans near Tolkachi. He served in Russia from October 1942 until March 1943 and then took his battalion into Sicily where he fought in the areas of Carlentini, Lenini and Fondaco. It was while fighting in Italy at Monet Cassino that he won the Knight's Cross.

Kratzert was taken prisoner by Soviet troops on 4th May 1945 but he managed to escape to Vienna and made his way home. He died on 16th January 1996 in Vienna, Austria at the age of ninety-seven.

OTHER AWARDS		PROMOTIONS		
00.00.1935	Cross of Honour for Frontline Combatants	17.08.1917	Leutnant (Heer)	
22.08.1941	War Service Cross 2nd Class + Swords	01.10.1940	Oberleutnant z.V. (Luftwaffe)	
00.11.1942	Eastern Front Medal	01.06.1941	Hauptmann z.V.	
05.04.1943	Iron Cross 2nd Class	01.12.1943	Major z.V.	
25.05.1943	Iron Cross 1st Class	-----		-----
27.10.1943	German Cross in Gold	-----		-----
15.01.1944	Luftwaffe Ground Assault Badge	-----		-----
07.10.1944	Luftwaffe Close Combat Clasp in Bronze	-----		-----

HEINZ KRINK

(25.03.1919 – 28.06.1975)   *Hauptmann*

(Wehrkundearchiv)

Knight's Cross: Awarded on 9th June 1944 as *Leutnant* and Adjutant in the II Battalion, 3rd *Fallschirmjäger* Regiment for outstanding bravery during the Third Battle of Cassino, where he had supported his commander in every way and the battalion had held a critical part of the front from Cavalry Mountain to the Colle San Angelo.

Heinz Krink was born on 23rd March 1919 in Berlin-Charlottenburg and entered the Luftwaffe in August 1939, and transferred to the parachute troops almost immediately and was assigned to the 6th Company. He underwent officer training in September 1941, and was commissioned as a *Leutnant* in April 1943.

From June 1943, he served as Ordnance Officer with the II Battalion of the 3rd *Fallschirmjäger* Regiment and saw heavy action in Russia where he earned something of a reputation for offensive operations. In February 1944, his regiment relieved the 211th Grenadier Regiment in Cassino, where he had proved himself a capable commander as well as a good adjutant, leading the battalion during the fighting withdrawal in Northern Italy. He was recommended for the Knight's Cross by the Commander of the 1st *Fallschirmjäger* Division *Generalleutnant* Richard Heidrich. A few weeks later Heidrich had the honour of presenting Krink with the award.

Krink was taken prisoner by the Allies on 2nd May 1945. He died on 28th June 1975 in Essen in the Ruhr area of Germany.

OTHER AWARDS		PROMOTIONS	
00.00.1939	Parachutist Badge	01.09.1940	Gefreiter
00.09.1942	Eastern Front Medal	01.09.1941	Obergefreiter
17.03.1943	Iron Cross 2nd Class	25.09.1941	Kriegsoffizieranwärter
10.08.1943	Iron Cross 1st Class	01.02.1942	Oberjäger
17.10.1943	German Cross in Gold	01.11.1942	Feldwebel
-----	-----	20.04.1943	Leutnant
-----	-----	20.06.1944	Oberleutnant
-----	-----	20.04.1945	Hauptmann

HANS "HANNE" KROH

(13.05.1907 – 18.07.1967)

Generalmajor

Generalmajor Hans Kroh (right) and General der Fallschirmtruppe Hermann-Bernhard Ramcke, sharing tea and biscuits, as prisoners of war, September 1944. (Author's Collection)

Knight's Cross: Awarded on 21st August 1941 as *Major* and Commander 1st Battalion of the 2nd *Fallschirmjäger* Regiment as part of the 7th Air Division for actions in Crete. He led his battalion during heavy fighting for an oil refinery near Stavromenos, and his troops fought back against Greek and British forces for ten days until they were relieved. The battle helped to secure the German victory in Crete.

Knight's Cross with Oakleaves: *Oberstleutnant* Kroh became the 443rd recipient of the Oakleaves on 6th April 1944 as Commander 2nd *Fallschirmjäger* Regiment for his part in the prevention of a breakout by a Soviet Corps during the defence of Nowo Andrejewka on 5th January 1944. He was presented with the Oakleaves personally by Hitler at the Berghof at a ceremony in the Great Hall in April 1944.

Knight's Cross with Oakleaves and Swords: Awarded as the 96th recipient on 12th September 1944 as *Oberst* and *Führer* 2nd *Fallschirmjäger* Division for actions during the bitter defensive fighting during the Battle of Brest.

Hans Kroh was born on 13th May 1907, in Heidelberg and entered the police service in Brandenburg-Havel as a cadet in April 1926. He was commissioned as a *Leutnant* in April 1933 and in August was appointed a platoon leader with the *Landespolizei Wecke*. In January 1934 he transferred to the *Landespolizeigruppe "General Göring"* and in October 1935 was appointed commander of the 2nd Company of the *"General Göring"* Regiment.

Kroh returned to military service with the Bundeswehr with the rank of Oberst in June 1956. In September 1957, he was promoted to Brigadegeneral and appointed commander of the 1st Air Landing Division, and in July 1959 he was promoted to Generalmajor. He retired on 30th September 1962, and died on 18th July 1967 in Braunschweig. (Wehrkundearchiv)

He transferred to the Luftwaffe in April 1936, and after completing his parachutist-rifle course he was appointed senior trainer at the Stendal Parachute School. He was promoted to *Hauptmann* in October 1937 and joined the 1st *Fallschirmjäger* Regiment in April 1938 as a battalion commander. In January 1939, he transferred to the 7th Air Division and by June 1940 had been appointed Operations Officer under *Generalleutnant* Kurt Student. He took command of the 1st Battalion of the 2nd *Fallschirmjäger* Regiment in August 1940 and was promoted to *Major* in March 1941. Kroh led a Battle Group that had been formed from his own command during the invasion of Crete in May, after its commander *Oberst* Alfred Sturm was taken prisoner. He led his unit to an oil refinery near Stavromenos where they managed to hold out against a far superior enemy. His men fought against Greek and British forces for ten days until troops of the German mountain infantry arrived to relive them. This battle helped to secure the area and to win the Battle of Crete and for this Kroh was awarded the Knight's Cross in August 1941.

In January 1943, Kroh was promoted to *Oberstleutnant* and in march he took over as commander of the 2nd *Fallschirmjäger* Regiment, part of General Ramcke's 2nd *Fallschirmjäger* Division in North Africa. He then transferred to the Russian Front where his troops suffered heavy losses as they weren't trained to stand and fight in such a way, but nevertheless they fought with bravery and tenacity. As a result of Kroh's leadership and skill he was awarded the Knight's Cross with Oakleaves on 6th April 1944. On 11th August, Ramcke took command of Fortress Brest and Kroh took over the 2nd *Fallschirmjäger* Division. On 12th September, Kroh was awarded the Knight's Cross with Oakleaves and Swords. Six days later Kroh was taken prisoner at Brest.

OTHER AWARDS		PROMOTIONS	
00.00.193_	Combined Pilots & Observers Badge	08.04.1926	Polizeianwärter
00.00.1936	Parachutist Badge	01.04.1933	Leutnant der Polizei
02.10.1936	Armed Forces Long Service Award 4th to 3rd Class	01.08.1933	Oberleutnant der Polizei
22.05.1940	Iron Cross 2nd Class	01.10.1937	Hauptmann (Luftwaffe)
22.05.1940	Iron Cross 1st Class	01.03.1941	Major
09.02.1942	Italian Medal of Honour in Silver	11.01.1943	Oberstleutnant
00.00.1942	Luftwaffe Ground Assault Badge	06.04.1944	Oberst
00.10.1942	Eastern Front Medal	13.09.1944	Generalmajor
24.12.1942	German Cross in Gold	-----	-----
00.05.1943	KRETA Cuff title	-----	-----
00.00.1943	AFRIKA Cuff title	-----	-----
00.00.194_	Wound Badge in Black	-----	-----

MARTIN KÜHNE

(01.11.1918 – 25.03.2003) *Major*

(Wehrkundearchiv)

Knight's Cross: Awarded on 29th February 1944 as *Hauptmann* and Commander I Battalion, 2nd *Fallschirmjäger* Regiment for his outstanding command and bravery during heavy action on the Island of Leros in the Aegean Sea. In December 1943, he led his battalion during the attack on Leros and his troops were up against a large enemy force of Italian soldiers (who had now changed sides) and British forces. After some fierce fighting the Germans took 5,000 Italian prisoners and over 2,000 British prisoners and for his leadership and skill Kühne was awarded the Knight's Cross.

Martin Kühne was born on 1st November 1918 in Langebrück, Dresden and entered the Luftwaffe in November 1937 with the 10th Anti-aircraft Regiment. He attended officer training school in Fürstenfeldbruck and from there transferred to the Parachute Training School in Wittstock in September 1939.

He was commissioned as a *Leutnant* in December, and in May 1940 he was appointed Platoon Leader in the 15th Company of the 1st *Fallschirmjäger* Regiment, and saw action in Holland. He saw action in the Moerdijk area where he was seriously wounded on 11th May, while taking a heavily-fortified bunker. He later saw action during the airborne invasion of Crete where he led a platoon of the 1st Company of the 2nd *Fallschirmjäger* Regiment. Near Corinth, he captured a British anti-aircraft battery which resulted in a recommendation of the Knight's Cross. During the invasion of Crete he was dropped between the city and airport of Rethymon where he and a few of his men defended their position bravely until reinforcements arrived. On 20th May 1941, Kühne was again seriously wounded. In October 1941, he was transferred to Russia where he served for a time as adjutant of the I Battalion of the 2nd *Fallschirmjäger* Regiment. In November 1942, he was transferred to Africa where he served with General Ramcke's Brigade and played a vital role in the unit's successful escape through enemy-held territory. His exploits and bravery were recognized when on 23rd July 1943, he was awarded the German Cross in Gold. From 1944 until the end of the war, he saw action in northern Italy and was promoted to *Major* in March 1945. Taken prisoner by the Allies in May 1945, he was released in 1946. He died on 25th March 2003 in Braunschweig in Lower Saxony.

OTHER AWARDS		PROMOTIONS	
28.04.1940	Parachutist Badge	01.11.1937	Fahnenjunker-Gefreiter
18.05.1940	Iron Cross 2nd Class	01.01.1939	Fähnrich
18.05.1940	Iron Cross 1st Class	01.08.1939	Oberfähnrich
00.06.1941	Wound Badge in Silver	28.12.1939	Leutnant
07.10.1941	Luftwaffe Honour Goblet	01.10.1941	Oberleutnant
01.11.1941	Armed Forces Long Service Award 4th Class	01.07.1943	Hauptmann
09.02.1942	Italian Medal of Honour in Silver	01.03.1945	Major
16.07.1942	Eastern Front Medal	-----	-----
11.02.1943	Commemorative Medal for the Campaign in Libya	-----	-----
26.05.1943	Luftwaffe Ground Assault Badge	-----	-----
23.07.1943	German Cross in Gold	-----	-----

KURT-ERNST KUNKEL
(13.01.1923 – 23.09.2012) *Oberleutnant*

Knight's Cross: Awarded on 30th April 1945 as *Leutnant* and Commander 2nd Company, 4th *Fallschirmjäger* Regiment after he proved himself as a company commander during the retreat near Bologna and during the fierce fighting in the Po Plain. However all research into his award has found no indication of an approved award in any archives. Apparently the award was approved by the Commanding General of the I. *Fallschirmjäger* Corps, *General der Fallschirmtruppe* Richard Heidrich and some sources state he was actually presented with the award but this seems highly unlikely.

Kurt-Ernst Kunkel was born on 13th January 1923 in Weißwasser, Oberlausitz and volunteered for active duty in November 1940 with the 63rd Luftwaffe Training Regiment in Straubling. After his parachutist training he was posted to the 4th *Fallschirmjäger* Regiment and saw action during the Battle of Sicily. He parachuted into the city on 14th July 1943 and saw action primarily in the area north of the Simeto and south of Catani. He was later wounded during the fighting and spent a number of weeks in hospital. He then saw action at Sulmena, Pizzo and Ferrato and later at Orsogna-Ortona in the Cassino area. There he led offensive patrols and his platoon formed the rearguard. His commanders saw officer qualities in him and he was sent on an officers training course in August 1944. Following his commission as a *Leutnant* in October he took command of the 2nd Company of the 4th *Fallschirmjäger* Regiment. He proved himself a most capable commander and recommended for the Knight's Cross.

Captured by British forces on 3rd May 1945, he was held as a prisoner of war until his release on 25th October 1947. He joined the *Bundeswehr* after the war and was promoted to *Oberstleutnant* in October 1977, and retired three years later. Kunkel died in Velten, Oberhavel in Brandeburg on 23rd September 2012.

OTHER AWARDS		PROMOTIONS	
00.00.1940	Parachutist Badge	00.00.1941	Gefreiter
17.08.1943	Iron Cross 2nd Class	00.00.1943	Feldwebel
00.11.1943	Wound Badge in Silver	28.10.1944	Leutnant
15.01.1944	Iron Cross 1st Class	00.00.1945	Oberleutnant

RUDOLF KURZ
(29.01.1916 – 12.06.1979)   *Leutnant*

(Wehrkundearchiv)

Knight's Cross: Awarded on 18th November 1944 as *Oberfähnrich* and *Führer* 2nd Company, (12th) *Fallschirmjäger* Assault Regiment for distinguishing himself in Italy. He took part in heavy fighting between August and September 1944 and later led his company during six days of fighting during the battle near Monghidoro and Pianoro.

Rudolf Kurz was born on 29th January 1916 in Kiel and after seeing service in the Reich Labour Service (*Reichsarbeitsdienst* or RAD), he joined the army in February 1938. He served as a Platoon Leader in the 257th Infantry Regiment from 1939, seeing action in France where he was awarded the Iron Cross 2nd Class.

In 1941, he volunteered for the parachute troops and saw action during the airborne invasion of Crete where in June he won the Iron Cross 1st Class. He went onto distinguish himself during the Russian campaign with the 1st *Fallschirmjäger* Regiment and after completing an officer candidate course he was made a Platoon Leader and served in Italy with the 12th *Fallschirmjäger* Assault Regiment where he saw heavy fighting during the months of August and September 1944 in defence of Viareggio on the Adriatic near Rimini. Kurz led his company during six hard days of fighting, with the regiment taking many losses. He distinguished himself repeatedly during the tank battle near Monghidoro and in the Battle of Pianoro. As a result the U.S. forces were met by tough resistance from the German *Fallschirmjäger* troops and their advance through Bologna and the Po Valley was delayed for several weeks. He was wounded during the American advance and awarded the Wound Badge in Gold. He died on 12th June 1979, in Cuxhaven, Lower Saxony.

OTHER AWARDS		PROMOTIONS	
07.07.1940	Iron Cross 2nd Class	00.00.1939	Gefreiter (Heer)
13.01.1941	Parachutist Badge	00.00.1940	Feldwebel
18.06.1941	Iron Cross 1st Class	00.00.1940	Unteroffizier
20.05.1943	KRETA Cuff title	00.00.1942	Feldwebel (Luftwaffe)
07.07.1943	Luftwaffe Ground Assault Badge	00.00.1943	Oberfeldwebel
12.07.1943	German Cross in Gold	00.00.1944	Oberfähnrich
20.04.1944	Wound Badge in Silver	01.01.1945	Leutnant
24.09.1944	Wound Badge in Gold	-----	-----

DR. CARL LANGEMEYER

(06.08.1907 – 25.07.1982)   *Oberstabsarzt*

(Wehrkundearchiv)

Knight's Cross: Awarded on 18th November 1944 as *Stabsarzt* and Commander *Fallschirm* Medical Training Battalion for his leadership and bravery in the Nancy-Luneville area of France. Although he was wounded during the battalion's last attack on 30th September 1944 he continued to lead his battalion from the front for three hours and repulsed all further attacks.

Carl Langemeyer was born on 6th August 1907 in Holzminden and studied medicine and joined the 65th Infantry Regiment after completing his military training. At the outbreak of war he joined the Luftwaffe as a doctor and served in the Polish campaign. He joined the parachute troops in 1940 and saw action during the invasion of Holland as part of the 1st *Fallschirmjäger* Regiment. There he had to operate and fight. He didn't wear the Red Cross insignia during this time and as a result of his bravery was awarded the Iron Cross 1st and 2nd Classes. He was attached to the 2nd Company of the 1st *Fallschirmjäger* Regiment during the airborne invasion of Crete where he won the Luftwaffe Honour Goblet. He led a medical company during the invasion of Russia and later served at the Luftwaffe University Hospital in Strasbourg where he was appointed Chief Physician. In April 1943, he was head of the 1st *Fallschirmjäger* Medical Battalion and for his efforts and bravery in the area near Rome he was awarded the German Cross in Gold. In April 1944, a month later became the 1st Fallschirmjäger Army's advising surgeon and was appointed the commanding officer of the Parachute Air Instruction Battalion. During this time he had been wounded twice but continued to serve at his post. He was wounded for the third time in September and was hospitalized for a short time. After his recovery, he served as Division Medical Officer of the 2nd *Fallschirmjäger* Division and saw heavy action in the Ruhr Pocket.

In late-April 1945, the Germans in the pocket were almost surrounded and Dr. Langemeyer managed to escape the pocket before he could be taken prisoner. He headed home to Minden to the house of his parents but a few days later he was captured there by U.S. troops. He spent time in a French prison in Metz and was finally released in October 1948. He would later serve in the *Bundeswehr*, rising to the rank of *Oberfeldarzt der Reserve*. He died at home on 25th July 1982 in Holzminden.

OTHER AWARDS		PROMOTIONS	
00.00.1939	Parachutist Badge	00.10.1939	Assistenarzt
00.00.1940	Iron Cross 2nd Class	00.00.1942	Stabsarzt
00.00.1940	Iron Cross 1st Class	01.11.1944	Oberstabsarzt
00.06.1941	Luftwaffe Honour Goblet	-----	-----
00.00.194_	KRETA Cuff title	-----	-----
12.12.1943	German Cross in Gold	-----	-----
00.12.1944	Wound Badge in Black	-----	-----

ERICH LEPKOWSKI

(17.09.1919 – 31.05.1975)   *Oberleutnant*

(Wehrkundearchiv)

Knight's Cross: Awarded on 8th August 1944 as *Leutnant* and *Führer* 5th Company, 2nd *Fallschirmjäger* Regiment for actions in Brest.

Erich Lepkowski was born on 17th September 1919, in Giesen, Treubing and after his schooling he joined the 1st Infantry Regiment in Königsberg. He transferred to the Luftwaffe on 1st September 1939 and trained as a radio operator. In August 1940 he joined the signals platoon of the 2nd *Fallschirmjäger* Regiment in Berlin. He saw action during the airborne attack on Crete and was taken prisoner, but was soon freed by forces under the command of *Major* Kroh. He was sent to Russia in April 1942, where he fought well and was awarded the Iron Cross 1st Class. During action in the swamps of the Volkho he went on thirty offensive patrols in forty-eight days. Promoted to *Leutnant* in April 1943, he took command of the 5th Company of the 2nd *Fallschirmjäger* Regiment in December 1943 after its commander had been killed in action. He took part in the defensive fighting on the hills near Peromasik and his unit managed to hold back an advance of seven Soviet tanks using only three assault guns.

During the fierce fighting in Brest-Lepkowski used three captured American tanks to bolster the rescue mission's firepower and American and French flags were flown from the vehicles to help trick the partisans. Also, as an added security measure, French-speaking soldiers were selected to drive the vehicles in case they were stopped and questioned. Nothing was left to chance. His men even had false release papers for the prisoners. In the early hours of 16th August the column of eighteen trucks and three tanks moved forward to its first challenge the U.S. perimeter. A diversionary attack was launched by the *Fallschirmjäger* troops and while the Americans were distracted by this Lepkowski and his men slipped through the lines and into French held territory. As the column neared the building where the German prisoners were being kept, Lepkowski's men leapt from their trucks and attacked. The prisoners inside, knowing what was happening, overpowered their guards and ran for freedom. Lepkowski's men swept aside the French partisans and broke through to the open road and headed back towards Brest. They blasted their way through a road block and onto the American perimeter where they found the U.S. troops still occupied by the diversionary attacks. The column slipped back into Fortress Brest without further trouble. It had been a great success; the column had travelled seventy-five miles and had rescued 130 prisoners and had captured fifteen French partisans, and for this Lepkowski was awarded the Knight's Cross.

Lepkowski was wounded in March 1944 and again in September for the sixth time, and was captured by the Americans on 20th September 1944. He remained in Allied captivity until 18th July 1947. He joined the *Bundswehr* in April 1960, was promoted to *Oberstleutnant* in October 1973, and retired on New Year's Eve 1974. He died on 31st May 1975 in Saarbrücken.

OTHER AWARDS		PROMOTIONS	
00.00.1939	Parachutist Badge	00.00.1940	Oberjäger
28.06.1941	Iron Cross 2nd Class	00.00.1941	Feldwebel

00.09.1942	Eastern Front Medal	01.04.1942	Oberfeldwebel
27.10.1942	Iron Cross 1st Class	20.04.1943	Leutnant
00.05.1943	KRETA Cuff title	01.07.1944	Oberleutnant
29.03.1944	German Cross in Gold	-----	-----
00.09.1944	Wound Badge in Silver	-----	-----

WALTER PAUL LIEBING

(12.08.1912 – 18.10.1998)   *Oberstleutnant*

(Wehrkundearchiv)

Knight's Cross: Awarded on 2nd February 1945 as *Major* and *Führer* 23rd *Fallschirmjäger* Regiment for actions in France. His unit while attached to a Battle Group in the Nancy area held the Mosel and Meurthe position as well as the Seulle sector against a vast superior enemy force and for this Liebing was awarded the Knight's Cross.

Walter Liebing was born on 12th August 1912 in Dresden and joined the Police in April 1932 as a cadet, and later attended an officer training course at Dresden Police Headquarters. In February 1933, he became a platoon leader in the Dresden Police Department's 4th Hundertschaft.

In September 1935, he transferred to the Luftwaffe and was made a *Leutnant*. He attended flying school and in November 1940 he assumed command of a reconnaissance unit and flew thirty-two missions in the east. After being awarded the Iron Cross in September 1941, he was promoted to *Hauptmann* and assigned to the 1st Luftwaffe Field Division in September 1942. Following his promotion to *Major* in February 1943, Liebing became a battalion commander in the newly formed 6th *Fallschirmjäger* Division. After his success in France, he was made commander of the 23rd *Fallschirmjäger* Regiment and saw action near Krefeld, at Fischeln and near Gennep against numerous armoured assaults by the enemy. At the Rhine Bridge at Uerdingen, Liebing held a bridgehead until the last German troops had crossed, he then blew up the bridge. For this he was recommended for the Oakleaves on 10th March 1945, but the request for this award was refused. He was taken prisoner on 26th April by U.S. forces. He died on 18th October 1998 in Düsseldorf.

OTHER AWARDS		PROMOTIONS	
21.07.1931	German Reich Sports Badge in Bronze	04.04.1932	Polizeianwärter
02.10.1936	Armed Forces Long Service Award 4th Class	01.10.1933	Polizei-Wachtmeister
10.06.1937	Military Pilots Badge	01.08.1934	Polizei-Fahnenjunker
30.07.1940	Iron Cross 2nd Class	01.08.1934	Polizei-Fähnrich
14.06.1941	Operational Flying Clasp for Reconnaissance Pilots	25.03.1935	Leutnant der Landespolizei
02.09.1941	Iron Cross 1st Class	01.09.1935	Leutnant (Luftwaffe)
20.03.1944	Infantry Assault Badge in Silver	31.07.1937	Oberleutnant
30.03.1944	Army Close Combat Clasp in Bronze	01.07.1940	Hauptmann
-----	-----	01.02.1943	Major
-----	-----	20.04.1945	Oberstleutnant

ROLF MAGER
(01.12.1917 – 01.01.1945)   *Hauptmann*

(Wehrkundearchiv)

Knight's Cross: Awarded on 31st October 1944 as *Hauptmann* and Commander II Battalion, 6th *Fallschirmjäger* Regiment for operations near Amsterdam, Holland. In September and October 1944, his unit fought at Schijndel and Alphen, south of Amsterdam, Holland, in a defensive role. His battalion stooped a strong armoured attack then launched a counterattack driving the enemy from the German trenches. *Hauptmann* Mager established a new defensive line at Boxtel, stopping an enemy breakthrough to Tilburg. During the counterattack, Mager himself was seriously wounded and evacuated to Germany. He died from his wounds in an American hospital in Aachen.

Rolf Mager was born on 1st December 1917 in Königstein, Saxony and joined the 2nd Air Signals Replacement Battalion in October 1936, and on the first day of 1941 he transferred to the parachute troops, being assigned to the 1st *Fallschirmjäger* Regiment. He first saw action during the invasion of Crete as an *Oberleutnant* and later won the Iron Cross 1st Class in the northern sector of the Eastern Front in April 1942. He then transferred to Italy and fought in the southeast sector of the country before seeing action during the fighting withdrawal to Rome and the north of the country. In 1944, he took command of the 2nd Battalion of the 6th *Fallschirmjäger* Regiment and from September to October he fought at Schijndel and Alphen during some tough defensive battles. His battalion stopped a strong armoured attack and then launched an attack against the enemy, driving them from their trenches.

He was wounded during the Ardennes Offensive and was evacuated to the hospital in Bogheim near Aachen. When the hospital was overrun by American troops he was one of the many patients taken prisoner. Despite an emergency operation by a U.S. surgeon, Mager succumbed to his wounds on 1st January 1945. Some sources state he was posthumously promoted to the rank of Major, although Scherzer makes no mention of this in his book *Die Ritterkreuzträger 1939-1945*.

OTHER AWARDS		PROMOTIONS	
00.00.193_	Parachutist Badge	01.10.1936	Fähnrich
01.10.1940	Armed Forces Long Service Award 4th Class	01.01.1938	Leutnant
17.06.1941	Iron Cross 2nd Class	01.08.1940	Oberleutnant
01.04.1942	Iron Cross 1st Class	01.02.1943	Hauptmann
00.00.194_	Army Close Combat Clasp in Bronze	00.00.1945	Major
00.00.1943	Army Ground Assault Badge	-----	-----
00.00.1943	Close Combat Clasp in Silver	-----	-----
00.04.1943	Wound Badge in Silver	-----	-----
00.05.1943	KRETA Cuff title	-----	-----
28.09.1944	German Cross in Gold	-----	-----
05.06.1943	Luftwaffe Salver of Honour	-----	-----
30.11.1944	Close Combat Clasp in Gold *	-----	-----

* He was one of only 631 recipients of this rare award

JOHANNES "HANNES" MARSCHOLEK

(13.02.1917 – 05.09.2004)   *Hauptmann*

(Author's Collection)

Knight's Cross: Awarded on 31st October 1944 as *Oberleutnant* and Platoon Leader in the 5th Battery, 5th Fallschirm-Flak Battalion for actions in France. During the fierce fighting in Normandy Marsholek led his battery during decisive stages of the fighting.

Johannes "Hannes" Marscholek was born on 13th February 1917 in Gleiwitz and joined the 20th Flak Regiment in Breslau in November 1936 after completing the obligatory service with the Reich Labour Service. He was to remain with the flak throughout his career as a soldier. After various courses and a promotion Marscholek joined the Linz Flak Battalion's 1st Battery in October 1938. He was promoted to *Leutnant* in March 1939 and saw action in the western campaign as commander of the 3rd Battery of the 371st Reserve Flak Battalion. In June 1940, he was transferred to the home front to guard important installations. He remained in this defensive post until January 1944. On 29th January, Marscholek became a member of the flak battalion designated for the 5th *Fallschirmjäger* Division and was made a Platoon Leader. Marscholek saw heavy fighting in the villages of La Monts, Houteville, La Butte, Marigny, St Lô, Dangy, La Salle and Avranches and during these battles the battalion commander *Major* Fritz Görtz was killed. Marscholek was appointed temporary battery commander and proved very capable. In just two days, his two anti-tank 88mm guns had knocked out twenty-eight Sherman tanks on the Cotentin Peninsula and had disabled four others. Of the twenty-eight tanks destroyed, Marscholek had personally destroyed twenty-one of them. He continued to command a battalion until the final day of the war.

He was captured at the end of the war and briefly kept in captivity by the Allies. He died on 5th September 2004 in Ludwigshafen.

OTHER AWARDS		PROMOTIONS	
16.12.1938	Commemorative Medal of 13th March 1938	01.10.1937	Gefreiter
26.08.1939	Commemorative Medal of 1st October 1938 + Bar	01.04.1938	Unteroffizier
17.12.1940	War Service Cross 2nd Class + Swords	01.10.1938	Wachtmeister
14.04.1942	Iron Cross 2nd Class	01.03.1939	Leutnant der Reserve
20.04.1942	Iron Cross 1st Class	23.01.1942	Oberleutnant der Reserve
16.06.1943	Luftwaffe Anti-Aircraft Badge	31.01.1944	Hauptmann (active)

EUGEN ALBERT MAX MEINDL

(16.07.1892 – 24.01.1951)   *General der Fallschirmtruppe*

(Author's Collection)

Knight's Cross: Awarded on 14th June 1941 as *Generalmajor* and Commander 1st Air-Landing Regiment for actions in Crete. In May, he led his assault regiment during the invasion of Crete, and was wounded shortly after parachuting into the area near Maleme airfield. Although he was unable to take full command during the early stages of the invasion because of his injury he did take part in the latter stages of the campaign and his bravery was recognised when he was awarded the Knight's Cross. Meindl continued to show great leadership qualities and in July 1943 he was appointed Inspector of all Luftwaffe Field Formations and was promoted to *Generalleutnant*. In November he was appointed Commanding General of the 2nd *Fallschirmjäger* Corps.

Knight's Cross with Oakleaves: Awarded as *General der Fallschirmtruppe* and Commanding General II *Fallschirm* Corps on 31st August 1944 to become the 564th recipient, for actions near Falaise on the Western Front. On the night of 19th/20th August, Meindl and his Chief of Staff, *Oberst* Ernst Blauensteiner, each led an assault group in a last chance bid to escape from the Falaise Pocket. After a desperate march through enemy territory they finally broke free of the encirclement and escaped the pocket – for this Meindl won the Oakleaves.

Knight's Cross with Oakleaves and Swords: Awarded on 8th May 1945 and *General der Fallschirmtruppe* and Commanding General II *Fallschirm* Corps. *However, there is no proof that the award was ever processed or approved. The award was made as a result of the "Dönitz Directive" which has been proved invalid and illegal. A list with Meindls name on for approval of the award was never signed by Dönitz, perhaps not even seen by him. The award sequence number was determined by the Award Association of the Knight's Cross of which Miendl was a member.*

A talented commander and highly decorated officer, Eugen Meindl played a major role during the invasion of Poland, Denmark, Norway and Crete. He entered military service in July 1912 as an officer candidate, and was commissioned as a *Leutnant* two years later. After the war, he remained in the army and served as a battery officer with the 13th Light Artillery and 5th Artillery Regiments. He served for a time in Stuttgart where he was responsible for training and then in 1925 he was transferred to the 5th Division as a staff officer. In October 1930, he was adjutant to the 5th Artillery Regiment under the command of *Oberst* Ludwig Beck (who later became Chief of the General Staff of the Army and an important figure in the resistance movement against Hitler).

On 15th October 1935, Meindl was appointed commander of the 1st Battalion, 5th Artillery Regiment, he was promoted to *Oberstleutnant* in August 1936 and took command of the 112th Mountain Artillery Regiment. In September 1939, he took part in the Polish Campaign and later played a vital role in the invasion of Denmark and Norway. On 9th April 1940, the 3rd Mountain Division under the command of Eduard Dietl were transported by destroyers to Narvik where they captured the town. The British counter-attacked and sunk the German destroyers; the survivors had to swim to safety. The Anglo-French forces began to attack Dietl's men. The fighting went on for weeks and the Allies recaptured Narvik on 28th May. Dietl's command was forced back against the Swedish border. Low on supplies and ammunition, Dietl needed reinforcements quick. On 7th June, Meindl volunteered to jump with the paratroopers, although he had no previous parachute training. However, because of the fall of France the British evacuated Narvik and Dietl's troops moved into the town once more. In August 1940, Meindl was rested and attached to the Commander of the Military District of Salzburg, the following month he was named commander of the 1st Parachute Air Landing Assault Regiment. In May 1941, he took over as commander of Battle Group West during the airborne invasion of Crete, where he won the Knight's Cross.

Eugen Meindl with Generalfeldmarschall Erwin Rommel. (Author's Collection)

In February 1942, Meindl's command was upgraded to a division and transferred to the Eastern Front. His division, which had been formed from 1st Parachute Air Landing Assault Regiment, had been established in northern Russia to control five *Luftwaffe* field regiments and a signals battalion. The main bulk of his command fought on the right flank of the Demjansk Salient while the other part fought in the south. In May the German forces finally broke the encirclement and the Luftwaffe ground troops played a major role in breaking through the Russian perimeter. In October, Meindl returned to Germany as the commanding General of the 13th Air Corps and supervised the formation of twenty-two new Luftwaffe Field Divisions. In July 1943, he was named Inspector of the *Luftwaffe* Field Formations and was promoted to *Generalleutnant*. In November he took command of the 2nd Parachute Corps and by February 1944 came under the control of the Commander-in-Chief West in Paris. After his promotion to *General der Fallschirmtruppe* in April, his command was placed at the disposal of *Generaloberst* Friedrich Dollmann's 7th Army. Following the Allied landings in Normandy, the 2nd *Fallschirmjäger* Corps along with the 3rd *Fallschirmjäger* Division and the 17th SS-Panzer Grenadier Division, was deployed to counter attack the US troops in the area around St. Lô. On the evening of 6th August, *Oberstleutnant* von Kluge, the son of *Generalfeldmarschall* von Kluge, visited Meindl's command post. He told Meindl that his father had ordered the 2nd Parachute Corps to hold its position, because a major panzer force was about to counterattack. Meindl was astonished by the order and he told the young officer that he felt Normandy could no longer he held and if the *Feldmarschall* knew the true situation he wouldn't issue such an order. Nevertheless Meindl obeyed and the counterattack took place. After about five miles, the panzer force ran out of fuel and the allies destroyed it. Hitler would not allow a retreat and because of this two German armies in the Falaise Pocket were virtually destroyed. Meindl said later that, "… it was heartbreaking to stand and watch!"

After the near disaster of the Falaise Pocket Meindls troops were sent to the Netherlands, to the Nijmegan area to counter the Allied airborne and ground offensive. The counterattack was a success and many prisoners were taken and the remainder of the Allies were pushed back. Later his forces saw action in Germany, on home soil against a far superior enemy, and here his troops suffered a heavy defeat. On 25th May 1945, Meindl and his troops finally surrendered and he was kept in various

Meindl surrendered to the Allies on 25th May 1945, and spent time in several prisons before eventually being released in September 1947. (Roger James Bender)

Eugen Meindl as depicted in a famous postcard by Wolfgang Willrich. (Author's Collection)

prison camps until his release in September 1947. He spent the remaining years of his life as an active member of the Knight's Cross Association, and it was while he was a member that he convinced the Association that he had been awarded the Knight's Cross with Oakleaves and Swords. He died in Munich on 24th January 1951.

OTHER AWARDS		PROMOTIONS	
00.00.1915	The Gallipoli Star (Turkish Half Moon)	27.07.1912	Fahnenjunker-Gefreiter
18.07.1915	Iron Cross 2nd Class	22.03.1913	Fähnrich
17.01.1916	Iron Cross 1st Class	17.02.1914	Leutnant
00.00.1917	Austrian Military Service Cross 3rd Class + War Decoration	18.04.1917	Oberleutnant
00.00.1918	Knight's Cross of the Royal Saxony Albrecht Order + Swords	01.08.1924	Hauptmann
00.00.1918	Knight's Cross of the Order of the Zähringer Lion 2nd Class + Swords	01.04.1934	Major (Luftwaffe)
00.00.1935	Cross of Honour for Frontline Combatants	02.08.1936	Oberstleutnant
02.10.1936	Armed Forces Long Service Award 4th to 1st Class	01.04.1939	Oberst
00.10.1939	Commemorative Medal of 1st October 1938	01.01.1941	Generalmajor
22.10.1939	Bar to the Iron Cross 2nd Class	01.02.1943	Generalleutnant
10.06.1940	Bar to the Iron Cross 1st Class	01.04.1944	General der Fallschirmtruppe
00.00.194_	Parachutist Badge	-----	-----
10.11.1940	Narvik Campaign Shield	-----	-----
25.10.1941	Wound Badge in Black	-----	-----
27.07.1942	German Cross in Gold	-----	-----
09.08.1942	Eastern Front Medal	-----	-----
25.05.1943	KRETA Cuff title	-----	-----

JOACHIM MEISSNER

(15.10.1911 – 25.07.1944)   *Hauptmann*

(Wehrkundearchiv)

Knight's Cross: Awarded on 12th May 1940 as *Leutnant der Reserve* and *Führer* Assault Group "*Essen*," Air-Landing Assault Battalion *Koch* for actions in France. He led his assault group occupied the village of Eben Emael and defended the bridgehead against enemy attacks until reinforcements arrived. His group killed 150 enemy soldiers and took 150 prisoner, while only suffering twenty-two dead themselves.

Joachim Meissner was born on 15th October 1911 in Freystadt, Lower Silesia and joined the Reichswehr in October 1929. In April 1934, he was made Department Chief of the Foreign Section of the Reich Director of Sport under Hans von Tschammer und Osten, for southern Europe.

On 26th August 1939, he was called up for active duty and joined the 8th Engineer Battalion in Neisse. In January 1940, he transferred to the parachute troops and in March was commissioned as a *Leutnant*. During the invasion of France Meissner flew into Canne with his Assault Group only to find that the enemy had already blown the bridge there. When the battalion commander was seriously wounded Meissner, as deputy commander took over and his group occupied the village of Eben Emael. They defended the bridgehead against heavy enemy attacks until reinforcements arrived. The following morning, Meissner led the remaining elements of Assault Group *Essen* to the eastern side of the canal; the group had suffered twenty-two dead and twenty-six wounded. In return, they had killed 150 enemy soldiers and had wounded approximately fifty and had taken 150 prisoners. For this great success Meissner was awarded the Knight's Cross personally by Hitler and received an early promotion to the rank of *Oberleutnant*.

In August, he joined the 2nd *Fallschirmjäger* Regiment and took part in the airborne invasion of Crete, jumping east of Rethymnon. He became an Ordnance Officer for the 2nd *Fallschirmjäger* Regiment in December 1941 and held this position until 10th July 1942, fighting in Russia. Promoted to *Hauptmann* in September 1942, he assumed command of the 6th Company of the 2nd *Fallschirmjäger* Regiment in April 1943. On 16th April 1944, Meissner became the acting commander of the 3rd Battalion of the 143rd *Fallschirmjäger* Regiment, part of the 5th *Fallschirmjäger* Division.

Joachim Meissner was killed in the battle for St. Lô on 25th July 1944. He is buried in the Military Cemetery in Marigny, and his grave is located in block 4, row 40, grave No: 1552.

Left to Right: Joachim Meissner, Rudolf Witzig and Walter Koch being congratulated by Hitler after receiving the Knight's Cross for their part in the successful attack on the Belgium fortress of Emael-Eben. (Author's Collection)

OTHER AWARDS		PROMOTIONS	
01.04.1939	Armed Forces Long Service Award 4th Class	01.10.1931	Oberschütze
00.10.1939	Commemorative Medal of 1st October 1938	01.10.1933	Gefreiter
00.00.1939	Parachutist Badge	01.11.1933	Unteroffizier-Anwärter
12.05.1940	Iron Cross 2nd Class	21.02.1938	Reserve-Offiziersanwärter
13.05.1940	Iron Cross 1st Class	14.04.1938	Unteroffizier der Reserve
04.07.1942	Eastern Front Medal	26.08.1939	Feldwebel der Reserve
26.10.1942	Luftwaffe Ground Assault Badge	20.03.1940	Leutnant der Reserve
-----	-----	16.05.1940	Oberleutnant der Reserve
-----	-----	30.09.1942	Hauptmann (active)

OTTO MENGES
(09.05.1917 – 24.05.1944)   *Leutnant*

(Wehrkundearchiv)

Knight's Cross: Awarded posthumously on 9th June 1944 as *Oberfeldwebel* and Platoon Leader in the 6th Company, 1st *Fallschirmjäger* Regiment for outstanding bravery while leading a counterattack north of Cassino.

Otto Menges was born on 9th May 1917 in Bechtolsheim, Bingen and joined the IV Parachute Rifle Battalion of the *General Göring* Regiment in October 1937 and in April 1938 he entered the 2nd Company of the 1st *Fallschirmjäger* Regiment. After completing the parachutist-rifleman course in Stendal in July he was promoted to *Oberjäger*. Menges went on to serve with distinction in the Norwegian Campaign, and jumped with his unit into Crete and was even captured by the British in May, being a prisoner-of-war for just a day.

He saw action in Russia and was promoted to *Oberfeldwebel* in March 1943. He was recommended for the German Cross in Gold by his regimental commander, *Oberst* Schulz in October 1943. In early-1944, he was transferred to Italy where he saw action at Monet Cassino, and on 8th February, the enemy launched an attack against the German troops northwest of Cassino and Menges on his own initiative led his company in a strong counter-attack and although the terrain was rough and the enemy strong his troops managed to push back the enemy attack. The official report on the counter-attack stated that, "... *the careful guidance and exemplary personal commitment by Menges was a crucial factor in the success of the counter-attack.*" On 11th February, the enemy drove into the German defensive positions between Hill 539 and the neighbouring hills. Menges once again seized the initiative and drove the enemy back. His commander Karl-Lothar Schulz recommended him for the Knight's Cross and promotion to the rank of *Leutnant*.

Menges was killed in action on 24th May 1944, while leading yet another counter-attack north of Cassino. He received the award and the promotion posthumously. He is buried in the War Cemetery in Pomezia, Italy, his body has not been identified and he is buried as an "Unknown Soldier."

OTHER AWARDS		PROMOTIONS		
00.12.1939	Commemorative Medal of 1st October 1938 + Bar	12.10.1939	Oberjäger	
18.04.1940	Iron Cross 2nd Class	12.11.1941	Feldwebel	
20.01.1941	Wound Badge in Black	04.03.1943	Oberfeldwebel	
29.06.1941	Iron Cross 1st Class	-----		-----
02.10.1941	Armed Forces Long Service Award 4th Class	-----		-----
01.10.1942	Luftwaffe Ground Assault Badge	-----		-----
20.05.1943	KRETA Cuff title	-----		-----
16.12.1943	Wound Badge in Silver	-----		-----
16.01.1944	German Cross in Gold			

GERHARD GEORG MERTINS

(30.12.1919 – 19.03.1993)   *Major*

(Wehrkundearchiv)

Knight's Cross: Awarded on 6th December 1944 as *Hauptmann* and *Führer* 5th *Fallschirm-Pioniere* Battalion for actions in France. Mertins led his battalion during the retreat in Normandy as part of the 9th Panzer Division, and he successfully brought his unit through to Nancy. During the heavy action he and his battalion blew up a total of 46 bridges and halted the allied advance.

Gerhard Mertins was born on 30th December 1919 in Berlin and joined the 208th Engineer Replacement Company's 1st Platoon in September 1939, and by the following year he had become leader of the Company Headquarters Squad.

Mertins took part in the Balkans campaign in March 1941, and later parachuted into Crete where he won the Iron Cross 1st and 2nd Classes. In October, he saw action on the Eastern Front where he took over command of the 4th Company from the wounded *Oberleutnant* Gerstner. It wasn't long before Mertins was wounded himself and had to be evacuated to an aid station. While recovering he was assigned to the headquarters of Air Fleet 3 and then in October 1942 he returned to action on the Eastern Front. During the heavy fighting near Strasnogorodka, his unit was encircled by Soviet forces, but Mertins managed to break out and during the course of the fighting was wounded twice. For his actions during the encirclement he was awarded the German Cross in Gold. After recovering in hospital from wounds received in Russia, he was transferred to the Colgne-Wahn, where he took over the 1st Company of the Parachute Engineer Replacement Battalion. He saw action during the retreat in Normandy where he won the Knight's Cross, and later during the Ardennes Offensive his unit prevented the enemy attempts to break through the German lines. His divisional commander, *Generalmajor* Heilmann, later described the 5th Parachute Engineer Battalion as the elite unit of his division. On 9th March 1945, Mertins was wounded for the fifth time and spent the remainder of the war recovering from his wounds. He died in Fort Lauderdale, Florida, in the United States, on 19th March 1993.

OTHER AWARDS		PROMOTIONS	
27.03.1941	Parachutist Badge	07.09.1939	Pionier
07.06.1941	Iron Cross 2nd Class	01.03.1940	Oberpionier
25.06.1941	Iron Cross 1st Class	11.06.1940	Gefreiter
08.02.1943	German Cross in Gold	01.01.1941	Unteroffizier
06.12.1944	Wound Badge in Silver	15.01.1941	Kriegsoffizieranwärter
06.12.1944	Luftwaffe Close Combat Clasp in Bronze	17.03.1941	Feldwebel
15.02.1945	Luftwaffe Close Combat Clasp in Silver	30.04.1941	Leutnant
09.03.1945	Wound Badge in Gold	01.03.1943	Oberleutnant
-----	-----	28.08.1944	Hauptmann
-----	-----	28.02.1945	Major

HEINZ MEYER

(09.04.1916 – 22.09.1987)   *Major*

(Wehrkundearchiv)

Knight's Cross: Awarded on 8th April 1944 as *Hauptmann* and Commander 8th Company, 4th *Fallschirmjäger Regiment* in recognition of his success in pushing back an Allied assault which posed a serious threat to the German positions at Monte Cassino.

Knight's Cross with Oakleaves: He became the 654th recipient of the Oakleaves on 18th November 1944 as *Hauptmann* and *Führer* 3rd Battalion, 15th *Fallschirmjäger Regiment* for his continued gallantry in action and inspiring leadership during the battles in Normandy and in Holland.

Heinz Meyer was born on 9th April 1916, in Magdeburg and joined the 14th Parachute Company of the *General Göring* Regiment in November 1937. In April 1938, he joined the 4th Company of the 1st *Fallschirmjäger* Regiment and in April 1940 was assigned to the Luftwaffe Officer Candidate School in Berlin-Gatow. After his promotion to *Leutnant* in August 1940, Meyer became a platoon leader in the 11th Company of the 3rd *Fallschirmjäger* Regiment. He took part in the operations in Holland, fought in Norway where he won the Iron Cross 1st Class and took part in the airborne invasion of Crete. Meyer then took part in the airborne reinforcement of General Dietl's mountain troops in northern Norway at Narvik. He then became a Platoon Leader in the 11th Company of the 3rd *Fallschirmjäger* Regiment and was promoted to *Leutnant* in August 1940. He parachuted into Prison Valley at Crete on 20th May 1941 during the German airborne invasion of the island and received the Iron Cross 1st Class a month later.

In October 1941, he saw action in Russia, along the Newa River east of Leningrad. In early 1942 he transferred to the 3rd Battalion of the 4th *Fallschirmjäger* Regiment and became acting commander of the regiment's 11th Company. Promoted to *Oberleutnant* in July he was again deployed to Russia in November, and was attached to the 9th Army near Rzez, where he won the German Cross in Gold. Meyer and his company then moved to the Italian Front, seeing action in Sicily. In November 1943, he was promoted to *Hauptmann* and for a brief period took command of the 3rd Battalion of the 3rd *Fallschirmjäger* Regiment during the defence of the Calvary Mountain near Cassino. On 21st February 1944, the 2nd Battalion of the 4th *Fallschirmjäger* Regiment moved into position on Calvary Hill, to the northwest of the Monastery. On 19th March, an Allied force attacked and although Meyer was taken by surprise his men sprang into action against the enemy forces. Six tanks were destroyed and another sixteen disabled. By halting this attack Meyer and his men had removed a dangerous threat to the Monastery, and for this he was awarded the Knight's Cross. He was then transferred to France where he saw action in Normandy during the fighting in the Falaise Pocket. Despite continued attacks by Allied aircraft, his unit had defended well against the U.S. 2nd Infantry Division. By August, the 5th *Fallschirmjäger* Division had almost been cut off in and barely escaped capture. Meyer's leadership and bravery was recognized when he was awarded the Knight's Cross with Oaklaves.

By March 1945, Meyer was commanding a Battle Group against the Americans in the Harz Mountain area. He was taken prisoner by the Americans on 8th May 1945, and was released on 20th December the same year. Meyer died in Viersen on 22nd September 1987.

OTHER AWARDS		PROMOTIONS	
23.05.1940	Iron Cross 2nd Class	01.10.1938	Gefreiter
21.06.1941	Iron Cross 1st Class	01.10.1939	Obergefreiter
02.11.1941	Armed Forces Long Service Award 4th Class	01.11.1939	Unteroffizier
20.09.1942	Luftwaffe Ground Assault Badge	27.04.1940	Reserve-Offiziersanwärter
00.00.1942	Eastern Front Medal	01.05.1940	Feldwebel
20.05.1943	KRETA Cuff title	01.08.1940	Leutnant der Reserve
21.06.1943	German Cross in Gold	01.07.1942	Oberleutnant der Reserve
20.02.1944	Wound Badge in Black	01.11.1943	Hauptmann der Reserve
-----	-----	21.10.1944	Major der Reserve

DR. JUR. WERNER WOLFGANG EBERHARD MILCH

(15.11.1903 – 17.11.1984)   *Major der Reserve*

Knight's Cross: Awarded on 9th January 1945 as *Hauptmann der Reserve* and Commander *Fallschirm*-Mortar Training and Testing Battalion for actions near Nancy, France, where his troops smashed the American bridgehead at Flavigny.

(Wehrkundearchiv)

Dr. Werner Milch, the brother of *Generalfeldmarschall* Erhard Milch, was born on 15th November 1903 in Wilhelmshaven. He joined the Reichswehr in April 1924 and served as a volunteer in the 6th Prussian Artillery Regiment in Minden. He was commissioned as a *Leutnant* in March 1939, and saw action during World War II with the 603rd Motorized Special Purpose Artillery Regiment during the Polish Campaign and then during the Western Campaign, where he won the Iron Cross 2nd Class. On 17th December 1941, Milch joined the 1st *Fallschirmjäger* Regiment as a battery commander and saw action on the Eastern Front. He later served in North Africa with the Ramcke Brigade from August to November 1942. His battery fought in a defensive role at Bab el Quattara where they destroyed a number of enemy tanks. In June 1943, he transferred to the 2nd *Fallschirmjäger* Division and took part in the Battle of Rome. In the winter of 1943, he returned to Russia where he commanded the II Battalion of the 2nd *Fallschirmjäger* Regiment during the difficult and bloody defensive battles there. He and his battery held Zhaikovka airfield and fought successfully at Juchnov.

Dr. Werner Milch's brother Generalfeldmarschall Erhard Milch with Albert Speer Reichsminister for Armaments and War Production and on the right Willy Messerschmitt, the famous aircraft designer. (Author's Collection)

Milch fought his last battle at Bad Zwischenahn airport where on 5th May 1945 his battalion repulsed a heavy attack by enemy tanks. Just three days later, he surrendered to the Allies. After the war, he acted as a co-counsel during the trial of his brother for war crimes at Nuremberg. He died on 17th November 1984 in Hemer, North-Rhine Westphalia. He is buried there at the local cemetery (Section D, Field 21, Grave 176-180).

OTHER AWARDS		PROMOTIONS	
02.10.1936	Armed Forces Long Service Award 4th to 3rd Class	01.03.1937	Gefreiter der Reserve
16.05.1940	Iron Cross 2nd Class	20.08.1937	Unteroffizier der Reserve
19.07.1941	Wound Badge in Black	16.09.1937	Wachtmeister der Reserve
18.02.1942	Iron Cross 1st Class	01.03.1939	Leutnant der Reserve
01.07.1942	Luftwaffe Ground Assault Badge	31.10.1941	Oberleutnant der Reserve
19.10.1942	Parachutist Badge	23.01.1943	Hauptmann der Reserve
15.12.1942	Eastern Front Medal	01.01.1945	Major der Reserve
05.03.1943	Italian-German Campaign Medal in Africa	-----	-----
01.05.1943	KRETA Cuff title	-----	-----
00.11.1943	Wound Badge in Silver	-----	-----
15.04.1944	German Cross in Gold	-----	-----

GERD PAUL LUDWIG MISCHKE

(16.03.1920 – 05.11.1992)   *Hauptmann*

(Wehrkundearchiv)

Knight's Cross: Awarded on 18th May 1943 as *Leutnant* and Platoon Leader in the 2nd Company, *Fallschirm-Flak* Machine-gun Battalion for action in northwest Africa. He was responsible, along with his company of halting the American advance south of Mateur in March 1943. During the German attack his company provided ant-tank defence and Mischke himself destroyed a heavy tank from a distance of forty metres. On 5th May his five anti-tank guns destroyed six enemy tanks and prevented another breakthrough by the enemy.

Gerd Mischke was born on 16th March 1920 in Wuppertal-Barmen and joined the 82nd Flight Training Regiment in Osnabrück in April 1939. After several other postings, he transferred to the 2nd Battery of the 7th Anti-aircraft Battalion in July 1940. He then transferred to the parachute troops and after completing his parachute-rifle training he joined the 2nd Company of the Parachute Anti-aircraft Machine-gun Battalion in Aschersleben in December 1940.

He first saw action during the invasion of Crete where he fought as a gun commander in the Rethymnon area. On 22nd May, his unit repulsed the enemy and Mischke led a counter-attack, winning the Iron Cross 1st Class and 2nd Classes. He later served on the Russian front where he led his battery with bravery and skill and was commissioned as a *Leutnant* on 19th June 1942. In 1943, he was transferred to Tunis and then to Northwest Africa where he won the Knight's Cross. In late-1944, he saw action in Brest and was awarded the German Cross in Gold in January 1945. Mischke died on 5th November 1992 in Wuppertal-Barmen.

OTHER AWARDS		PROMOTIONS	
20.10.1940	Parachutist Badge	01.04.1940	Gefreiter
13.06.1941	Iron Cross 2nd Class	15.03.1941	Kriegsoffizieranwärter
28.06.1941	Iron Cross 1st Class	01.04.1941	Unteroffizier
18.07.1942	Luftwaffe Ground Assault Badge	01.02.1942	Feldwebel
12.11.1942	AFRIKA Cuff title	01.04.1942	Oberfeldwebel
04.04.1943	Italian-German Campaign Medal in Africa	19.06.1942	Leutnant der Reserve
01.01.1945	German Cross in Gold	10.05.1944	Oberleutnant der Reserve
-----	-----	13.09.1944	Hauptmann der Reserve
-----	-----	01.01.1945	Hauptmann (active)

KARL NEUHOFF

(24.04.1915 – 25.12.2001)   *Oberleutnant*

(Wehrkundearchiv)

Knight's Cross: Awarded on 9th June 1944 as *Oberfeldwebel* and Assault Detachment Leader in the 6th Company, 3rd *Fallschirmjäger* Regiment for actions at Cassino. On 15th March 1944, Neuhoff and his men managed to stop the New Zealand 24th Battalion from entering the city of Cassino.

Karl Neuhoff was born in Gevelsberg, a small town in North Rhine-Westphalia on 24th April 1915 and entered military service in November 1937 when he joined the III Battalion of the 17th Infantry Regiment. In May 1938, he transferred to the parachute troops, and after he had completed his training was appointed Squad Leader in the 10th Company of the 17th Infantry Regiment. He took part in the Polish Campaign and in 1940 he joined the 7th Air Division's Parachute Replacement Battalion. In April 1941, he served with the 3rd Fallschirmjäger Regiment during the airborne invasion of Crete where he won the Iron Cross 1st and 2nd Classes. He was then transferred to Russia where he took part in heavy fighting and was wounded, and the following month he was again wounded.

He then saw action during the Battle of Sicily, it was in a defensive role in the Lentini area under the command of the Schmalz Brigade. He was one of the last soldiers to cross over to the mainland in August 1943. In March 1944, he saw action with New Zealand troops in the area around Cassino where he won the Knight's Cross. He was wounded once again on 23rd March and in June he was commissioned as a *Leutnant* and on 29th December he was promoted to *Oberleutnant*. He continued to command the 1st Battalion of the 3rd *Fallschirmjäger* Regiment until the end of the war. He surrendered to U.S. troops on 2nd May 1945. After the war, he migrated to the United States where he died on Christmas Day 2011 in Kentucky. He is buried the Resthaven Cemetery in Corbin, Knox County, Kentucky.

OTHER AWARDS		PROMOTIONS	
30.07.1938	Parachutist Badge	01.10.1938	Gefreiter
23.06.1941	Iron Cross 2nd Class	01.09.1939	Oberjäger
22.06.1941	Iron Cross 1st Class	01.12.1940	Feldwebel
10.01.1942	Wound Badge in Black	23.12.1942	Oberfeldwebel
01.10.1942	Luftwaffe Ground Assault Badge	22.06.1944	Leutnant
20.05.1943	KRETA Cuff title	29.12.1944	Oberleutnant
27.10.1943	German Cross in Gold	-----	-----
30.03.1944	Wound Badge in Silver	-----	-----

DR. HEINRICH NEUMANN

(17.02.1908 – 19.05.2005)   *Oberstarzt*

Knight's Cross: Awarded on 21st August 1941 as *Oberstabsarzt* and Regimental Doctor of the 1st Air-Landing Assault Regiment, at the same time was *Führer* of 1st Battalion, 1st Air-Landing Assault Regiment for actions in Crete. During the airborne invasion of Crete he assumed command of the I Battalion after *Major* Koch had been wounded. He led the battalion into action and stormed Hill 107, from which the enemy was firing on Malemes airfield. Neumann led the battalion with great skill and bravery; – his achievement was more remarkable because Neumann was not a natural commander, he was the regimental doctor.

Neumann returned to active service in 1959 with the Bundeswehr and served as Oberstarzt der Reserve with the Parachute Troops until July 1962 when he was appointed Senior Instructor at the Parachute School in Altenstadt. He retired in 1964. Dr. Heinrich Neumann died on 19th May 2005 in Düsseldorf. (Private Source)

(Author's Collection)

Heinrich Neumann was born on 17th February 1908 in Berlin-Steglitz and joined the 9th Infantry Regiment in January 1933. In June he transferred to the 6th Prussian Medical Battalion in Braunschweig and in March 1934 transferred to the Luftwaffe. On 18th June, he graduated from the University of Münster as a doctor of medicine.

Neumann then transferred to Berlin as an aviation station medical officer and in July 1937 went to Staaken for flight training. In April 1938, he was assigned to the 1st Luftwaffe Administration Command (*Luftgau*) Medical Battalion in Königsberg and a few months later served in the Reich Air Ministry under *Generalmajor* Student. On 19th February 1939, he attended his parachute-rifle training in Stendal and from there joined the Luftwaffe Medical or First-aid Echelon in Frankfurt on the Oder and from there went to Magdeburg. Neumann joined the parachute troops as commander of the 7th Luftwaffe Medical Company in Gardelegen. He became commanding officer of the 7th Parachute Medical Battalion, and on 15th October 1940 he was appointed regimental medical officer of the 1st Parachute Assault Regiment. Neumann later took part in the invasion of Fortress Holland where he was awarded the Iron Cross 1st Class. He took command of the 1st Battalion when *Major* Koch was wounded and stormed Hill 107 and for this he was awarded the Knight's Cross.

He went on to serve in Russia where he was able to rescue 5,000 wounded soldiers from the Juchnov Pocket. Promoted to *Oberstarzt* in September 1943, he served as the Divisional Doctor of the 6th *Fallschirmjäger* Division from June 1944 and ended the war as Doctor of the II Parachute Corps.

OTHER AWARDS		PROMOTIONS	
00.00.1935	Observers Badge	01.05.1933	Unterarzt
02.01.1937	Armed Forces Long Service Award 4th Class	19.08.1933	Assistenzarzt
09.11.1938	German Red Cross Award 2nd Class	01.06.1934	Oberarzt
31.03.1939	Parachutist Badge	01.08.1935	Stabsarzt
06.06.1939	Spanish Cross in Silver + Swords	31.05.1939	Oberstabsarzt
06.06.1939	Medal for the Spanish Campaign	06.02.1942	Oberfeldarzt
06.06.1939	Spanish War Cross	01.09.1943	Oberstarzt
26.06.1939	Commemorative Medal of 1st October 1938 + Bar	-----	-----
20.05.1940	Iron Cross 2nd Class	-----	-----
20.05.1940	Iron Cross 1st Class	-----	-----
00.00.1942	Eastern Front Medal	-----	-----
00.10.1942	Luftwaffe Ground Assault Badge	-----	-----
00.05.1943	KRETA Cuff title	-----	-----

HEINRICH ORTH

(14.01.1916 – 10.03.1942)   *Leutnant*

(Wehrkundearchiv)

Knight's Cross: Awarded posthumously on 18th March 1942 as *Oberfeldwebel* and Platoon Leader in the 4th Company, 1st Air-Landing Assault Regiment for actions in Russia. On 10th March 1942, Orth led his platoon into an enemy held village near Zhaikovska, and he and his troops were immediately fired upon. The Soviets held the village with stubborn resistance and the German troops managed to drive out the enemy from the village, but during the fierce fighting Orth was killed.

Heinrich Orth was born on 14th January 1916 in Dudweiler-Herrensohr, Saarbrücken, and he entered the Luftwaffe in October 1935. He joined the I Battalion of the 4th Anti-aircraft Regiment in Dortmund, and in April 1938 volunteered to join the parachute service. He completed his parachutist-rifleman course and after was assigned to the 1st Company of the 1st *Fallschirmjäger* Regiment. He served as an *Oberjäger* and squad leader during the invasion of Poland and proved that he was a fighter. In February 1940, he was transferred to the 17th Company and fought bravely in the battles for the Belgian frontier fortress Eben Emael and the bridges over the Albert Canal. He freed two squads which had been surrounded by the enemy and for this he won both the Iron Cross 1st and 2nd Classes and was promoted to *Feldwebel*.

In August 1940, he was made Platoon Leader in the 4th Company of the 1st Parachute Assault Regiment and later saw action during the invasion of Russia. He led his platoon with great bravery, and during the bloody fighting near the village of Zhaikovska Orth was killed. Before he died, he had led his platoon and occasionally the company against strong and stubborn resistance and had driven the enemy out of the village. For this he was honoured posthumously with the Knight's Cross.

He was buried in the Paratroopers Cemetery in Schaikowka together with another Knight's Cross holder, *Oberleutnant* Helmut Arpke, who was killed at the same place on 16th January 1942.

OTHER AWARDS		PROMOTIONS	
00.00.1938	Parachutist Badge	01.12.1936	Gefreiter
02.10.1939	Armed Forces Long Service Award 4th Class	01.12.1937	Oberjäger
00.12.1939	Commemorative Medal of 1st October 1938 + Bar	13.05.1940	Feldwebel
13.05.1940	Iron Cross 2nd Class	01.07.1941	Oberfeldwebel
13.05.1940	Iron Cross 1st Class	04.08.1942	Leutnant

GERHARD PADE

(21.06.1912 – 20.10.1983) *Major*

(Wehrkundearchiv)

Knight's Cross: Awarded on 30th April 1945 as *Major* and Commander 1st Battalion, 4th *Fallschirmjäger* Regiment. *There is no proof in surviving records in the Federal Archives of the Knight's Cross being officially awarded. Not a legally valid award by the Commanding General of the I Fallschirm-Corps, General der Fallschirmtruppe Richard Heidrich*

Gerhard Pade was born on 21st June 1912 in Berlin and entered the police service on 1st October 1932. He completed a police training course at the Brandenburg-Havel Police School and became a police *Wachtmeister*.

In July 1937, he transferred to the Luftwaffe and was assigned to the parachute troops. After completing his parachutist-rifleman's course he joined the 1st Battalion of the 1st *Fallschirmjäger* Regiment on 1st April 1938. He completed a senior NCO course in early-1939 and was well known as an athlete and won sporting titles as a hammer thrower. He didn't see action during the Polish Campaign but did fight in the Western Campaign and saw action in Fortress Holland. There he distinguished himself in battle and won the Iron Cross 1st and 2nd Classes.

On 1st June 1941, he became a wartime officer candidate and following an officer course he joined the 2nd Company of the 1st *Fallschirmjäger* Regiment. He was made a Platoon Leader and played a leading role in the defensive actions in Russia, where for a time he led the 1st Company. In March 1942, he was commissioned as an *Oberleutnant* and within a year had been promoted to *Hauptmann*. From May 1942 to January 1943, he commanded the 14th Anti-tank Company of the 1st *Fallschirmjäger* Regiment and on 28th January he attended a company commander's course in Versailles. In July 1944, he was given temporary command of the I Battalion of the 1st *Fallschirmjäger* Regiment and saw action in Italy where he won the German Cross in Gold. He continued to see action during the fierce fighting near Bologna and Imola, and from 8th December 1944 led I Battalion of the 4th *Fallschirmjäger* Regiment. He held the defensive positions and guarded the crossings of the Po and the Schio Rivers and was recommended for the Knight's Cross.

He surrendered to Allied troops in May 1945 and was released in early 1946. Pade died on 20th October 1983 in Berlin.

OTHER AWARDS		PROMOTIONS	
02.01.1937	Armed Forces Long Service Award 4th Class	01.09.1933	Polizei-Wachtmeister
00.00.1939	Commemorative Medal of 13th March 1938	16.03.1936	Oberjäger
15.04.1940	Iron Cross 2nd Class	01.04.1938	Feldwebel
22.05.1940	Iron Cross 1st Class	01.08.1939	Hauptfeldwebel
30.05.1940	Wound Badge in Black	01.06.1941	Kriegsoffizieranwärter
01.10.1942	Luftwaffe Ground Assault Badge	01.03.1942	Leutnant
20.05.1943	KRETA Cuff title	01.03.1942	Oberleutnant
20.08.1944	German Cross in Gold	01.04.1943	Hauptmann
00.00.1944	War Service Cross 2nd Class + Swords	01.01.1945	Major

HUGO PAUL
(01.02.1913 – 12.03.1993)   *Major*

(Author's Collection)

Knight's Cross: Awarded on 18th November 1944 as *Hauptmann* and *Führer* of the Parachute Battalion *Paul* for actions in the Western Campaign. He took part in heavy action near Overloon and Venlo in the Netherlands, where his troops pushed back several attacks made by enemy tanks. Through his leadership and skill as a battalion leader the enemy was driven out of Overloon and several enemy tanks were destroyed during the fierce fighting.

Hugo Paul was born on 1st February 1913 in Villingen, Gießen and he joined the 15th Regiment in Marburg-Lahn in April 1931. By October, he had become a squad leader in the 1st Company and in April 1934 had become a section leader in the 12th Company of the 115th Infantry Regiment, with the rank of *Unteroffizier*. In April 1937, he became Platoon Leader with the 12th Company and by August had been promoted to *Feldwebel*. From June 1937 until April 1938 he attended the Hannover Cavalry School and spent the next two years in the reserves.

In June 1940, he became an *Oberfeldwebel* and reported to Parachute School III in Braunschweig for parachute training. In August he was assigned to the 12th Company of the 1st *Fallschirmjäger* Regiment. After passing through Luftwaffe Officer Candidate School in Berlin-Gatow in March 1941, he now saw action in Crete. When his company commander was killed during the early stages of the invasion, Paul took over command of the 4th Company. He won both the Iron Cross 1st and 2nd Classes and in September 1941 was commissioned as an *Oberleutnant*, bypassing the rank of *Leutnant*.

In Russia, he saw action at Anisovo-Gorodische and in January 1942 was one of the most successful patrol leaders of his regiment, inflicting serious defeats on the enemy. He even received a letter of congratulations from the Commanding General of the VIII Air Corps, *Generaloberst* Wolfram von Richthofen. He was wounded in March 1942, and after recovering from his wounds saw action in Tunisia. He served as company commander with the 5th *Fallschirmjäger* Division until April 1943 when he was again wounded. He returned to active duty as a *Hauptmann* in October and served again briefly with the 5th *Fallschirmjäger* Regiment but fell ill and returned to Germany. From December 1943 until April 1944, he served as an instructor at the Panzer School in Paris. He later served as an Ordnance Officer with Parachute Battalion *Schirmer,* and after attending a battalion training course he took command of Parachute Battalion "Paul," with which he saw action near Overloon and Venlo. It was here that he was awarded the Knight' Cross, and it was presented to him while in hospital by *Generalleutnant* Wolfgang Erdmann.

He was promoted to *Major* in February 1945, and he commanded the 3rd Battalion of the 21st Fallschirmjäger Regiment in Holland until the end of the war. He rejoined the *Bundeswehr* in March 1956 with the rank of Major and served until December 1969 after being promoted to *Oberstleutnant*. Hugo Paul died on 12th March 1993 in Worms.

OTHER AWARDS		PROMOTIONS	
20.07.1936	Armed Forces Long Service Award 4th Class	01.04.1933	Obergrenadier
14.01.1941	Parachutist Badge	01.08.1934	Unteroffizier
12.06.1941	Iron Cross 2nd Class	01.08.1937	Feldwebel
24.06.1941	Iron Cross 1st Class	01.06.1940	Oberfeldwebel
18.03.1942	Wound Badge in Black	01.08.1940	Offiziersanwärter
21.09.1942	Eastern Front Medal	01.09.1941	Oberleutnant
18.03.1943	Luftwaffe Ground Assault Badge	01.04.1943	Hauptmann
20.05.1943	KRETA Cuff title	01.02.1945	Major
30.07.1943	AFRIKA Cuff title	-----	-----
28.08.1943	Italian-German Campaign Medal in Africa	-----	-----

HERBERT PEITSCH

(26.01.1926 – 30.07.1944) **Gefreiter**

(Wehrkundearchiv)

Knight's Cross: Posthumously awarded on 29th October 1944 as *Gefreiter* and Rifleman of the 7th Company, 6th *Fallschirmjäger* Regiment for actions on the western front. During the Allied invasion of France Peitsch served with great bravery and took part in a successful breakout and he played a vital role in the halting of the enemy advance in the Battle of Ste. Mère Eglise. Peitsch was a tower of strength in the fighting at Coutances and Poncey and during the attack near Perrou he was killed. Again he was recommended for the Knight's Cross and finally in October it was posthumously awarded to him.

Herbert Peitsch was born on 26th January 1926 in Pollnow, Schlawe and joined the 5th Company of the 205th Infantry Replacement Regiment on 7th August 1941. He saw action during the Russian campaign where he won the Iron Cross 2nd Class.

After his fourth application to the parachute troops, Peitsch was transferred to the 6th *Fallschirmjäger* Regiment, that had been formed by *Major* Friedrich-August von der Heydte in January 1944. He joined the unit in May and saw action in Normandy. On 6th June 1944, D-Day, Peistch was in action in the Carentan area. He witnessed American paratroops of the 101st Airborne Division dropping into the area and he rounded up the troops who had scattered all over the area and brought them back to his regimental headquarters as prisoners. For this act his battalion commander recommended him for the Knight's Cross but it was refused. He was however awarded the Iron Cross 1st Class in July.

He later took part in halting an enemy advance, and during bitter fighting at Coutances and Poncey, he was killed on 30th July 1944 (although some sources claim the date was 6th or 7th August) while defending an American attack.

OTHER AWARDS		PROMOTIONS	
00.00.194_	Parachutist Badge	30.12.1942	Gefreiter
17.04.1943	Iron Cross 2nd Class	-----	-----
01.07.1944	Iron Cross 1st Class	-----	-----

ERICH PIETZONKA

(04.10.1906 – 18.12.1989)   *Oberst*

(Wehrkundearchiv)

Knight's Cross: Awarded on 5th September 1944, as *Oberstleutnant* and Commander 7th *Fallschirmjäger Regiment* for his leadership and bravery during the heavy fighting around the area of Shitomir and Kirvograd, Russia.

Knight's Cross with Oakleaves: He became the 584th recipient of the Oakleaves on 16th September 1944 as *Oberst* and Commander 7th *Fallschirmjäger Regiment* in recognition of his success and leadership during the fierce fighting around Fortress Brest. His counter-attacks halted the enemy forces and his troops destroyed forty-three tanks as well as the capturing over 300 prisoners.

Erich Pietzonka was born in Plümkenau, Oppeln, on 4th October 1906, and he entered the army with the 14th Company of the 7th Prussian Infantry Regiment in Silesia on 1st November 1924. In January 1932, he transferred to the 2nd Company as a Platoon Leader and in December 1933 was promoted to *Oberfeldwebel*. After completing his officers' courses at Hildesheim and Braunschweig Flying School, he was commissioned as a *Leutnant* in April 1935. After promotion to *Hauptmann* he served as chief of staff with III./KG 355, which later became known as the KG 53 "Legion Condor."

In February 1938, he was appointed commander of the 1st Company of the Luftwaffe Watch Battalion in Berlin before joining the 9th Company of the 1st *Fallschirmjäger* Regiment *"General Göring"* seven months later. On 15th July 1940, following his parachute training Pietzonka was made commander of the 2nd Battalion of the 2nd *Fallschirmjäger* Regiment. On 26th April 1941, he participated in the parachute operation against the Corinth Canal as a *Major* with the 2nd *Fallschirmjäger* Regiment. Pietzonka was unfortunately seriously wounded on landing and didn't take part in the battle. However, he soon recovered and rejoined his battalion in December and took part in the defensive actions at the Volkhov and the Mius in 1942-1943, and here won the German Cross in Gold.

In June 1943, he took temporary command of the 2nd *Fallschirmjäger* Regiment and led them with great skill during the German occupation of Rome. During the winter of 1943, he saw action against the Red Army at Zhitomir and Kirovograd and it was here that he won the Knight's Cross. Promoted to *Oberstleutnant* in March 1944, and to *Oberst* in September 1944, he saw action in Normandy and finally in Fortress Brest where he won the Knight's Cross with Oakleaves. Three days after being presented with the Oakleaves, he was captured by U.S. troops and he remained in captivity until 6th May 1946. Erich Pietzonka died in Bad Sassendorf on 18th December 1989.

OTHER AWARDS		PROMOTIONS	
00.00.1936	Reich Sports Badge in Bronze	01.11.1926	Schütze
02.10.1936	Armed Forces Long Service Award 4th Class	01.11.1928	Gefreiter
17.12.1936	Armed Forces Long Service Award 3rd Class	01.11.1929	Unteroffizier
00.00.1938	Parachutist Badge	20.05.1931	Oberfeldwebel-Anwärter
28.05.1940	Iron Cross 2nd Class	01.11.1931	Unterfeldwebel
28.05.1940	Iron Cross 1st Class	01.12.1933	Oberfeldwebel

21.07.1941	Wound Badge in Black	01.04.1935	Leutnant
09.02.1942	Italian Medal of Honour in Bronze	01.04.1935	Oberleutnant
22.06.1942	Infantry Assault Badge in Silver	01.04.1936	Hauptmann
14.07.1942	Eastern Front Medal	26.03.1941	Major
04.08.1942	German Cross in Gold	01.03.1944	Oberstleutnant
06.11.1942	Luftwaffe Ground Assault Badge	08.09.1944	Oberst

FRITZ PRAGER

(17.12.1905 – 03.12.1940) *Major*

Knight's Cross: Awarded on 24th May 1940 as *Hauptmann* and Commander 2nd Battalion, 1st *Fallschirmjäger* Regiment for actions in Holland. After being wounded in Holland after leading his troops in the storming of Mooerdijk Bridge he remained with his battalion, which held the bridge until relieved by tanks of the 9th Panzer Division.

Fritz Prager with his son shortly after being awarded the Knight's Cross, May 1940. (Author's Collection)

(Author's Collection)

Fritz Prager was born on 17th December 1905 in Chemnitz and he entered the *Reichswehr* in November 1923 and was assigned to the 10th Infantry Regiment. In July 1938, now a *Hauptmann* he joined the parachute troops and after completing his parachutist-rifleman course in Stendal he was appointed commander of the II Battalion of the 1st *Fallschirmjäger* Regiment in Braunschweig.

In September 1939, his battalion was one of the first to enter Poland, where it captured Wola Gulowska airfield. On 13th October 1939, Prager was decorated with the Iron Cross 2nd Class by *Generalmajor* Kurt Student. In April 1940, he underwent an operation, but this did not keep him from jumping with his battalion over Holland. He led his troops during the storming of Moerdijk Bridge where he was seriously wounded. On 10th May 1940, he was awarded the Iron Cross 1st Class and two weeks later came the award of the Knight's Cross. While recovering from his wound, he heard that his battalion was to be deployed to relieve the mountain infantry near Narvik where he led the II Battalion of the 3rd *Fallschirmjäger* Regiment.

However, he became ill towards the end of 1940 and was diagnosed with cancer; he died in hospital on 3rd December 1940.

OTHER AWARDS		PROMOTIONS	
02.10.1936	Armed Forces Long Service Award 4th to 3rd Class	01.06.1930	Leutnant
00.00.1938	Parachutist Badge	01.07.1933	Oberleutnant
13.10.1939	Iron Cross 2nd Class	01.04.1937	Hauptmann
10.05.1940	Iron Cross 1st Class	19.06.1940	Major

HERMANN-BERNHARD "GERHARD" RAMCKE

(24.01.1889 – 04.07.1968) *General der Fallschirmtruppe*

(Private source)

Knight's Cross: Awarded on 21st August 1941 for his heroic action in Crete, while serving as *Generalmajor* and Commander of the Supplementary Troops of the XI Air Corps and at the same was *Führer* of the Air Landing Assault Regiment. On 21st May, the airborne invasion of Crete began, the following day Ramcke was dropped by parachute into Crete with 500 troops. They landed west of Tavronitis and east of the airfield at Malem. Once landed Ramcke took command of the Air Landing Assault Regiment after its commander had been seriously wounded. Ramcke led the fighting along the coast road culminating in the capture of Canea on 27th May. Five days later, the last of the British troops who had not already been evacuated surrendered to the Germans. The award was presented to Ramcke personally by *Reichsmarschall* Hermann Göring at Hitler's Military Headquarters the Wolfs Lair.

Knight's Cross with Oakleaves: He became the 145th recipient of the Oakleaves on 13th November 1942 as *Generalmajor* and Commander of *Fallschirmjäger Brigade Ramcke* in North Africa. In October 1942, the British 8th Army began its offensive and the German-Italian front almost collapsed. However, Ramcke's command held out and without vehicles he began to fight a retreat on foot to the west, and on 6th November his men attacked an entire British supply column, capturing their vehicles. He then travelled almost 200 miles through enemy held territory joining Rommel's Panzer Army. In December, Ramcke was summoned to Hitler's headquarters in East Prussia where he was decorated with the Oakleaves and promoted to *Generalleutnant*. In February 1943, Ramcke was appointed commander of the 2nd *Fallschirmjäger* Division, seeing action during the occupation of Rome. In early September, Ramcke was seriously wounded when his staff car was attacked by an Allied fighter plane, he spent several weeks in hospital in Dresden.

Knight's Cross with Oakleaves and Swords: Awarded on 19th September 1944, he became the 99th recipient, as *Generalleutnant* and as commander of Fortress Brest. In July Ramcke had transferred to France following the Allied invasion of Normandy. The 2nd *Fallschirmjäger* Division arrived in Brittany and started to defend the port of Brest from possible Allied air landings. Later that same month, the Americans attacked from the Normandy beachhead and entered Brittany in August; their objective was to seize the fortified Port of Brest. On 11th August, Ramcke arrived to take command of what was now Fortress Brest, relinquishing his command of the 2nd *Fallschirmjäger* Division to *Oberst* Hans Kroh. Ramcke now had over 35,000 troops under his command and held the city for over a month.

Knight's Cross with Oakleaves, Swords and Diamonds: Awarded on 19th September 1944, to become the twentieth recipient as *Generalleutnant* and Commander of Fortress Brest. On the same day he surrendered to the Americans, he was informed by radio that he had been awarded the Swords and the Diamonds simultaneously, a rare event. He was presented with both awards, while a prisoner at Trent Park, by a representative of the Red Cross.

One of the bravest and most highly decorated German soldiers of World War II, and the only member of the *Fallschirmjäger* to be awarded the Knight's Cross with Oakleaves, Swords and Diamonds, Hermann-Bernhard Ramcke was born on 24th January 1889 in Schleswig-Friedrichsberg, Prussia and started his military career in the Imperial Germany Navy.

During World War I, he served aboard the cruiser *Prinz Adalbert* in the Baltic and North Sea, and when she was badly damaged in 1915. Fearing that the war might end before the ship could be repaired, he transferred to the marines. For Ramcke it was a lucky move his ship returned to duty a few months later and he later heard via a telegram that it had been sunk with the loss of 672 of her crew. In September 1915, he was promoted to *Feldwebel* and attached to a Replacement Battalion in Bruges, Belgium. In early-1916, he was appointed Platoon Leader in the 12th Company of the 2nd Matrosen-Regiment in Flanders. On 26th January, he was wounded when a grenade exploded and a fragment struck his right thigh. In July 1917, he was transferred to an assault battalion of the Flanders Naval Corps and a year later commissioned as a *Leutnant*. After a defensive action against three British attacks, Ramcke was awarded the Prussian Military Service Cross in Gold, the highest decoration for non-commissioned officers in the Imperial Armed Forces. He also took part in the withdrawal from Flanders and led an assault battalion in house-to-house fighting along the Ghent-Bruges Canal. His bravery resulted in him being recommended for the Knight's Cross with Swords of the Prussian Royal Hohenzollern House Order, but the war ended before the award could be approved.

Ramcke remained in the army after the war serving as a company leader with the *Freikorps* in the Baltic. In April 1919, he was shot in the right shoulder and sent back to Germany. While recovering from the injury, he trained himself to use his left hand to shoot and also throw grenades. He spent the next few years in various infantry regiments and had, by September 1934, been promoted to *Major*. In November 1935, he transferred to the Army Command Center where he became an instructor, training the Silesian Border Defence Units. In July 1936, he joined the infantry, and in March 1937 was promoted to *Oberstleutnant*. At the outbreak of World War II, in September 1939, he transferred as an observer to the 14th Army. He was part of the training and planning unit for the campaign in Poland and during the early stages of the campaign he captured 109 Polish soldiers, including nine officers together with eighteen vehicles and explosives, taking them all to the German lines. In July 1940, he joined the 7th Air Division and started his paratrooper training at the Parachute School in Braunschweig. In August, he transferred from the Army to the Luftwaffe and was assigned

(Wehrkundearchiv)

to the 1st *Fallschirmjäger* Regiment, and made responsible for the development and training of the parachute troops in the use of heavy weapons.

Ramcke with General Student. (Author's Collection)

On 21st May 1941, the airborne invasion of Crete began with the 2nd Air Corps dropping two massive waves of paratroopers and glider troops onto the island. The following day, Ramcke, who had been appointed commander of Battle Group West, was dropped by parachute into Crete along with 550 reinforcements. They landed west of Tavronitis and east of the airfield at Malem, once landed Ramcke took command of the 1st *Fallschirmjäger* Assault Regiment after the commander *Generalmajor* Meindl had been seriously wounded. Advancing with elements of *Generalmajor* Julius Ringel's 5th Mountain Division, Ramcke led his assault group in some bitter fighting along the coast road that culminated in the capture of Canea on 27th May. Five days later, the last of the British troops who had not been evacuated surrendered to the Germans. Ramcke was praised by Meindl and senior commanders and was awarded the Knight's Cross.

In March 1942, he was transferred to the Headquarters Staff of the Italian Armed Forces to assist with the training of the *Enrico Frattini's Folgore Fallschirmjäger* Division, for the proposed German-Italian invasion of Malta. However, the planned invasion of Malta was called off by Hitler in May; he had decided to wait until Egypt fell to the Axis before attempting an invasion of Malta. In July, Ramcke was transferred from Greece to Libya and the 1st *Fallschirmjäger* Regiment took up defensive positions on the El Alamein front. In October, the British 8th Army began its El Alamein offensive and the German-Italian front nearly collapsed. However, Ramcke's command held out and without vehicles he began to fight a retreat on foot to the west, and by 6th November his men highjacked an entire British supply column and captured their vehicles. For this, he was awarded the Knight's Cross with Oakleaves, personally presented to him by Hitler.

On 13th February 1943, Ramcke was appointed Commander of the 2nd *Fallschirmjäger* Division and in the summer he led his division during the occupation of Rome. Ramcke's division had begun to arrive in Rome in July, and after the announcement of Italy's armistice with the

Allies on 8th September the Germans took control of the country and Ramcke's command seized the capital along with the 3rd Panzer Grenadier division and took part in heavy fighting against Italian troops. Finally, by the 10th September, German troops had taken key positions from the Italian forces and 2,500 prisoners had been taken from one Italian headquarters. A few days later, Ramcke was seriously wounded when his staff car was attacked by an Allied fighter plane. As a result, Ramcke spent several weeks in a military hospital in Dresden. He returned to command the 2nd *Fallschirmjäger* Division on 17th February 1944, and found that his division had been deployed to the southern sector of the Russian Front. During his absence, his division had been under the command of *Generalmajor* Gustav Wilcke, and had been busy helping stop the massive Soviet attacks aimed at reaching the Dniester River. When Ramcke took over it had fallen back across the Bug River and he for a time managed to contain the enemy bridgeheads on the Dniester River until it could hold out no longer. On 17th March, Ramcke fell ill and returned to Germany where he oversaw the formation and rebuilding of the 2nd *Fallschirmjäger* Division.

While making ready to return to Russia, the division was ordered to France following the Allied invasion of Normandy. The 2nd *Fallschirmjäger* Division arrived in Brittany a few weeks after the invasion and started defending the port of Brest from possible Allied air landings. Then came the breakout by the Americans from the Normandy beachhead in late-July, when the Americans captured Avranches at the base of the Cotentin Peninsula. They

(Author's Collection)

Ramcke at Trent Park in 1946.
(Private source)

carried on west and entered Brittany in August, their objective being to seize the fortified port of Brest. Ramcke's division arrived at Brest as the U.S. 6th Armoured Division approached the city from the north and managed to contain the German garrison. On 11th August, Ramcke assumed command of what was now "Fortress Brest," and handed command of the 2nd *Fallschirmjäger* Division to *Oberst* Hans Kroh. Ramcke now had over 35,000 Army, Luftwaffe and Kriegsmarine troops at his disposal and he told his men to defend the city to the "last grenade," in an effort to tie down American forces for as long as possible. Ramcke's men held on for a month before, finally, on 19th September 1944, they surrendered. The Americans later found, in Ramcke's command bunker, a vast store of alcohol and large quantities of food and other plunder. On that same day, Ramcke was informed by radio that he been awarded not only the Knight's Cross with Oakleaves and Swords, and simultaneously the Knight's Cross with Oakleaves, Swords and Diamonds. A few days later, the awards were presented to Ramcke while at Trent Park interrogation and prison camp in England, by a representative of the Red Cross.

In May 1946, he was handed over to the French authorities, who charged him with organizing and permitting the murder of French citizens and for plundering property and for taking part in the torture of prisoners of war. Most thought the charges were false; he was sentenced in March 1951 to five years imprisonment. He was released three months later, with time already served. He returned home and later wrote his memoirs. He died on 4th July 1968 in Kappeln, Schlei.

OTHER AWARDS		PROMOTIONS	
17.04.1916	Iron Cross 2nd Class	26.09.1902	Matrose
27.01.1917	Iron Cross 1st Class	01.07.1909	Obermatrose
03.11.1918	Prussian Military Service Cross in Gold	01.04.1912	Bootsmannsmaat
03.11.1919	Wound Badge in Gold	19.07.1915	Oberbootsmannsmaat
05.11.1919	Baltic Cross	11.09.1915	Feldwebel
26.01.1935	Cross of Honour for Frontline Combatants	05.12.1916	Offiziers-Stellvertreter
02.10.1936	Armed Forces Long Service Award 4th to 1st Class	18.07.1918	Leutnant der Marine-Infanterie
01.10.1939	Bar to the Iron Cross 2nd Class	15.01.1921	Oberleutnant
00.00.193_	Combined Pilots & Observers Badge in Gold + Diamonds	31.01.1927	Hauptmann
01.08.1940	Parachutist Badge	01.09.1934	Major
23.05.1941	Bar to the Iron Cross 1st Class	16.03.1937	Oberstleutnant
00.00.1942	Luftwaffe Ground Assault Badge	29.02.1940	Oberst
00.00.1942	Italian Medal of Honour in Silver	22.07.1941	Generalmajor
00.00.1943	AFRIKA Cuff title	21.12.1942	Generalleutnant
00.05.1943	KRETA Cuff title	14.09.1944	General der Fallschirmtruppe

SIEGFRIED RAMMELT

(18.12.1914 – 21.03.1944)   *Oberleutnant*

(Wehrkundearchiv)

Knight's Cross: Awarded posthumously on 11th June 1944 as *Leutnant* and *Führer* Regimental Engineer Platoon, 3rd *Fallschirmjäger* Regiment for actions at Monte Cassino, Italy. He distinguished himself in battle repeatedly and successfully led one of the most difficult offensive patrols of the campaign. Recommended for the Knight's Cross shortly afterwards, it wasn't officially awarded until several months after his death.

Siegfried Rammelt was born in Falkenberg, Liebenwerda on 18th December 1914 and after a five month stint with the Reich Labour Front he joined Army in November 1935. He was assigned to the 32nd Infantry Regiment's 6th Company in Eilenburg. In October 1937, with the rank of *Unteroffizier* he was also a reserve officer candidate and was released to work as an aviation electrician with the Junkers works in Dessau. He successfully passed the engineering school in Weimar in a year, and in May 1938 took part in his first reserve exercise with his old regiment.

In October 1939, he was called up for active service with the 81st Infantry Regiment and he immediately volunteered for the parachute troops and on completion of his parachutist-rifleman's course he joined the 11th Company of the 3rd *Fallschirmjäger* Regiment. He took part in the airborne invasion of Crete where he was awarded both classes of the Iron Cross in June 1941. On 30th August, he completed training as a platoon leader in Döberitz. In October, during the early stages of the Russian Campaign, Rammelt was seriously wounded during the fighting at the Neva River.

He was considered officer material by his regimental commander and was sent for further training, which included assignment to the Luftwaffe School of Warfare at Gross-Born in February 1942. Promoted to *Oberleutnant* in April 1943, he went on to distinguish himself during the fierce fighting at Monte Cassino where he was awarded the Knight's Cross, but not until several months after his death.

OTHER AWARDS		PROMOTIONS	
02.11.1939	Armed Forces Long Service Award 4th Class	01.09.1936	Reserve-Offiziersanwärter
12.06.1941	Iron Cross 2nd Class	01.10.1936	Gefreiter
22.06.1941	Iron Cross 1st Class	01.09.1937	Unteroffizier
01.10.1942	Luftwaffe Ground Assault Badge	25.05.1938	Feldwebel
20.05.1943	KRETA Cuff title	01.06.1942	Leutnant
05.02.1944	German Cross in Gold	20.04.1943	Oberleutnant

DR. JUR. ERNST-WILHELM RAPRÄGER

(15.09.1918 – 16.02.2008)   *Major*

(Wehrkundearchiv)

Knight's Cross: Awarded on 10th May 1943 as *Oberleutnant* and *Führer* of a Battle Group of the II Battalion, Luftwaffe Regiment *Barenthin* for actions in North Africa. He successfully repelled several enemy attacks in the northern sector of the Tunisian theatre.

Ernst-Wilhelm Rapräger was born on 15th September 1918, in Straßburg, Alsace. After the completion of his service with the Reich Labour Service, he joined the Luftwaffe. He was assigned to the 12th Anti-aircraft Regiment in Berlin-Lankwitz in November 1937 and from there was transferred to the 4th Battery of the 33rd Anti-aircraft Battalion in July1938.

When war broke out in September 1939, Rapräger was stationed in the Westwall as a deputy platoon leader with the Reserve Fortress Anti-aircraft Battalion 332. He was commissioned as a *Leutnant* on 1st February 1940, and in July joined the parachute troops and completed the parachutist-rifleman course at Parachute School III in Braunschweig. He went on to serve as a platoon leader in various companies and was promoted to *Oberleutnant* in April 1942. On 19th May, he was transferred to the officer reserve of IV Battalion of the 1st *Fallschirmjäger* Regiment. Following a transfer to the Rocket Batteries Testing Battalion, part of the Parachute Instruction Regiment in October 1942, he became commander of the 15th Battery of the 1st Parachute Artillery Regiment.

When the Allies landed in Northwest Africa, Rapräger was sent to Africa as part of the XI Air Corps and was made commander of a battle group. He successfully repelled many enemy attacks while in Tunisia and was awarded the Knight's Cross. He was promoted to *Hauptmann* on 10th May 1944. On 15th July, he took over the 21st Parachute Rocket Battalion south of Nimwegen, where on 17th September he repulsed several strong attacks by American forces. He was severely wounded while leading an offensive patrol near Riethorst on 17th September 1944.

Rapränger was made a prisoner of war in May 1945, while still recovering in hospital. He died on 16th February 2008 in Saarbrücken-Dudwiler.

OTHER AWARDS		PROMOTIONS	
00.00.1940	West Wall Medal	01.10.1938	Gefreiter
01.03.1941	Parachutist Badge	01.10.1938	Reserve-Offiziersanwärter
21.07.1942	Luftwaffe Ground Assault Badge	01.04.1939	Unteroffizier
21.01.1943	Wound Badge in Black	01.10.1939	Wachtmeister
29.01.1943	Iron Cross 2nd Class	01.02.1940	Leutnant der Reserve
17.03.1943	Iron Cross 1st Class	01.04.1942	Oberleutnant der Reserve
-----	-----	01.07.1943	Hauptmann der Reserve
-----	-----	10.05.1944	Hauptmann (active)
-----	-----	30.01.1945	Major

ADOLF REININGHAUS

(06.12.1915 – 12.08.1996)   *Oberfeldwebel*

(Wehrkundearchiv)

Knight's Cross: Awarded on 13th September 1944 as *Oberfeldwebel* and Platoon Leader of the 14th Company, 7th *Fallschirmjäger* Regiment for actions on the Western Front. During the Battle of Normandy he led his company during a three-day battle with American forces. His troops destroyed thirty-two enemy tanks and prevented the 2nd *Fallschirmjäger* Regiment from being completely wiped out.

Adolf Reininghaus was born on 6th December 1915 in Remscheid and entered the Luftwaffe on 1st November 1936. He completed a NCO training course in August 1937 and joined the 1st *Fallschirmjäger* Regiment in January 1940. After completing his parachute training he was promoted to *Oberjäger* in May 1940.

In March 1941, he won the Iron Cross 2nd Class during the Balkans campaign. He then transferred to Russia where he saw action on the northern sector of the Eastern Front, where he was decorated with the Iron Cross 1st Class. On 1st January 1944, he joined the 7th Fallschirmjäger Regiment and later saw action during the Battle of Normandy. When allied forces broke through near Avranches, the 2nd *Fallschirmjäger* Division under *Generalleutnant* Ramcke was sent to the western theatre. The 7th *Fallschirmjäger* Regiment under Oberst Pietzonka moved up the Sizun road into the Commana, where it halted the Americans, and into the Huelot area. It was here that Reininghaus distinguished himself during the three days of fighting, where his platoon played a vital role in destroying thirty-two enemy tanks. For his leadership and bravery, he was awarded the Knight's Cross.

Oberfeldwebel Reiningahus was taken prisoner by the Americans on 19th September 1944 and was released in 1947. He died on 12th August 1996, in Remscheid.

OTHER AWARDS		PROMOTIONS	
00.00.1940	Parachutist Badge	01.10.1937	Gefreiter
17.03.1941	Iron Cross 2nd Class	01.10.1938	Obergefreiter
18.12.1941	Iron Cross 1st Class	01.05.1940	Oberjäger
-----	-----	01.04.1942	Feldwebel
-----	-----	05.02.1944	Oberfeldwebel

PAUL-ERNST RENISCH

(02.07.1917 – 25.01.1998)   *Major*

(Wehrkundearchiv)

Knight's Cross: Awarded on 31st October 1944 as *Hauptmann* and Commander III Battalion, 1st *Fallschirmjäger* Regiment for actions in Italy. He took part in the heavy fighting on the Adriatic at Pesaro, Cattolica and Rimini. His battalion managed various times to outflank the enemy and hold them back. His bravery and leadership won him the Knight's Cross.

Paul-Ernst Renisch was born on 2nd July 1917, in Brussels, Belgium, and, after a five-month period with the Reich Labour Service, he joined the Luftwaffe in November 1936. He was assigned to the 26th Anti-aircraft Regiment in Dessau. In October 1937, he moved to the 7th Anti-aircraft Regiment in Wolfenbüttel and, in December 1938, he was commissioned with the rank of *Leutnant* and joined the 340th Motorized Searchlight Battalion as a signals officer.

He didn't see action during the Polish campaign and served with the 30th Anti-aircraft Regiment in France in May 1940. On 1st October 1941, Renisch joined the parachute troops, where he was promoted to *Oberleutnant*. After attending the usual training, he was assigned to the 2nd Company of the 1st *Fallschirmjäger* Regiment in April 1942. He was placed in charge of the company and later made official company commander. In the autumn of 1942, he led his company during the fighting in Russia.

Renisch led troops in the bitter winter fighting in the Orel bend and participated in the recapture of the village of Stonotische and the defence of Hills 266 and 262.3. He then fought against heavy Russian attacks and was awarded the Iron Cross 1st Class. On 28th January 1943, he took command of I Battalion of the 1st *Fallschirmjäger* Regiment after the battalion commander was wounded. He later achieved two major successes near Ortona during the heavy fighting on the Italian mainland and in the second battle of Cassino where he was awarded the German Cross in Gold. After his promotion to *Hauptmann* in June 1944, he saw action on the Adriatic at Pesaro, Cattaolica and Rimini and here won the Knight's Cross.

Promoted to *Major* in January 1945, he was captured by British forces on 2nd May and remained in captivity until early-1946. He died on 25th January 1986, in Ettlingen.

OTHER AWARDS			PROMOTIONS	
23.03.1942	Parachutist Badge		14.03.1938	Reserve-Offiziersanwärter
00.10.1942	Eastern Front Medal		01.04.1938	Unteroffizier
21.12.1942	Iron Cross 2nd Class		01.10.1938	Wachtmeister der Reserve
25.03.1943	Iron Cross 1st Class		01.12.1938	Leutnant der Reserve
09.11.1943	Luftwaffe Ground Assault Badge		01.09.1939	Leutnant (active)
00.00.194_	Wound Badge in Black		01.12.1941	Oberleutnant
22.04.1944	German Cross in Gold		21.06.1944	Hauptmann
-----	-----		01.03.1945	Major

RUDOLF RENNECKE
(19.06.1915 – 03.03.1986)   *Oberstleutnant*

(Wehrkundearchiv)

Knight's Cross: Awarded on 9th June 1944 as *Hauptmann* and *Führer* II Battalion, 3rd *Fallschirmjäger Regiment* in recognition of his outstanding leadership as Battle Commandant of Cassino. From February 1944 he was responsible for the defence of the city and with his battalion he proved a capable commander and made a courageous effort in defending the city.

Knight's Cross with Oakleaves: He became the 664th recipient of the Oakleaves on 25th November 1944 as *Major* and *Führer* 1st *Fallschirmjäger Regiment* in recognition of his leadership and bravery during the heavy fighting near Lake Trasimeno, Italy and in the defensive battles near Bologna.

Rolf Rennecke was born on 19th June 1915, in Leipzig, and joined the 32nd Infantry Regiment in November 1937 as a company commander. He completed his army parachute-rifleman course in August 1938 and transferred to the Parachute Infantry Regiment in October. He took part in the first parachute troops' battle of war in Poland when his battalion saw action during the battle at Wola Gulowska airfield on 24th September 1939. He was promoted to *Feldwebel* in March 1940, and in May parachuted into Fortress Holland near the Moerdijk bridges. There he eliminated a machine-gun nest and took a number of prisoners while storming a farm with only two companions.

On 10th May 1940, Rennecke took part in the airborne invasion of Crete and here he fought with great bravery as a Platoon Leader with the 6th Company of the 1st *Fallschirmjäger* Regiment. On 16th May, he was simultaneously awarded both the Iron Cross 2nd Class and 1st Class. He was promoted to *Leutnant* on 11th July 1940. He then transferred to the northern sector of the Eastern Front, where he was seriously wounded on 4th November 1941, near Leningrad. From February 1942, he served as battalion adjutant while attached to the 3rd *Fallschirmjäger* Regiment, and from December 1942 until February 1944, he was appointed Regimental Adjutant.

On 5th June 1944, Rennecke was promoted to *Major* and appointed Commander of the 1st *Fallschirmjäger* Regiment and saw heavy action in Italy, seeing action in the bitter fighting in the Rimin area and near Bologna, where he was awarded the Knight's Cross with Oakleaves. Promoted to *Oberstleutnant* in January 1945 he continued to command the 1st *Fallschirmjäger* Regiment in Italy until the end of the war. He died on 3rd March 1986 in Bayerisch Gmain, Bavaria.

OTHER AWARDS		PROMOTIONS	
27.08.1938	Army Parachutist Badge	01.10.1938	Gefreiter and Reserve-Offiziersanwärter
03.11.1939	Commemorative Medal of 13th March 1938	20.04.1939	Oberjäger
03.11.1939	Commemorative Medal of 1st October 1938	29.03.1940	Feldwebel
16.05.1940	Iron Cross 2nd Class	11.07.1940	Leutnant der Reserve
16.05.1940	Iron Cross 1st Class	22.07.1942	Oberleutnant der Reserve
07.11.1941	Wound Badge in Black	16.06.1943	Oberleutnant (active)
01.10.1942	Luftwaffe Ground Assault Badge	22.12.1943	Hauptmann
00.12.1942	Eastern Front Medal	05.06.1944	Major
20.05.1943	KRETA Cuff title	30.01.1945	Oberstleutnant
12.12.1943	German Cross in Gold	-----	-----

HELMUT RINGLER

(04.10.1915 – 22.06.1962)   *Hauptmann der Reserve*

(Wehrkundearchiv)

Knight's Cross: Awarded on 15th May 1940 as *Leutnant der Reserve* and Heavy Machine-gun Platoon Leader in the Assault Group "*Stahl*," Air-Landing Assault Battalion *Koch* for actions in Holland. He and his platoon jumped into Fortress Holland and their objective was the capture of the Veldwezelt bridge over the Albert Canal. They landed under heavy fire but still managed to overpower the enemy with strong flanking fire and played a major role in the German assault. Ringler's great bravery helped the Germans secure a victory.

Helmut Ringler was born in Wollstein, Witzenhausen, on 4th October 1915, and joined the 9th Anti-aircraft Regiment in Münster, in November 1935. In August 1939, he joined the 1st *Fallschirmjäger* Regiment on the day the regiment was mobilized for war. He was assigned to the Koch Parachute Assault Battalion, where on 11th April 1940, he became a platoon leader in the 4th Company.

On 10th May 1940, he parachuted into Fortress Holland as part of Assault Group *Stahl* under the command of *Oberleutnant* Altmann. Their objective was the capture of the Veldwezelt Bridge over the Albert Canal and Ringler, with his platoon, jumped in the second wave to reinforce the assault group, which was in the midst of heavy fighting. On landing, Ringler assembled his men and overpowered the enemy troops who had been manning a section of trench directly in front of them. Ringler distinguished himself in battle and was wounded during the action. He received the Iron Cross 2nd Class on 12th May, the Iron Cross 1st Class the day after, and on the 14th came the award of the Knight's Cross.

However, in October 1942, he was taken off frontline duty due to the wounds he received during the fighting in Holland. He then served in the parachute officer reserves. He became commander of a training company in Stendal and served in similar posts in Germany. He finally returned to active duty as Commander of the II Battalion of the 2nd *Fallschirmjäger* Regiment in the west.

Ringler died on 22nd June 1962 in Bonn.

OTHER AWARDS		PROMOTIONS	
00.00.1938	Parachutist Badge	01.10.1937	Feldwebel der Reserve
00.11.1939	Armed Forces Long Service Award 4th Class	01.10.1939	Leutnant der Reserve
12.05.1940	Iron Cross 2nd Class	20.05.1940	Oberleutnant der Reserve
13.05.1940	Iron Cross 1st Class	01.10.1942	Hauptmann der Reserve

ARNOLD VON ROON

(19.07.1914 – 24.10.1990) *Major im Generalstab*

(Author's Collection)

Knight's Cross: Awarded on 9th July 1941 as *Oberleutnant* and Commander 3rd Company, 2nd *Fallschirmjäger* Regiment for actions in Crete. He led his company upon landing near his objective – Rethymnon airfield, and took a vineyard hill and fought his way through to the center of Rethymnon airfield and captured the enemy-occupied Hill 156 on 27th May.

Arnold von Roon was born on 19th July 1914, in Berlin-Friedenau, and entered the 3rd Mounted Regiment, part of the 1st Cavalry Division in Rathenow, on 1st April 1934. In January 1935, he attended the infantry school at Dresden and in November he transferred to the Luftwaffe. After completing his flight training, he joined Air Group Prenlau. He was commissioned as a *Leutnant* on 20th April 1936 and served as an observer with A/88, the long-range reconnaissance squadron of the Legion Condor during the Spanish Civil War.

In May 1938, he was attached to the Air Ministry, and in October he served as Operations Officer of the 7th Air Division under *Generalleutnant* Kurt Student. From there, he reported to the parachute troops and had completed the parachutist-rifleman course in Stendal by March 1939. He saw action during the Polish Campaign as *Führer* of the 3rd Company of the 2nd *Fallschirmjäger* Regiment. In April 1940, he became company commander and saw action with his unit in Holland. However, most of his company was dropped in the wrong place. Nevertheless, Roon managed to reach the headquarters of the 22nd Airborne Division and was awarded the Iron Cross 1st and 2nd Classes.

During the campaign in the Balkans, he saw action at the Corinth Canal and jumped during the second wave at Crete. His company landed about four miles west of Rethymnon airfield but managed to fight their way through to the center of the airfield on 27th May and captured Hill 156. For this feat Roon was awarded the Knight's Cross. In March 1943, Roon was promoted to *Major* in the General Staff and served as Operations Officer in the 4th *Fallschirmjäger* Division and from January 1945 until the end of the war he served as Operations Officer in the 1st Parachute Army.

He died in Miesbach on 24th October 1990.

OTHER AWARDS		PROMOTIONS	
17.04.1936	Observers Badge for Reconnaissance Flyers	20.04.1936	Leutnant
00.00.1936	Pilots Badge	30.10.1938	Oberleutnant
01.12.1938	Spanish War Cross	19.09.1941	Hauptmann
28.03.1939	Parachutist Badge	01.03.1943	Major im Generalstab
01.04.1939	Armed Forces Long Service Award 4th Class	-----	-----
06.06.1939	Spanish Cross in Gold + Swords	-----	-----
15.05.1940	Iron Cross 2nd Class	-----	-----
15.05.1940	Iron Cross 1st Class	-----	-----
15.06.1943	KRETA Cuff title	-----	-----

WALTER SANDER

(25.07.1914 – 28.04.1981)   *Oberleutnant der Reserve*

(Wehrkundearchiv)

Knight's Cross: Awarded on 28th February 1945 as *Leutnant der Reserve* and *Führer* 1st Company, 5th *Fallschirm-Pioniere* Battalion for actions during the Ardennes Offensive. He led his company deep into the enemy rear and captured a signals battalion of the American 28th Division, and took 200 prisoners in Wiltz.

Walter Sander was born on 25th July 1914 in Völksen, Springe an der Deister and joined the Armed Forces in October 1935. He served for two years and then left the armed forces with the rank of *Unteroffizer*. He returned to active duty on 30th August 1919, joining the 4th Company of the Parachute Engineer Battalion.

Sander took part in either the Polish or the French Campaigns and finally saw action during the airborne invasion of Crete. Here he won the Iron Cross 1st and 2nd Classes and was promoted to *Feldwebel* in October 1941. He was seriously wounded on the Neva front in northern Russia on 30th October 1941. But despite this, he was present during the battalion's second tour of duty in Russia. During the fierce fighting in the Lake Ilmen area, from October 1942 to January 1943, Sander proved himself while leading many patrols. In February 1943, his leadership during the patrols was rewarded with the German Cross in Gold. Then in April, he was sent as a wartime officer candidate to Dessau-Rosslau for an officer course. He later parachuted into Sicily, and in January 1944 was commissioned as a *Leutnant der Reserve*.

In Normandy, he led the 5th Parachute Engineer Battalion's 4th Company and held its sector for sixteen days against heavy enemy attacks. He later distinguished himself further during the Ardennes Offensive where he won the Knight's Cross after his unit captured a signals battalion and took 200 prisoners. He ended the war as an *Oberleutnant der Reserve* and was captured by U.S. troops in April 1945.

Sander died on 28th April 1981 in Springe an der Deister.

OTHER AWARDS		PROMOTIONS	
02.10.1939	Armed Forces Long Service Award 4th Class	01.10.1936	Gefreiter
27.07.1940	Iron Cross 2nd Class	06.10.1937	Unteroffizier
27.07.1940	Iron Cross 1st Class	01.10.1941	Feldwebel
01.02.1941	Parachutist Badge	11.01.1943	Kriegsoffizieranwärter
01.12.1941	Wound Badge in Black	01.01.1944	Leutnant der Reserve
03.10.1942	Luftwaffe Ground Assault Badge	18.12.1944	Oberleutnant der Reserve
00.11.1942	Eastern Front Medal	-----	-----
08.02.1943	German Cross in Gold	-----	-----
20.05.1943	KRETA Cuff title	-----	-----
00.00.1944	Luftwaffe Close Combat Clasp in Bronze	-----	-----

BRUNO SASSEN

(13.03.1918 – 19.06.2006)   *Leutnant*

(Author's Collection)

Knight's Cross: Awarded on 22nd February 1942, as *Feldwebel* and Platoon Leader in the 10th Company, 3rd *Fallschirmjäger* Regiment for actions in the Soviet Union. From October to November 1941, his company pushed back the enemy advances on the German positions in the Vyborgaskaya bridgehead. Sassen and his two machine-guns halted the enemy there for thirty-three days. When the Russians captured the anti-tank ditch in front of his position on 15th November, he and five comrades counterattacked and drove the enemy away.

Bruno Sassen was born on 13th March 1918 in Nüttermoor, Leer and after spending five months in the Reich Labour Front he joined the 13th Cavalry Regiment, serving in the 2nd Squadron in November 1937. In October of the following year, he became a reserve veterinary officer candidate and was sent to the army's veterinary academy in Hannover. On 27th September 1939, his studies came to an abrupt end when he was called to active service.

Left to right: Oberfeldwebel Karl Rothert, Leutnant Bruno Sassen, Oberfeldwebel Paul Volke and Oberjäger Kurt Fielitz.
(Author's Collection)

In June 1940, he reported to the Luftwaffe's parachute troops, and after his parachute training he was assigned to the 10th Company of the 3rd *Fallschirmjäger* Regiment. He saw action in Crete southwest of Chania. He and thirty men stormed a British tent camp, but Sassen was wounded and taken prisoner, though he was freed seven days later. He received the Iron Cross 1st and 2nd Classes for his actions in Crete. In October, he was transferred to the Russian Front and he saw action at the Neva River where he was promoted to *Feldwebel* and where he was awarded the Knight's Cross.

On 27th March 1943, he was seriously wounded while storming a vital hill during the fighting east of Twery in the central sector of the Eastern Front. Here he won the German Cross in Gold. Once out of hospital, he didn't return to combat, but instead was given a training command and shortly before the end of the war became special duties officer on the staff of the Leer Station Commander.

Bruno Sassen died in Bad Pyrmont on 19th June 2006. (Wehrkundearchiv)

OTHER AWARDS		PROMOTIONS	
00.00.1935	Golden Hitler Youth Badge of Honour	01.10.1938	Gefreiter
00.00.1939	Parachutist Badge	31.03.1939	Unteroffizier der Reserve
16.06.1941	Iron Cross 2nd Class	01.10.1941	Feldwebel der Reserve
28.08.1941	Iron Cross 1st Class	10.03.1942	Kriegsoffizieranwärter
00.11.1942	Eastern Front Medal	01.10.1942	Leutnant (active)
00.04.1943	Wound Badge in Silver	-----	-----
00.05.1943	KRETA Cuff title	-----	-----
12.07.1943	German Cross in Gold	-----	-----

GERHARD SCHACHT
(06.04.1916 – 07.02.1972)

Major im Generalstab

(Wehrkundearchiv)

Knight's Cross: Awarded on 12th May 1940 as *Leutnant* and *Führer* Assault Group "*Beton*" in the Air-Landing Assault Battalion *Koch* for actions during the Western Campaign. His battalion prevented the Vroenhaven Bridge from being blown. The enemy troops guarding the bridge were overpowered and taken prisoner.

Gerhard Schacht was born on 6th April 1916, in Berlin-Steglitz, and volunteered to joined the Reichswehr in November 1934. He served for almost twelve months with the 3rd Motorized Reconnaissance Battalion in Wünsdorf before leaving the army with the rank of *Gefreiter*. He returned to the army with his old battalion in November 1936, and after he attended the Officer Candidate School in Dresden, he transferred to the Luftwaffe in October 1937.

Schacht joined the 1st *Fallschirmjäger* Regiment, and in January 1938 was commissioned as a *Leutnant*. In January 1940, he was assigned to the "Friedrichshafen Test Battalion" (this was the cover name for the Koch Assault Battalion). He led the Assault Group "Beton" during the attack on Holland and his objective was to seize and hold the Vroenhaven Bridge over the Albert Canal. He was dropped with his assault group on 10th May 1940, and although they failed to secure the bridge they took 300 prisoners. For his leadership and success, he was awarded the Iron Cross 1st and 2nd Classes and the Knight's Cross, all on the same day.

In December 1940, he was transferred to the staff of the 7th Air Division under *Generalleutnant* Richard Putzier. In April 1941, he was assigned to the XI Air Corps where he served as Operations Officer during the Crete operation. He was promoted to *Hauptmann* in February 1942, and from July, served as Operations Officer of the *Ramcke* Parachute Brigade in North Africa. A year later in July 1943, he was assigned to the 2nd *Fallschirmjäger* Division as Intelligence Officer (Ic). He was promoted to *Major* in May 1944 and continued to serve in various staff appointments until the end of the war.

After a brief period of captivity, he left the armed forces in June 1945. He joined the Bundswehr in June 1956 and continued to serve as a staff officer in various posts. He was promoted to *Oberst* in September 1964, and from September 1968 served as Military Attaché to Tehran until he was dismissed from this post and served as deputy commander of the 1st *Fallschirmjäger* Division in Bruchsal until his retirement in January 1972. He died on 7th February 1972 in Dortmund.

OTHER AWARDS		PROMOTIONS	
08.12.1938	Observers Badge	30.09.1935	Gefreiter der Reserve
02.10.1939	Commemorative Medal of 13th March 1938	02.11.1936	Fahnenjunker-Gefreiter
02.11.1939	Armed Forces Long Service Award 4th Class	01.01.1938	Leutnant
12.05.1940	Iron Cross 2nd Class	16.05.1940	Oberleutnant
12.05.1940	Iron Cross 1st Class	25.02.1942	Hauptmann
26.06.1940	Wound Badge in Black	01.05.1944	Major im Generalstab
01.09.1940	Commemorative Medal of 1st October 1938 + Bar	-----	-----
06.01.1943	KRETA Cuff title	-----	-----
26.03.1943	AFRIKA Cuff title	-----	-----
21.12.1944	German Cross in Gold	-----	-----
18.03.1945	Tank Combat Badge in Bronze (Heer)	-----	-----
18.03.1945	Luftwaffe Close Combat Clasp in Bronze	-----	-----
18.03.1945	Wound Badge in Silver	-----	-----

MARTIN SCHÄCHTER

(14.03.1915 –)   *Major*

(Author's Collection)

Knight's Cross: Awarded on 12th May 1940 as *Leutnant* and *Führer* Assault Group "*Eisen*" in the Air-Landing Assault Battalion *Koch* for actions in France and Belgium. He led his assault battalion in a mission to seize the bridge over the Albert canal at Canne. However the enemy had already blown up the bridge and during the heavy fighting he was wounded in the leg. His battalion played a major role in the attack on Eben Emael and the clearing of the enemy trenches in the landing area.

Martin Schächter was born in Petershagen, in the district of Minden, North Rhine-Westphalia, on 14th March 1915. He entered the Army on 1st April 1934, as an officer candidate with the 18th Engineer Battalion. A year later, he transferred to the Luftwaffe and began observer training. Commissioned as a *Leutnant* in April 1937, he spent several years in various bomber units which included KG 152 and the KG 355.

In January 1939, Schächter joined the 1st *Fallschirmjäger* Regiment and fought in Poland in September. He then joined the secret Assault Detachment Koch, and in March 1940 he had been appointed acting commander of the engineer company. On 10th May 1940, Schächter took off as part of a glider mission to seize the bridge over the Albert Canal. However, one of the gliders was released too early and did not have enough height or speed to reach the landing zone. As the other assault groups had already landed, the Belgians realized what was happening and blew up the bridge. The glider of the 9th Squad landed 220 yards south of the bridge at the village of Eben Emael, while gliders carrying the 6th and 7th Squads landed on the middle high ground instead of the northern, as planned. The paratroopers began clearing trenches in the landing area of defending troops and Schächter was wounded during the fighting. As a result of his leadership, he was awarded the Iron Cross 1st and 2nd Classes and the Knight's Cross on the same day.

After recovering from his wounds, he joined the 1st *Fallschirmjäger* Regiment in February 1941. He took part in the Crete invasion, and on 20th May, he was again wounded in action. He was promoted to *Hauptmann* in February 1942 and was attached to the Luftwaffe headquarters in Berlin until September 1943. He now joined the 3rd *Fallschirmjäger* Division and was again wounded when U.S. artillery struck the division headquarters. On 15th March 1945, he was captured while serving as the Second General Staff Officer (Ib) of the 3rd *Fallschirmjäger* Division in the Ruhr Pocket.

OTHER AWARDS		PROMOTIONS	
00.04.1936	Observers Badge for Bombers	01.04.1935	Fahnenjunker-Gefreiter
00.05.1937	Parachutist Badge	00.00.1936	Fähnrich
00.04.1939	Armed Forces Long Service Award 4th Class	01.01.1938	Leutnant
12.05.1940	Iron Cross 2nd Class	16.05.1940	Oberleutnant
12.05.1940	Iron Cross 1st Class	01.02.1942	Hauptmann
15.09.1940	Wound Badge in Silver	01.01.1945	Major
00.00.1943	KRETA Cuff title	-----	-----

DIPL. ING. RICHARD SCHIMPF

(16.05.1897 – 30.12.1972)   *Generalleutnant*

(Wehrkundearchiv)

Knight's Cross: Awarded on 6th October 1944 as *Generalleutnant* and Commander 3rd *Fallschirmjäger* Division for actions during the breakout from the Falaise Pocket in Normandy.

Richard Schimpf was born in Eggenfeld, Bavaria, on 16th May 1897 and he joined the 9th Royal Bavarian Infantry Regiment as a *Fahnenjunker* in February 1915. He saw action on the Western Front during World War I, serving as a platoon leader, company leader and as battalion adjutant. He was commissioned as a *Leutnant* in March 1916, and after the war he stayed in the army and served with the 23rd Reichswehr Brigade.

In April 1925, he began training as a pilot before changing his mind and trained as a staff officer. In September, he joined the staff of the VII Military District in Munich and later served with the Scientific Research and Testing Institute in Lipezk. In October 1930, he transferred to the Army Weapons Office and began studying engineering at the Berlin-Charlottenburg Technical College. He was promoted to *Hauptmann* in April 1932, and passed his exams and was awarded a diploma in engineering in January 1935. The following month he entered the Luftwaffe and was assigned to the Air Ministry and in April was appointed a Squadron Commander with the Air Reconnaissance Group in Münster. In March 1936, he became head of the Aerial Photographic and Survey section in the Air Ministry, and in October 1939 he was assigned to Army Group A, as Operations Officer and later saw action during the French Campaign.

In January 1941, Schimpf was transferred to the General Government of Poland and appointed Chief of Staff to Air Region Command VIII. In December, Air Region Command Kiev, was formed in southern Russia with its headquarters in Kharkov, and Schimpf became Chief of Staff. In September 1942, he was given temporary command of the Luftwaffe Field Division *"Meindl,"* a unit formed from staff of the 1st Parachute Landing Assault Regiment. Later it became known as Luftwaffe Field Division Nr.21, and Schimpf took over as commander and led the unit in Russia. In January 1943, it absorbed the Luftwaffe Field *Jäger* Regiment and became the largest Luftwaffe Field Division. In March, Schimpf was replaced as commander by *Generalmajor* Rudolf-Eduard Licht and was put on the reserve list.

On 17th February 1944, Schimpf returned to active service as commander of the 3rd *Fallschirmjäger* Division, while attached to the 7th Army in France. After the Allies landed in Normandy on 6th June, the 2nd Parachute Corps, 3rd *Fallschirmjäger* Division and the 17th SS-Panzer Grenadier Division "Götz von Berlichingen" were deployed from Brittany to counter the American advance in the area of St. Lô. The 2nd Parachute Corps, under the command of Meindl, remained heavily engaged with U.S. forces for the next two months; and the German 5th Panzer Army and 7th Army were almost completely encircled at Falaise by the advancing American-Anglo forces. Meindl's forces managed to hold open a narrow corridor that allowed thousands of German troops to escape. On 20th August 1944, Schimpf was severely wounded in the leg during the breakout and had to be carried out by his men. However, in recognition of his efforts and personal bravery he was awarded the Knight's Cross.

In early January 1945, Schimpf returned to command the 3rd *Fallschirmjäger* Division and was now attached to *General der Panzertruppe* Hasso von Manteuffel's 5th Panzer Army. He was now engaged in delaying the Allied advance along the Siegfried Line. On 1st March, the U.S. 12th Army Group resumed its offensive, a two-pronged advance to clear the southern Rhineland up the Rhine River, the U.S. 1st Army advanced on Cologne while the U.S. 3rd Army under General Patton cleared the Eifel to the south. Schimpf was not allowed to breakout or fall back. Hitler made it clear there would be no retreat. On 8th March, Schimpf was captured near Bad Godesberg along with his troops by the advancing Americans.

Schimpf remained in Allied captivity until December 1947. He entered the Bundeswehr in 1957 and joined the air force, serving as a *Generalmajor* and commander of Military District III, until his retirement in July 1962. He died on 30th December 1972 in Düsseldorf.

OTHER AWARDS		PROMOTIONS	
00.00.191_	Iron Cross 2nd Class	11.02.1915	Fahnenjunker
00.00.191_	Iron Cross 1st Class	25.10.1915	Leutnant
00.00.1917	Wound Badge in Black	01.04.1925	Oberleutnant
00.00.1918	Bavarian Military Service Order 4th Class + Swords	01.04.1932	Hauptmann
00.00.1935	Cross of Honour for Frontline Combatants	01.04.1935	Major (Luftwaffe)
02.10.1936	Armed Forces Long Service Award 1st Class	01.04.1937	Oberstleutnant
05.08.1940	Bar to the Iron Cross 2nd Class	01.10.1939	Oberst im Generalstab
17.02.1941	Bar to the Iron Cross 1st Class	18.03.1943	Generalmajor
00.00.194_	Hungarian Pilots Badge	01.08.1943	Generalleutnant
00.09.1942	Eastern Front Medal	-----	-----
26.08.1944	German Cross in Gold	-----	-----
00.09.1944	Wound Badge in Silver	-----	-----

HORST SCHIMPKE

(10.11.1920 – 06.03.1980)   *Leutnant*

(Wehrkundearchiv)

Knight's Cross: Awarded on 5th September 1944 as *Leutnant* and Platoon Leader in the 1st Company, 1st *Fallschirm-Panzer Jäger* Battalion for actions at Monte Cassino, Italy. During the Third Battle of Cassino Schimpke and his company knocked out over 20 enemy tanks and repulsed several enemy attacks.

Horst Schimpke was born on 10th November 1920, in Berlin-Schöneberg, and he entered the army in September 1939, joining the 206th Anti-tank Replacement Company in Allenstein. He transferred to the Luftwaffe in August 1940 before being assigned to the 3rd Company of the *Fallschirm-Panzer-Jäger Battalion*.

In May 1941, Schimpke jumped into Crete during the invasion and saw action at Máleme, Khaniá and Suda Bay. He was wounded in action, and in June was awarded the Iron Cross 1st and 2nd Classes. From January to March 1942, he fought in North Africa as part of the defensive fighting at Maramarica and Cyrenaika. He was promoted to *Feldwebel* in August 1942, and from July until October 1942 he conducted security duties as part of the 3rd Air Fleet. Towards the end of 1942, he was transferred to Russia and fought there until the spring of 1943. In August, he was commissioned as a *Leutnant*. In February 1944, he became acting commander of the 1st Company of the Parachute Anti-tank Detachment. The following month he saw action during the fighting at Cassino and his company destroyed over twenty tanks and Schimpf was awarded the Knight's Cross.

During the final stages of the war, he was placed in command of the 10th Parachute Anti-tank Battalion which he led from March 1945 until the end of the war. Schimpf died on 6th March 1980 in Bochum-Gerthe. He is buried at the Hiltrop Cemetery. (Section 72, Grave 155-156).

OTHER AWARDS		PROMOTIONS	
00.09.1940	Parachutist Badge	01.03.1940	Oberschütze
08.06.1941	Iron Cross 2nd Class	01.09.1940	Gefreiter
21.06.1941	Iron Cross 1st Class	19.12.1940	Unteroffizier-Anwärter
04.07.1941	Wound Badge in Black	01.10.1941	Oberjäger
00.00.1942	KRETA Cuff title	01.08.1942	Feldwebel
-----	-----	01.10.1942	Kriegsoffizieranwärter
-----	-----	01.04.1943	Oberfeldwebel
-----	-----	01.08.1943	Leutnant

GERHART SCHIRMER

(09.01.1913 – 05.09.2004)   *Oberstleutnant*

Knight's Cross: Awarded on 14th June 1941 as *Hauptmann* and Commander 6th Company, 2nd *Fallschirmjäger Regiment* for his part in the capitulation of British forces during the invasion of Greece. His company forced the surrender of over 1,250 troops, which included seventy-two officers. Schirmer was presented with the Knight's Cross at Führer headquarters *Wolfschanze*, Rastenburg, on 18th July 1941.

(Author's Collection)

(Wehrkundearchiv)

Knight's Cross with Oakleaves: He became the 657th recipient of the Oakleaves on 18th November 1944 as *Oberstleutnant* and Commander 16th *Fallschirmjäger Regiment* for his leadership during the occupation of the city of Vilnius in July 1944, and during the fighting near the Memel Bridgehead at Tilsit.

In December 1986, Schirmer was arrested in Germany for writing an article stating that he had been held in the former concentration camp at Sachsenhausen in October 1945, while there he was forced by the Soviets to build a gas chamber and execution room, to show the world what the Nazis had done. He also said that nearly 25,000 prisoners died at Sachsenhausen during the time it was being used as a NKVD Soviet prison camp. Gerhart Schirmer died on 5th September 2004 in Lauf-Aubach in Offenburg at the age of ninety-one. (Author's Collection)

Gerhart Schirmer was born on 9th January 1913, in Chemnitz and he entered the Landespolziei in Saxony in April 1932. He served in various posts in the police and attended the Officer Training Schools at both Dresden and Munich in 1933 and 1934. In September 1935, he transferred to the Luftwaffe as a *Leutnant* and attended the Pilot Training School in Upper Silesia. He was promoted to *Oberleutnant* in October 1937, and on 1st May 1939 he transferred to the Parachute Troops where he was appointed company commander with the 2nd *Fallschirmjäger* Regiment. During the invasion of Poland his unit was tasked with establishing and holding an important bridgehead on the Vistula. He was promoted to *Hauptmann* in June 1940, taking part in the Balkans Campaign as well as in the parachute operation at the Corinth Canal and during the fight to occupy the airfield there. After *Hauptmann* Pietzonka was wounded on landing, Schirmer took command of the 2nd Battalion, and pursued the enemy across the Peloponnese, taking seventy-two British officers and 1,200 soldiers, as well as, 9,000 Greek troops prisoner. Later, during the Crete operation, his troops captured Hill 296 and for this he was awarded the Knight's Cross.

In 1943, now with the rank of *Major*, Schirmer led the 3rd Battalion of the 5th *Fallschirmjäger*

Regiment during the heavy offensive fighting in Tunisia and later assumed command of the regiment after *Oberstleutnant* Koch had been seriously wounded. In January 1944, he was made commander of the 16th *Fallschirmjäger* Regiment, and had great success in the East during the retreat into the positions guarding East Prussia and in the Memel Bridgehead. He and his regiment were named in the Official Armed Forces Communiqué of 25th August 1944.

On 7th November 1944, Schirmer was arrested by the Gestapo in connection with the July 20 assassination plot on Hitler. He was interrogated and it was found that he had only corresponded with the Stauffenberg family and had no connection with the assassination attempt. In January 1945, he was released from prison. From February until March, he served as a consultant on airborne defences while on the staff of *Generalfeldmarschall* Model. He ended the war as a prisoner of the Soviets and was imprisoned in a labour camp until January 1956. He joined the Bundeswehr in December that same year and served until his retirement in April 1971 as an *Oberst*.

OTHER AWARDS		PROMOTIONS	
00.06.1939	Parachutist Badge	01.10.1934	Leutnant der Landespolizei
02.10.1939	Armed Forces Long Service Award 4th Class	01.08.1935	Leutnant (Luftwaffe)
00.10.1939	Return of Memel Commemorative Medal	01.10.1937	Oberleutnant
00.11.1939	Commemorative Medal of 1st October 1938	01.06.1940	Hauptmann
28.05.1940	Iron Cross 2nd Class	01.06.1943	Major
28.05.1940	Iron Cross 1st Class	01.01.1944	Oberstleutnant
05.07.1940	Luftwaffe Honour Goblet	-----	-----
17.07.1942	KRETA Cuff title	-----	-----
00.10.1942	Eastern Front Medal	-----	-----
26.11.1942	Luftwaffe Ground Assault Badge	-----	-----
13.06.1943	German Cross in Gold	-----	-----
15.08.1943	Italian-German Campaign Medal in Africa	-----	-----
15.08.1943	AFRIKA Cuff title	-----	-----

ALFRED SCHLEMM

(18.12.1894 – 24.01.1986)   *General der Fallschirmtruppe*

(Wehrkundearchiv)

Knight's Cross: Awarded on 11th June 1944, as *General der Flieger* and Commanding General of the I *Fallschirm* Corps for his leadership during the Battle of Anzio. During the Allied invasion his command responded immediately to the Allied beachhead at Anzio and Schlemm led his forces against the British and Americans for three days until relieved by troops of the 14th Army.

Alfred Schlemm was born on 18th December 1894 into an Evangelical, middle-class family in Rudolstadt, Thüringen. He entered military service as an officer candidate in March 1913, and after attending the Danzig War School he was commissioned as a *Leutnant* in June 1914. He saw action during World War I, with the 56th Field Artillery Regiment. He ended the war as a battery commander and as an *Oberleutnant*.

Schlemm stayed in the army after the war and in October 1919 he joined the staff of the artillery commander of the 5th *Reichswehr* Brigade. A year later, he served with the 3rd Prussian Artillery Regiment and later transferred to the Reich Defence Ministry in October 1924. He served as a staff officer for the next ten years, and by June 1934 had been promoted to *Major*.

Schlemm with General der Fallschirmtruppe (later Generaloberst) Kurt Student. (Author's Collection)

In February 1938, he transferred to the Luftwaffe with the rank of *Oberst* and was assigned to the General Staff. In December 1940, now a *Generalmajor*, he was appointed Chief of Staff of the XI Air Corps under *General der Flieger* Kurt Student. In May 1941, he took part in the German airborne invasion of Crete. In February 1942, Schlemm was briefly attached to the staff of the VIII Air Corps on the Eastern Front. On 12th February, he was appointed commander of Battle Group *Schlemm*, a formation assigned to the XXXX Panzer Corps where he saw action on the Eastern Front. In June, he was promoted to *Generalleutnant* and assumed command of the 1st Air Division and was responsible for all Luftwaffe air and ground support units. In October, he was made Commanding General of the II Luftwaffe Field Corps on the Eastern Front as part of the 3rd Panzer Army. In February 1943, he took part in

Operation *Kugelblitz* (Ball Lightning) against the partisan region of Surazh Rayon. On 6th October, the 2nd Luftwaffe Field Division was attacked by two Russian armies and destroyed, which resulted in a ten mile gap in the German lines and the capture of Nevel. In November, Schlemm's Corps lost its four divisions to the LIII and IX Army Corps and began its transfer to Italy.

In January 1944, the II Luftwaffe Field Corps was redesignated the I *Fallschirm* Corps and Schlemm now took control of over 24,000 troops in the area around Rome. Within forty-eight hours of taking command, he received orders to respond immediately to the Allied beachhead at Anzio. Schlemm led his command against huge British and American forces for three days, until the 14th Army took over. For this he was rewarded with the Knight's Cross. In November, he was appointed Commander-in-Chief of the 1st Parachute Army and was engaged in fierce fighting against British and Canadian troops on the Maas and Waal Rivers.

On 8th February 1945, the Canadian 1st Army launched an offensive to clear German forces between the Maas and Rhine Rivers. It was near the Nijmegan area that the Anglo-Canadian forces met with fierce opposition from Schlemm's infantry entrenched in the West Wall positions of the Reichswald. Schlemm maintained an unbroken front but suffered heavy loss, and when the American 9th Army advanced over the Roer it condensed Schlemm's forces into a small bridgehead on the west bank of the Rhine. Schlemm had other worries. Hitler had issued one of his Führer Orders, stating that German commanders would need his explicit permission before one soldier or one piece of equipment could be evacuated from the west bank to the east. Hitler also made it clear that he wanted the bridges across the Rhine destroyed before they could fall into the hands of the Allies. Any commander who failed to destroy a bridge or blew it up too early would be executed. Schlemm later said to an American interrogator: *"Since I had nine bridges in my area, I could see my hopes for a long life rapidly dwindling."*

On 7th March 1945, Schlemm began to destroy the bridges in his area. By 9th March, seven of the nine bridges had been destroyed. Schlemm had set up a special bridge command with a team of officers at each bridge with demolition teams linked by radio and linked to Schlemm's headquarters so he could personally give the order to demolish. Throughout the night of 9th/10th March, Schlemm kept a close watch on the bridges making sure that the last troops and armour got across the Rhine. At 7:00am on 10th March, the two remaining bridges were destroyed. On 21st March, his headquarters took a direct hit from Allied bombers and Schlemm was wounded and taken to hospital. On 8th May, Schlemm surrendered to British forces of the 21st Army Group.

In July 1947, Schlemm was sent to Island Farm Special POW Camp and in October he was transferred to a holding camp in Hamburg, and in March 1948 he was released. He died on 24th January 1986 in Ahlten near Hannover.

OTHER AWARDS		PROMOTIONS	
00.00.191_	Iron Cross 2nd Class	08.03.1913	Fahnenjunker-Unteroffizier
00.00.191_	Iron Cross 1st Class	20.10.1913	Fähnrich
00.05.1917	Wound Badge in Black	19.06.1914	Leutnant
00.12.1934	Cross of Honour for Frontline Combatants	16.09.1917	Oberleutnant
02.10.1936	Armed Forces Long Service Award 4th to 2nd Class	01.06.1925	Hauptmann
08.03.1938	Armed Forces Long Service Award 1st Class	01.06.1934	Major
10.08.1940	Bar to the Iron Cross 2nd Class	01.09.1935	Oberstleutnant im Generalstab
22.06.1941	Bar to the Iron Cross 1st Class	01.02.1938	Oberst im Generalstab
00.00.1942	KRETA Cuff title	01.06.1940	Generalmajor
04.08.1942	German Cross in Gold	01.06.1942	Generalleutnant
00.10.1942	Eastern Front Medal	30.01.1943	General der Flieger
00.00.1942	Luftwaffe Ground Assault Badge	04.11.1944	General der Fallschirmtruppe
00.04.1945	Wound Badge in Silver	-----	-----

HERBERT SCHMIDT

(03.10.1912 – 16.06.1944)   *Major.i.G*

Herbert Schmidt was killed by a shot from behind by a French sniper while sitting in a motor vehicle beside his divisional commander, Generalleutnant Bernhard-Hermann Ramcke, whilst travelling from Vannes to Pontivy, France on 16th June 1944. (Wehrkundearchiv)

Knight's Cross: Awarded on 29th May 1940 as *Oberleutnant* and Commander 1st Company, 1st *Fallschirmjäger* Regiment for actions in Norway.

Herbert Schmidt was born on 3rd October 1912 in Courbière Fortress in Graudenz, Prussia and he joined the Police as an officer candidate in April 1932. After training at the Brandenburg-Havel Police School he joined the Police Battalion *Wecke* a year later, and in October 1934, it was renamed the General Göring State Police Group. In July 1935, he underwent officer training at Berlin-Gatow, and in October 1936, he served as a Platoon Leader in the 2nd Company of Regiment *"Hermann Göring."* He then joined the Luftwaffe and on completing his parachutist-rifleman course at Stendal he was commissioned as a *Leutnant* in April 1937. In December 1938, he officially transferred to the Luftwaffe and was appointed Company Officer in the I Battalion of the 1st *Fallschirmjäger* Regiment.

In September 1939, now an *Oberleutnant,* he became Company Commander in the 1st Fallschirmjäger Regiment in Operation Weserübung, the codename given to the German attack on Denmark and Norway in April 1940. His company was dropped into Norway on the evening of the 14th April. He landed eight kilometres south of Dombas, and for five days his troops prevented the British 148th Infantry Brigade from linking up with Norwegian forces. Schmidt and his thirty-eight surviving men were taken prisoner by the Norwegians but were soon freed. For his efforts and leadership, Schmidt was awarded the Knight's Cross. During the fighting, however, Schmdit had been severely wounded and for the rest of his career he became a staff officer.

On 25th September 1940, still recovering from his wounds he joined the staff of the Inpsector-General of the Luftwaffe, *Generalfeldmarschall* Erhard Milch. He later became Operations Officer of the 1st Luftwaffe Field Division and the 2nd *Fallschirmjäger* Division.

OTHER AWARDS		PROMOTIONS	
00.00.1937	Reich Sports Badge in Bronze	01.04.1933	Polizei-Wachtmeister
00.06.1937	Parachutist Badge	01.10.1934	Polizei-Truppwachtmeister
00.08.1939	Armed Forces Long Service Award 4th Class	10.03.1935	Offiziersanwärter
00.11.1939	Commemorative Medal of 1st October 1938	01.10.1935	Fahnenjunker-Unteroffizier
13.05.1940	Iron Cross 2nd Class	20.04.1936	Fähnrich
16.05.1940	Iron Cross 1st Class	01.10.1936	Oberfähnrich
00.06.1940	Wound Badge in Black	20.04.1937	Leutnant
00.12.1942	Eastern Front Medal	12.12.1938	Leutnant (Luftwaffe)
-----	-----	01.10.1939	Oberleutnant
-----	-----	01.10.1942	Hauptmann
-----	-----	01.08.1943	Major im Generalstab

LEONHARD SCHMIDT

(09.12.1916 – 12.08.2006)   *Hauptmann*

(Wehrkundearchiv)

Knight's Cross: Awarded on 30th April 1945 as *Hauptmann* and *Führer* II Battalion, 1st *Fallschirmjäger* Regiment for actions in Italy. *There is no proof in surviving records of this award. No legally valid award by the Commanding general of the Fallschirm Corps, General der Fallschirmtruppe Richard Heidrich.*

Leonhard Schmidt was born on 9th December 1916 in Weißenstadt, Wunsiedel, Bavaria, and he joined the 2nd Company of Regiment "General Göring" in November 1937. In the spring of 1938, he attended a NCO course at Stendal and then joined the 2nd Company of the 1st *Fallschirmjäger* Regiment on 1st June 1938. He was deployed to Poland but saw no action. In 1940, the 3rd Company, to which he was now assigned, jumped into Stavanger, Norway to seize a key airfield at Stola where he won the Iron Cross 2nd Class. On 10th May, Schmidt saw action at Dordrecht, Holland where they seized key bridges over the Maas River and Schmidt won the Iron Cross 1st Class. From 4th June to 6th July 1940, Schmidt led his forces to Narvik where they reinforced General Dietl's mountain troops.

On 20th May 1941, Schmidt, together with the 3rd Company of the 1st *Fallschirmjäger* Regiment, jumped into Crete as part of the German airborne invasion. He was wounded on the same day. Schmidt and the regiment deployed to Russia in September 1941 and fought east of Leningrad until November. Schmidt was again wounded and spent time in a field hospital where he was promoted to *Feldwebel* in January 1942. He returned to Russia in October 1942 and remained there until July 1943. During this time, Schmidt's platoon distinguished itself in combat southwest of Orel in an attack on Promklewo. There was a recommendation submitted to give Schmidt a war-time commission and on 20th April 1943 he was promoted to *Leutnant*.

In December 1943, Schmidt returned to Italy where he became acting commander of the 3rd Company of the 1st *Fallschirmjäger* Regiment. In January 1944, Schmidt led his company during close combat northwest of Ortona in fighting against the British 8th Army. He was then deployed to Cassino, where, on 18th February, he fought in close combat on Hills 593 and 450 against the Gurkhas of the 4th Indian Division. In July, Schmidt was made adjutant of the 2nd Battalion of the 1st *Fallschirmjäger* Regiment. In December he assumed temporary command of the 2nd Battalion, and in April 1945, he was promoted to *Hauptmann*. He was recommended for the Knight's Cross, but it was never officially awarded before the war ended. He was taken prisoner on 2nd May 1945, and had spent almost seven years in the same *Fallschirmjäger* Regiment. He died on 12th August 2006 in Marktredwitz, Bavaria.

OTHER AWARDS		PROMOTIONS	
29.05.1938	Parachutist Badge	01.10.1938	Gefreiter
18.04.1940	Iron Cross 2nd Class	01.10.1939	Obergefreiter
25.05.1940	Iron Cross 1st Class	01.11.1939	Oberjäger
01.03.1941	Narvik Campaign Shield	01.01.1942	Feldwebel
15.07.1941	Wound Badge in Black	20.04.1943	Leutnant
01.10.1942	Luftwaffe Ground Assault Badge	01.07.1944	Oberleutnant
00.10.1942	Eastern Front Medal	20.04.1945	Hauptmann
20.05.1943	KRETA Cuff title	-----	-----
24.06.1943	German Cross in Gold	-----	-----
01.04.1945	Luftwaffe Close Combat Clasp in Bronze	-----	----- .

WERNER HERBERT SCHMIDT

(01.10.1906 – 17.08.1970)   *Oberstleutnant*

(Wehrkundearchiv)

Knight's Cross: Awarded on 5th April 1944 as *Major* and Commander 1st *Fallschirm* Machine-gun Battalion for actions in Cassino. He led his troops during the defence of the slopes around the monastery and they repulsed an assault by the 4th Indian Division.

Werner Schmidt was born in Posen, on 1st October 1906 and entered Brandenburg Havel Police School in April 1927. After various training courses, he joined the Police Battalion Wecke in March 1933 and was promoted to *Leutnant der Landespolizei* the following year. In October 1935, he transferred to the Luftwaffe and served in the Regiment *"General Göring"* and in March 1938 it was renamed and Schmidt became company commander in the 1st *Fallschirmjäger* Regiment.

In May 1940, he saw action in Holland and in September he was named company commander in the 1st Parachute Machine-gun Battalion and saw action during the airborne invasion of Crete. He won the Iron Cross 1st and 2nd Classes and was promoted to *Major*. In February 1942, he became the commanding officer of the 1st Parachute Machine-gun Battalion and led his troops in the central sector of the Eastern Front, where he received the German Cross in Gold.

In July 1942, following the Allied invasion of Sicily Schmidt and his battalion were flown to Catania airfield and took up position near Primasole, where it opposed a landing by the British 1st Parachute Brigade and inflicted heavy losses on it. He then took his troops to Cassino where they defended the slopes around the monastery and took part in fierce fighting and pushed back an assault made by the 4th Indian Division. During the fighting, Schimdt was wounded and later awarded the Knight's Cross.

In September 1944, Schmidt arrived at the Mallersdorf Reserve Hospital where he stayed for many months, he knew the war was over for him. He spent the remainder of the war attached to the reserves. He died on 17th August 1970 in Freudenstadt a small town in Baden-Württemberg, southern Germany.

OTHER AWARDS		PROMOTIONS	
00.00.1936	Parachutist Badge	05.10.1927	Polizeianwärter
02.10.1939	Armed Forces Long Service Award 4th to 3rd Class	13.10.1928	Polizei-Wachtmeister
00.11.1939	Commemorative Medal of 1st October 1938 + Bar	18.10.1930	Polizei-Oberwachtmeister
12.06.1941	Iron Cross 2nd Class	20.04.1934	Leutnant der Landespolizei
17.06.1941	Iron Cross 1st Class	29.06.1935	Hauptmann der Landespolizei
24.04.1942	German Cross in Gold	01.10.1935	Oberleutnant (Luftwaffe)
00.09.1942	Eastern Front Medal	01.03.1938	Hauptmann
00.00.1943	KRETA Cuff title	01.10.1941	Major
-----	-----	01.12.1944	Oberstleutnant

WOLF-WERNER GRAF VON DER SCHULENBURG

(14.09.1899 – 14.07.1944)   *Oberstleutnant z.V*

(Wehrkundearchiv)

Knight's Cross: Awarded on 20th June 1943 as *Major z.V.* and Commander I Battalion, 1st *Fallschirmjäger* Regiment for actions on the Eastern Front. He distinguished himself during numerous attacks by the Red Army south of Orel and helped to push back the advance on the 2nd Panzer Army.

Wolf-Werner Graf von der Schulenburg was born on 14th September 1899 in Bad Muskau, Rothenburg, a spa town in Upper Lusatia. His father served as the chief of staff in World War I for an army group commanded by the Crown Prince. The younger Schulenburg joined the Army in 1917 and was seriously wounded. As a result, operations left one of his legs two inches shorter than the other, but this didn't stop him from serving at the front and was commissioned as a *Leutnant* a few months before the armistice.

Schulenberg returned to active service in August 1939 and volunteered to join the Parachute troops of the Luftwaffe. He was assigned to the 1st *Fallschirmjäger* Regiment as an Ordnance Officer and was promoted to *Oberleutnant* in April 1940. He first saw action when his unit jumped into Moerdijk-Dordrecht, Holland, in May 1940, where he received thc Iron Cross 1st and 2nd Classes. On 20th May 1941, he took part in the airborne invasion of Crete. In September 1941, his regiment was deployed to Russia and fought east of Leningrad until November. Promoted to *Hauptmann* in November, he was named as acting commander of the 1st Battalion of the 1st *Fallschirmjäger* Regiment in February 1942. He returned to Russia with his unit in October, and in February 1943, he distinguished himself during the heavy fighting south or Orel and was awarded the Knight's Cross. He remained in Russia until July 1943, and then he and his unit were deployed to Italy and fought at Tarent and Ortona. From November 1943 until January 1944, he served as acting commander of the 1st *Fallschirmjäger* Regiment, before returning to command the 1st Battalion at Cassino.

In April 1944, he assumed command of the 13th *Fallschirmjäger* Regiment and saw action in Normady. Shortly after the Allied invasion, his regiment served as a battle group of the 17th SS Panzer Grenadier Regiment east of Marigny, France. On 13th July 1944, a massive Allied armoured attack inflicted heavy losses on his troops, and the following day Schulenburg moved to the front to make a personal assessment of the situation. While leading one of his battalions, an American infantryman spotted him and fired his machine-gun. Schulenburg was struck several times and killed instantly. He was posthumously promoted to *Oberstleutnant* and is buried at the German Military Cemetery at Marigny, France (Section 2, Row 22, Grave 821).

OTHER AWARDS		PROMOTIONS	
00.00.191_	Wound Badge in Silver	20.08.1917	Gefreiter
00.00.1939	Parachutist Badge	26.09.1917	Unteroffizier
23.05.1940	Iron Cross 2nd Class	25.07.1918	Fähnrich
23.05.1940	Iron Cross 1st Class	01.09.1918	Leutnant
00.00.1942	Eastern Front Medal	01.04.1940	Oberleutnant der Reserve (Luftwaffe)
01.10.1942	Luftwaffe Ground Assault Badge	01.11.1940	Hauptmann z.V.
20.05.1943	KRETA Cuff title	19.12.1941	Major z.V.
-----	-----	23.07.1944	Oberstleutnant z.V.

KARL-LOTHAR SCHULZ

(30.04.1907 – 26.09.1972)   *Generalmajor*

Knight's Cross: Awarded on 24th May 1940 as *Hauptmann* and Commander III Battalion, 1st *Fallschirmjäger* Regiment for actions in Rotterdam. During the attack on Holland his battalion captured the city airport at Rotterdam which was essential to the success of the campaign – the ground troops could now be supplied with food, ammunition and reinforcements. After the defeat of France in July 1940, Schulz was promoted to *Major* and took part in the aerial invasion of Crete in May 1941. His troops encountered fierce fighting and due to a shortage of ammunition

Schulz was promoted to Generalmajor in January 1945 and was captured by U.S. forces on 2nd May 1945. He was released on 17th October 1947, and he returned to Germany where he lived with his wife in Wiesbaden until his death on 26th September 1972. (Author's Collection)

(Wehrkundearchiv)

were forced to abandon the city shortly afterwards. Schulz nevertheless held positions near Heraklion and again his skills as a successful commander helped to secure the victory. He later saw action on the eastern front, and in April 1942, he was appointed temporary commander of the 1st *Fallschirmjäger* Regiment seeing action in Leningrad.

Knight's Cross with Oakleaves: Awarded on 20th April 1944, to become the 459th recipient as *Oberst* and Commander 1st *Fallschirmjäger* Regiment for his bravery and leadership during the battles around Monte Cassino. On 18th November 1944, he took command of the 1st *Fallschirmjäger* Division succeeding *Generalmajor* Hans Korte. From November 1944 until April 1945, he saw action during the defensive fighting in the sector near Imola, Italy.

Knight's Cross with Oakleaves and Swords: He became the 112th recipient of the Swords on 18th November 1944 as *Oberst* and *Führer* 1st *Fallschirmjäger* Division for further actions in northern Italy. His award came with the promotion to *Generalmajor*.

Karl-Lothar Schulz distinguished himself as a brave and courageous soldier during battle in Holland, Crete, Monte Cassino, and the Eastern Front. He was born on 30th April 1907 in Königsberg and upon completion of his schooling he entered the artillery in June 1924. His time as a soldier was short when he transferred to the police service in October 1925 and later served with the Security Police in Berlin. In February 1933, he joined the *Landespolizei* Wecke as a platoon leader and in January 1934 this unit became the *Landespolziei "Hermann Göring."*

In October 1935, he transferred to the Luftwaffe and was appointed Company commander in the 1st Battalion of the Regiment *"General Göring."* He then underwent a parachutist training course and in March 1937 he was promoted to *Hauptmann*. He saw action during the Polish Campaign and in January 1940 Schulz was appointed commander of the 3rd Battalion of the 1st *Fallschirmjäger* Regiment and saw action during the Western Campaign. His battalion captured the airport at Rotterdam which was essential to the campaign, the ground troops could now be supplied with food, ammunition, and reinforcements by air. For this he was awarded the Knight's Cross.

Schulz was promoted to *Major* in July 1940, after the victory celebrations after the defeat of France. He took part in the aerial invasion of Crete in May 1941 when he parachuted into Heraklion with his troops. They encountered heavy fighting and due to a shortage of ammunition his troops were forced to abandon the city shortly afterwards. Schulz nevertheless held positions near Heraklion and again his leadership skills helped secure a victory. In September 1941, his command was transferred to the Eastern Front where it saw action near Leningrad. He then led his forces at the Neva River at great cost. In April 1942, he was made temporary Chief of Operations of the 7th Air Division serving under *Generalleutnant* Erich Petersen. In June 1942, he took over as commander of the 1st *Fallschirmjäger* Regiment and saw action in Russia in the areas around Volkov, Rshev and Orel. He was promoted to *Oberstleutnant* in October 1942 and *Oberst* the following year. In April 1944, he was awarded the Oakleaves for actions following the Allied landings in Italy.

On 18th November 1944, Schulz took command of the 1st *Fallschirmjäger* Division when he succeeded *Generalmajor* Hans Korte. It was while commanding this unit, during the Battle of Monte Cassino, that Schulz earned the support and respect of his men and his superiors. His command spent November 1944 to April 1945 defending a sector near Imola, part of the 10th Army. In recognition of his bravery, he was awarded the Knight's Cross with Oakleaves and Swords on 18th November 1944.

OTHER AWARDS		PROMOTIONS	
00.10.1936	Parachutist Badge	01.04.1927	Polizei-Wachtmeister
00.06.1939	Armed Forces Long Service Award 4th to 3rd Class	01.08.1930	Polizei-Oberwachtmeister
12.05.1940	Iron Cross 2nd Class	20.04.1934	Leutnant der Polizei
12.05.1940	Iron Cross 1st Class	01.09.1935	Oberleutnant der Polizei
00.00.194_	Wound Badge in Black	01.10.1935	Oberleutnant (Luftwaffe)
26.02.1942	German Cross in Gold	01.03.1937	Hauptmann
00.00.1942	Luftwaffe Ground Assault Badge	19.07.1940	Major
00.10.1942	Eastern Front Medal	26.10.1942	Oberstleutnant
00.05.1943	KRETA Cuff title	21.10.1943	Oberst
-----	-----	17.01.1945	Generalmajor

ERICH JOHANNES SCHUSTER

(06.11.1919 – 11.01.1943)   *Oberleutnant*

Killed in action on 11th January 1943, during the advance over Hill 311, Tunisia, Erich Schuster was posthumously promoted to the rank of Oberleutnant. (Author's Collection)

Knight's Cross: Awarded on 21st August 1941 as *Feldwebel* and Section Leader in the 3rd Company, 1st Air-Landing Assault Regiment for actions during the campaign in Crete. His section was responsible for eliminating an anti-aircraft battery at Malemes airfield.

Erich Schuster was born on 6th November 1919, in Morbach, Bernkstel-Cues, and he joined the parachute troops as a volunteer on 3rd October 1938. He completed his parachutist-rifleman's training course in December 1939 and was assigned to the 1st Company of the 1st *Fallschirmjäger* Regiment in Stendal. In November 1939, Schuster was transferred to the Koch Parachute Assault Battalion.

On 10 May 1940, he saw his first action of the war during the French Campaign, his group's objective was Veldwezelt Bridge. He distinguished himself during the fighting and was awarded the Iron Cross 1st and 2nd Classes. On 20th May 1941, he took part in the airborne invasion of Crete, and his squad landed with the glider group at Malemes airfield. His platoon leader, *Feldwebel* Arpke, had been seriously wounded when his glider crash landed, so Schuster assumed command. His troops eliminated an anti-aircraft battery and occupied the western end of Malemes airfield. For this action and for his leadership he was awarded the Knight's Cross.

In July 1941, Schuster was promoted to *Feldwebel* and in January 1942 he saw action in Russia as a platoon commander. His company took part in the defence of Anisovo-Gorodische airfield. His friend, *Leutnant* Arpke, took part in the counterattack too, and when he was killed Schuster assumed commander of the 3rd Company. In November 1942, with the formation of the 5th *Fallschirmjäger* Regiment, Schuster, who had been promoted to *Leutnant,* took command of the 1st Company, which he led in action in Tunisia.

OTHER AWARDS		PROMOTIONS	
07.09.1939	Parachutist Badge	13.05.1940	Oberjäger
00.11.1939	Commemorative Medal of 1st October 1938 + Bar	25.07.1941	Feldwebel
13.05.1940	Iron Cross 2nd Class	01.07.1942	Leutnant
13.05.1940	Iron Cross 1st Class	08.04.1943	Oberleutnant
03.03.1942	Wound Badge in Black	-----	-----
25.09.1942	Eastern Front Medal	-----	-----

KARL ALFRED MARKUS SCHWARZMANN

(23.03.1912 – 11.03.2000) *Major der Reserve*

(Private source)

Knight's Cross: Awarded on 29th May 1940 as *Oberleutnant* and Platoon Leader in the 8th Company, 1st *Fallschirmjäger* Regiment for actions in the Western Campaign. He led his platoon in the invasion of Holland where they came under heavy fire but they managed to hold their positions until reinforcements arrived

Karl Schwarzmann was born in Fürth, East Franconia, a city in northern Bavaria on 23rd March 1912. He joined the 13th Company of the Nuremberg Infantry Regiment in April 1933. In 1936, he was a member of the German Gymnastics team in the Olympic Games in Berlin, where he won three Gold medals and two Bronze medals.

From June 1938, he served as an army sports instructor and was commissioned as a *Leutnant* with the Luftwaffe the same month. In January 1939, he was assigned to the II Battalion of the 1st *Fallschirmjäger* Regiment in Stendal and later at Braunschweig. He saw action during the Polish Campaign and fought near Wolo Gulowska. Promoted to *Oberleutnant* in March 1940, the following month he became commander of a machine-gun platoon in the 8th Company of the 1st *Fallschirmjäger* Regiment. In May 1940, Schwarzmann together with his company parachuted into Holland and took up a key position on the coast. This they held until relief forces arrived, however, during the fighting, Schwarzmann was badly wounded when a bullet pierced a lung. For his leadership and bravery, he was awarded the Iron Cross 1st and 2nd Classes and four days later he received the Knight's Cross.

In 1941, he took part in the airborne invasion of Crete seeing action in the Heraklion area. He was promoted to *Hauptmann* in June 1942 and made acting commander of the 8th Company of the 3rd *Fallschirmjäger* Regiment; the command was confirmed in October. He saw action in Russia until early 1943. In March, he became commander of the headquarters of the 7th Air Division, and from June 1943, served in the same position with the 1st *Fallschirmjäger* Division. In Mach 1944, he was forced to enter the Luftwaffe hospital in Munich because of his old wound. He remained in hospital for several months, and was promoted to *Major,* shortly before being captured by British forces in May 1945.

Scharzmann took part in his second Olympic Games in Helsinki in 1952, as a forty-year old, and won a silver medal. He died in Goslar on 11th March 2000.

OTHER AWARDS		PROMOTIONS	
00.04.1937	Armed Forces Long Service Award 4th Class	01.10.1934	Gefreiter
18.01.1939	Army Parachutist Badge	01.05.1935	Unteroffizier
25.05.1940	Iron Cross 2nd Class	27.06.1938	Leutnant
25.05.1940	Iron Cross 1st Class	11.03.1940	Oberleutnant der Reserve
29.05.1940	Wound Badge in Silver	14.07.1942	Hauptmann der Reserve
00.00.1942	Eastern Front Medal	20.04.1945	Major der Reserve
20.05.1943	KRETA Cuff title	-----	-----
12.12.1943	Luftwaffe Parachutist Badge	-----	-----

GÜNTHER SEMPERT

(20.10.1918 – 16.03.2009)   *Major*

(Private source)

Knight's Cross: Awarded on 30th September 1944 as *Hauptmann* and *Führer* 1st *Fallschirm-Panzer Jäger* Battalion in recognition of his heroism and achievements during the battles at Cassino, where his unit was credited with destroying a total of 120 enemy armoured vehicles.

Günther Sempert was born on 20th October 1918 in Wechselburg an der Mulde near Leipzig, Saxony. He entered the German Army in November 1927 as an officer candidate with the 4th Anti-tank Detachment. He began his training as an officer in November 1938 and saw action during the invasion of Poland in September 1939. He was commissioned as a *Leutnant* in December that same year and assumed duties as a recruiting officer in Spremberg but wanted to see more action and volunteered for airborne training.

After the completion of his parachute training, he transferred to the Luftwaffe in August 1940 and became a platoon leader in the 3rd Company of the 7th *Fallschirm-Panzer-Jäger* Detachment. On 20th May 1941, he jumped into Crete as part of the German airborne invasion. He was wounded the same day, but later fought at Máleme, Khaniá, and Suda Bay. For his leadership in Crete, he was awarded the Iron Cross 1st and 2nd Classes and promoted to *Oberleutnant* in December 1941. He later saw action in North Africa from January to March 1942 as part of the defensive fighting at Maramarica and Cyrenaika. In April, he assumed command of the 5th Company of the 7th *Fallschirm-Panzer-Jäger* Detachment. While on a visit to the invasion site at Dieppe, when the fighting was over, he was a victim of an accident when a round of ammunition exploded, causing the loss of an an eye.

He was deployed to Russia in October 1942 and remained there until March 1943, where his troops destroyed sixty-seven enemy bunkers. He was then transferred to Italy where he became the commander of the 4th Company of the 1st *Fallschirm-Panzer-Jäger* Detachment in June 1943, where he and his troops played a key role in the rescue of Mussolini. For the liberation of the "Duce" and for the destruction of sixteen enemy tanks, he was awarded the German Cross in Gold. He was again wounded in action in November. He then saw action at Cassino where he served as acting commander of the 1st *Fallschirm-Panzer-Jäger* Detachment. He distinguished himself in battle during the 3rd Cassino Battle. His anti-tank detachment destroyed 120 enemy tanks, and upon recognizing the enemy breakthrough towards his right flank, he skilfully used his anti-tank weapons and sealed it off. For these accomplishments and his leadership qualities, he was awarded the Knight's Cross.

On 30th January 1945, Sempert was promoted to *Major* and in April was wounded yet again. In May 1945, he was taken prisoner by U.S. forces and remained in allied captivity until 13th September 1945. Günther Sempert died on 16th March 2009 in Vire, France.

OTHER AWARDS		PROMOTIONS	
09.09.1939	Wound Badge in Black	01.04.1938	Fahnenjunker-Gefreiter
00.10.1940	Parachutist Badge	05.08.1938	Fahnenjunker-Unteroffizier
11.06.1941	Iron Cross 2nd Class	05.04.1939	Fähnrich

05.07.1941	Iron Cross 1st Class	22.12.1939	Leutnant
01.10.1942	Luftwaffe Ground Assault Badge	07.10.1940	Leutnant (Luftwaffe)
00.11.1942	Eastern Front Medal	01.12.1941	Oberleutnant
20.05.1943	KRETA Cuff title	05.05.1944	Hauptmann
14.06.1944	German Cross in Gold	30.01.1945	Major
00.04.1945	Wound Badge in Silver	-----	-----

HUBERT SNIERS
(06.04.1915 – 11.11.1999) *Oberleutnant*

(Wehrkundearchiv)

Knight's Cross: Awarded on 24th October 1944 as *Leutnant* and *Führer* III Battalion, 15th *Fallschirmjäger* Regiment for his bravery and leadership during tough defensive actions on the invasion front in France.

Hubert Sniers was born on 6th April 1915, in Rheydt, part of Mönchengladbach in the west of North Rhine-Westphalia. He joined the German Navy (*Kriegsmarine*) in October 1936 after a brief period with the labour service. He was trained as a radio operator and served aboard the *Admiral Scheer* as a *Gefreiter*. In October 1938, he was transferred to the flying boat base at Parnow where he became a radio technician.

On 3rd July 1941, he transferred to the parachute troops and once he had completed his parachutist-rifleman's course, he was assigned to the 4th *Fallschirmjäger* Regiment. In March 1942, he was sent to the Luftwaffe officer candidate school in Gross-Born, where he was commissioned as a *Leutnant* in April 1942. In June 1943, he finally saw action in Russia as a signals and operations officer with the 3rd Battalion of the 4th *Fallschirmjäger* Regiment. He transferred to the 15th *Fallschirmjäger* Regiment in January 1944, and by the end of the month, he had received the Iron Cross 1st Class for actions in Italy.

On 21st June 1944, he led the 9th Company of the 15th *Fallschirmjäger* Regiment on the invasion front. He now saw heavy action as part of the 353rd Infantry Division in the Cotentin area from 10th July. During the action Sniers, now an *Oberleutnant,* was wounded. He remained at the front and assumed command of the battalion at the beginning of August when its commander was seriously wounded. With his own wound to contend with, he led the battalion with outstanding skill and bravery and achieved great success in a defensive role; and was awarded the Knight's Cross. In January 1945, he became the official commander of the 3rd Battalion of the 15th *Fallschirmjäger* Regiment and was now fighting within the Reich itself, where in April he was taken prisoner. He died on 11th November 1999 in Heiden, Borken.

OTHER AWARDS		PROMOTIONS	
00.00.1940	Parachutist Badge	01.10.1937	Gefreiter
00.00.1942	Eastern Front Medal	01.10.1938	Obergefreiter
07.09.1943	Iron Cross 2nd Class	01.11.1939	Unteroffizier
29.01.1944	Iron Cross 1st Class	20.05.1941	Kriegsoffizieranwärter
-----	-----	20.04.1942	Leutnant
-----	-----	22.10.1944	Oberleutnant

ALBERT STECKEN

(24.01.1915 – 24.08.2011)   *Major.i.G*

Knight's Cross: Awarded on 28th April 1945 as *Major.i.G* and Chief of Operations (Ia) of the 8th *Fallschirmjäger* Division during a major counter-attack offensive against strong enemy attacks in the area of the Lower Rhine.

Albert Stecken was born on 24th January 1915 in Münster, North Rhine-Westphalia and he joined the State Police in Duisburg-Hambörn in October 1934. In July 1935, he entered the Air School at Potsdam-Eiche as an Officer Candidate, the following year he transferred to the Anti-aircraft Artillery School at Wüstrow.

On 1st October 1936, he joined the 1st Battalion of the 8th Anti-aircraft Regiment, and saw action during the Spanish Civil War as part of the Legion Condor. He had by now been commissioned as a *Leutnant* and took part in the fighting during the second Ebro offensive, and the first and second Mediterranean offensives. In January 1939, he was transferred to the I Battalion of the 32nd Anti-aircraft Regiment stationed in Berlin. He attended an Anti-aircraft course in Mecklenburg in September 1940, and was assigned to the Luftwaffe War School in Berlin-Gatow in December 1941. He held a number of staff positions, which included Operations Officer on the staff of II. Luftwaffe Field Corps before entering the Luftwaffe General Staff in June 1943.

Promoted to *Major* in July 1943, he served as Operations Officer with the 23rd Anti-aircraft Division from November 1943 until October 1944, seeing action on the Eastern Front. He was assigned to the staff of the Head of the Luftwaffe's Technical Equipment Branch on 11th January 1945. Then, just four days later, he took over as Operations Officer of the 8th *Fallschirmjäger* Division. He saw heavy action on the Lower Rhine front and led a hastily assembled group of forces in a counterattack against enemy forces which had broken through near Empel-Millingen, and managed to hold off the enemy attack. For this feat, Stecken was awarded the Knight's Cross, following a recommendation from General Meindl.

On 5th May 1945, he was taken prisoner by British troops, and remained in Allied captivity until 10th July 1945. He joined the Bundeswehr in 1956 and was promoted to *Generalmajor* in October 1969, and appointed Commander of the 4th Luftwaffe Division at the same time. He retired from service on 31st March 1971. He died on 24th August 2011, in Münster at the age of ninety-six.

OTHER AWARDS		PROMOTIONS	
14.02.1939	Armed Forces Long Service Award 4th Class	05.10.1934	Fahnenjunker der Landespolizei
04.05.1939	Medal for the Spanish Campaign	01.04.1935	Fahnenjunker-Truppenwachtmeister
04.05.1939	Spanish War Cross	01.06.1935	Fahnenjunker-Oberwachtmeister
06.06.1939	Spanish Cross in Gold + Swords	01.08.1935	Fahnenjunker-Unteroffizier (Luftwaffe)
24.04.1940	Iron Cross 2nd Class	01.04.1936	Fähnrich
28.06.1940	Iron Cross 1st Class	01.08.1936	Leutnant
30.01.1941	Narvik Campaign Shield	01.03.1939	Oberleutnant
00.00.1942	Eastern Front Medal	01.11.1941	Hauptmann
00.00.1944	Luftwaffe Anti-Aircraft Badge	01.07.1943	Major im Generalstab

EDUARD LEOPOLD EDGAR STENTZLER

(27.03.1905 – 19.10.1941)   *Major*

(Wehrkundearchiv)

Knight's Cross: Awarded on 9th July 1941 as *Major* and Commander 2nd Battalion, 1st *Fallschirmjäger* Assault Regiment for actions during the invasion of Crete. He took part in the capture of Hill 107 and took command of the regiment when its commander was wounded.

Edgar Stentzler was born on 27th March 1905 in Dortmund. He joined the 1st Mounted Regiment in April 1923. He was promoted to *Leutnant* in May 1929, transferred to the 15th Mounted Regiment in March 1930, and in October 1931, joined the 2nd Company of the regiment's Anti-tank Squadron. In October 1933, he attended the Observer School in Braunschweig and shortly after he left the army and joined the Luftwaffe. He was assigned to the Celle Flying School in July 1934, and in August 1935, he transferred to the Grossenhain Flying Squadron. The following year, now with the rank of *Hauptmann,* he was attached to the 121st Reconnaissance Group in Neuhaus. In July 1938, he was transferred to the staff of Air Region Commando XI in Hannover under the command of *Generalmajor* Ludwig Wolff.

In June 1940, he completed a course at the Academy of Air Warfare and joined the *Fallschirmjäger* Replacement Battalion as a volunteer. He completed his parachute training, and in July 1940, became commander of the 2nd Battalion of the Parachute Replacement Battalion in Quedlinburg. On 20th May 1941, he took part in the airborne invasion of Crete where he and his battalion landed east of Malemes airfield. He took part in the capture of Hill 107 where they were attacked by enemy forces as well as partisans. In the evening, Stentzler assumed command of the regiment after its commander, *Generalmajor* Meindl, had been wounded. He then took his battalion in pursuit of the enemy south of Pyrgos and took part in some of the bloodiest fighting of the campaign. His battalion had borne the brunt of the fighting, and with the support of heavy weapons, had pushed the enemy forces back and secured the Hill 107. It was later stated that if it hadn't been for the skill and leadership of Stentzler, the highly important high ground would not have been taken. As a result, his bravery and leadership was recognized when he was awarded the Knight's Cross.

In the summer of 1941, Stentzler and his battalion was transferred to Russia where they took part in the fighting on the Neva front. Here he was seriously wounded during an assault from the Petrushino bridgehead on 3rd October. He was evacuated to a hospital in Königsberg, East Prussia where he died on 19th October 1941.

OTHER AWARDS		PROMOTIONS	
00.00.1935	Pilots Badge	01.09.1927	Fähnrich
00.05.1936	Armed Forces Long Service Award 4th to 3rd Class	01.08.1928	Oberfähnrich
05.05.1940	Iron Cross 2nd Class	01.05.1929	Leutnant
00.08.1940	Parachutist Badge	01.04.1933	Oberleutnant
24.05.1941	Iron Cross 1st Class	01.08.1935	Hauptmann
-----	-----	19.07.1940	Major

KURT ARTHUR BENNO STUDENT

(12.05.1890 – 01.07.1978)   *Generaloberst*

(Author's Collection)

Knight's Cross: Awarded on 12th May 1940 as *Generalleutnant* and Commander 7th Air Division (*Parachute*) for the successful air and land operations at Eben-Emael on the Belgium border. It was Student who formulated the plan and together with *Oberst* Bruno Bräuer of the 1st *Fallschirmjäger* Regiment, Students troops landed near the fortress in gliders.

Knight's Cross with Oakleaves: He became the 305th recipient of the Oakleaves on 27th September 1943, as *General der Fallschirmtruppe* and Commanding General XI Air Corps (Air-Landing Corps) for actions in and around Sicily and for his part in the rescue of Mussolini from Italian partisans.

Kurt Student was born on 12th May 1890, in Birkholz, a village in the area of Züllichau-Schwiebus now in Poland. In March 1910, he and his four brothers entered cadet school and the young Kurt was assigned to the 1st Jäger Battalion. A year later, almost to the day, he was commissioned as a *Leutnant* and two months later underwent his pilot training, gaining his licence in August 1913. In February 1914, he was attached to the Flying Station in Posen where he flew as a reconnaissance pilot, then as a bomber pilot and finally as a fighter pilot. In October 1915, he was appointed as a squadron commander. In May 1917, he was wounded in aerial combat and after he recovered he took command of the 3rd Fighter Group, operating on the Western Front.

(Author's Collection)

In October 1919, he joined the *Reichswehr* and was attached to the Air Ministry and for the next few years he held various posts. Two years later, he was assigned to the staff of the Replacement Battalion of the 2nd Infantry Regiment, and in January 1929, was appointed a battalion commander and was promoted to *Major* a year later. He transferred to the Luftwaffe in September 1935 and was made commander of the test center for flying equipment, and at the same time was appointed as airfield commandant at Rechlin. In March 1937, he was made commander of the Aviation Weapons School and was also made Chief of Staff to the commander of the Flying Schools in the Reich. Promoted to *Generalmajor* in April 1938, he took command of the 7th Air Division, and it was at this time that Student became totally devoted to the concept of airborne warfare. In

July, he was appointed as commander of all parachute troops, he now oversaw its creation; he made sure that they were well equipped and well trained.

Left to right: Oberst Richard Heidrich, commander of the 3rd Fallschirmjäger Regiment, General der Fallschirmtruppe Kurt Student, Major Ludwig Heilmann, commander of the 3rd Battalion, 3rd Fallschirmjäger Regiment and Hauptmann Gerhart Schirmer, commander of the 6th Company of the 2nd Fallschirmjäger Regiment, seen here shortly after receiving the Knight's Cross from Student on 14th June 1941. (Wehrkundearchiv)

In September 1939, World War II began, but Student's troops were not used during the invasion of Poland. In October, Student met with Hitler and was told that his paratrooper troops would be used during the Western Campaign. Their mission was to take the Belgian fortress of Eben Emael and then to seize the bridges across the Albert Canal and hold them. Student went away to formulate his plan. Together with *Oberst* Bruno Bräuer's 1st *Fallschirmjäger* Regiment, Student troops landed near the fortress in gliders. Student used 500 glider troops and on 10th May 1940, almost four hundred parachute troops descended on the fort and within twenty-fur hours the fort had been captured. The objectives on the Albert Canal had been achieved and every bridge had been taken. Student later in a post-publication said of the operation, *"It was a deed of exemplary daring and decisive significance."* Also on 10th May, Students troops landed in Rotterdam and The Hague and here Student personally directed his troops. The Dutch counterattack failed and four days later Rotterdam capitulated. Hitler was overjoyed and awarded Student with the Knight's Cross on 12th May. Student was seriously wounded when a stray bullet struck him in the head while he was negotiating the Dutch surrender. It was thought that the bullet was fired by troops of the 1st SS Panzer Regiment. Student nevertheless spent several months in hospital and did not return to active duty until January 1941.

He now held the rank of *General der Fallschirmtruppe* and assumed command of the 11th Air Corps. On 20th April 1941, Hitler's fifty-second birthday, Student was summoned to Hitler's headquarters to discuss the plan for the invasion of Crete. Hitler was impressed by the plan and agreed to the operation. On 23rd May, Student flew with his staff to Crete to personally supervise the battle. Within seven days, Crete was overrun but Student's troops had suffered heavy losses. These huge losses caused Hitler to drop any idea of further action using paratroopers, and when Student proposed an air invasion of Malta, Hitler quickly rejected it.

Student continued to direct all airborne forces of the Reich and was greatly involved in the plan to rescue Mussolini from the Campo Imperatore Mountain Hotel on the Gran Sasso, Italy, in September 1943. It was his idea to land forces by gliders under the command of *SS-Sturmbannführer* Otto Skorzeny. On 27th September, Hitler awarded Student the Knight's Cross with Oakleaves after the success of the rescue.

General Student with Major i.G. Arnold von Roon. (Author's Collection)

In March 1944, Student was appointed Commander-in-Chief of the 1st *Fallschirm*-Army and saw action during the occupation of Rome, Monte Cassino and the attempted defence against the Allied landings at Anzio. In August, he was promoted to *Generaloberst* and was at his command post when the Allies launched Operation Market Garden, the airborne invasion of Holland on 17th September 1944. Student led his troops against the American 101st Airborne Division. One of the reasons that the U.S. objective failed was due to the skill of Student.

On 28th May 1945, Student surrendered to British troops and was imprisoned in the "London Cage" (MI9 prison facility located on Kensington Palace Gardens, London). He was later charged with war crimes that had taken place on Crete, and was sentenced to five years imprisonment. The Greek authorities requested his extradition to face trial in Athens for crimes committed in Greece, but this was refused due to Student's ill health. He was released early from prison due to his 1940 head wound, and he returned to Germany. He became the President of the Association of German Parachute Troops until his death in Lemgo in July 1978.

Wartime postcard of Student. (Author's Collection)

OTHER AWARDS			PROMOTIONS	
27.02.1914	Pilots Badge		03.03.1910	Fähnrich
26.09.1914	Iron Cross 2nd Class		20.03.1911	Leutnant
21.06.1915	Knight's Cross of the Saxony Albrecht Order 2nd Class + Swords		18.06.1915	Oberleutnant
29.08.1915	Iron Cross 1st Class		20.06.1918	Hauptmann
05.06.1917	Knight's Cross of the Royal House Order of Hohenzollern		01.01.1930	Major
10.09.1919	Fliers Commemorative Badge		01.01.1934	Oberstleutnant
30.01.1935	Cross of Honour for Frontline Combatants		01.10.1935	Oberst
21.05.1935	Military Pilots Badge		01.04.1938	Generalmajor
02.10.1936	Armed Forces Long Service Award 4th to 1st Class		01.01.1940	Generalleutnant
05.06.1939	Commemorative Medal of 1st October 1938 + Bar		29.05.1940	General der Flieger
20.09.1939	Bar to the Iron Cross 2nd Class		00.08.1940	General der Fallschirmtruppe
20.09.1939	Bar to the Iron Cross 1st Class		13.07.1944	Generaloberst
00.06.1940	Wound Badge in Silver		-----	-----
02.09.1940	Combined Pilots & Observers Badge in Gold + Diamonds		-----	-----
20.05.1943	KRETA Cuff title		-----	-----

ALFRED STURM

(23.08.1888 – 08.03.1962)   *Generalleutnant*

(Author's Collection)

Knight's Cross: Awarded on 9th July 1941 as *Oberst* and Commander 2nd *Fallschirmjäger* Regiment for actions during the invasion of Crete. He led his regiment with great skill and prevented 10,000 British and Greek troops from escaping to Crete.

Alfred Sturm was born in Saarbrücken, on 23rd August 1888, and entered army service as a pupil at the NCO School in Bieberich in October 1905. He entered World War I as a Vizefeldwebel, attached to the 144th Infantry Regiment on the Western Front. Wounded in January 1915, and once recovered he decided to train as a pilot with the 4th Flying Replacement Battalion and was assigned as a fighter pilot to the 5th Fighter Squadron. In April 1917, he scored his first victory and in June he was shot down himself. Having won both classes of the Iron Cross, he ended the war with the 89th Fighter Squadron.

Strum served for a time in the Defence Ministry and in May 1920 he was taken into the 10th Infantry Regiment. In January 1921, he was commissioned as a *Leutnant* and was again attached to the Defence Ministry before being transferred to the 8th Prussian Infantry Regiment in January 1926. In March, he was promoted to *Hauptmann,* and two years later, he left the infantry to begin his training once again as a pilot. In August 1930, he returned to his old regiment where he served until October 1933 when he was transferred to the Ministry of Aviation (*Reichsluftfahrministerium*), and served as a staff officer until December when he was transferred to the Fighter Air School in Schleißheim. In January 1935, Strum was appointed commander of the Air School in Magdeburg and in April was promoted to *Major*. From January 1936 until March 1939, he served as Air Base Commander at Detmold, and was now an *Oberst*. He then served with the Air Ministry until June 1940 when he was posted to the Wittstock Parachute Training School where, although fifty-two years old, he underwent parachute training.

In July 1940, he was appointed commander of the 2nd *Fallschirmjäger* Regiment and took part in the airborne invasion of Crete in May 1941. On the second day of the invasion, Strum was taken prisoner by the British but was freed a few days later. As a consequence, his regiment was led by *Major* Kroh and was extremely successful. On 20th May, he was appointed acting commander of the 7th Air Division after its commander *Generalleutnant* Wilhelm Süßmann was killed. For his regiment's success during the first days of the campaign, Strum was awarded the Knight's Cross. In October, now a *Generalmajor*, Strum was transferred to Russia where he saw action in the area around Leningrad as part of the 18th Army. For the next two months, the Soviets fought against the *Fallschirmjäger* regiments, but without success and in December, Strum and his regiment were sent back to Germany to rest. However, within a few weeks, Strum was made commander of a Battle Group formed from elements of his 2nd *Fallschirmjäger* Regiment together with units of the anti-tank and machine gun battalions and were sent to the Ukraine to bolster Army Group South. It defended a sector along the River Mius near the town of Charzysk throughout the winter of 1941 and into early-1942 with little success.

In August 1942, Strum became seriously ill and was taken off frontline duty and ordered to rest. In October, he was transferred to the eastern front to command the Ground Combat Schools of the Luftwaffe where he stayed until January 1945, when he was named Head of the Wehrmacht Motor Transport. It was a transport service with little or no petrol; and very few vehicles. For the last few weeks of the war, he commanded a Battle Group and was taken prisoner by Allied troops on 23rd April 1945. Held in captivity without cause, and it seems held illegally as a prisoner of war, being he was finally released on 5th June 1947. Alfred Strum died in Detmold on 8th March 1962.

OTHER AWARDS		PROMOTIONS	
00.00.1915	Prussian Pilots Badge	01.08.1913	Vizefeldwebel
18.06.1916	Iron Cross 2nd Class	01.01.1915	Offiziers-Stellvertreter
17.01.1917	Iron Cross 1st Class	05.06.1919	Leutnant
00.00.191_	Wound Badge in Silver	15.01.1921	Oberleutnant
00.12.1934	Cross of Honour for Frontline Combatants	01.03.1926	Hauptmann
00.00.1935	Pilots Badge	21.04.1935	Major
02.10.1936	Armed Forces Long Service Award 4th to 1st Class	02.08.1936	Oberstleutnant
00.10.1939	Commemorative Medal of 1st October 1938 + Bar	01.10.1938	Oberst
00.07.1940	Parachutist Badge	01.08.1941	Generalmajor
28.10.1940	Bar to the Iron Cross 2nd Class	01.08.1943	Generalleutnant
25.06.1941	Bar to the Iron Cross 1st Class	-----	-----
00.00.1943	KRETA Cuff title	-----	-----

KARL STEFAN (TYCZKA) TANNERT

(22.12.1910 –)   *Oberstleutnant*

(Wehrkundearchiv)

Knight's Cross: Awarded on 5th April 1944, as *Hauptmann* and Commander III Battalion of the 2nd *Fallschirmjäger* Regiment for actions near the city of Kirovograd on the southern sector of the Eastern Front.

Karl Tannert (known as Karl Tyczka from 18th February 1942), was born on 22nd December 1910 in Psaar near Loben, Upper Silesia. He served in the border protection services from 1933 and was made deputy company leader of the Border Protection Regiment "Gleiwitz" in February 1934. He attended an air-raid and gas course in April 1937 and was transferred to the Regiment SA-Standarte "*Feldherrnhalle*" in Berlin in July 1938. He then attended various military courses before becoming the commander of the 78th Infantry Regiment in August. Commissioned as *Leutnant* in September 1938 he served as adjutant to the 2nd Battalion of the Regiment SA-Standarte "*Feldherrnhalle*."

He volunteered for the airborne troops in June 1939 was officially accepted into the Luftwaffe as reservist. On 15th August, Tannert joined the 1st Battalion of the 1st *Fallschirmjäger* Regiment and saw action during the Polish Campaign. He later saw action in Denmark, where he took part in the capture of the bridges near Masnedö. He parachuted into Holland as commander of the leading platoon of 1st Company of the 1st *Fallschirmjäger* Regiment, taking part in the attack on the bridges at Dordrecht. In April, he saw action during the fighting near Narvik, Norway, winning the Iron Cross 1st and 2nd Classes. At Narvik, his aircraft was shot down, and Tannert helped to save several crewmen in the deep snow, suffering frostbite before being rescued several days later. Promoted to *Oberleutnant* in July 1940 he assumed command of the 1st Company of the 1st *Fallschirmjäger* Regiment in September.

On 20th May 1941, his company jumped into action east of Heraklion during the German airborne invasion of Crete. The following day, he was seriously wounded as his unit attempted to seize the airfield near the city. He returned to his unit just as they were being deployed to Russia, and saw action near Gorodok and Wyborg in November where he was once again wounded. He remained with his troops at this time and helped to prevent a Russian breakthrough, and the following month he was recommended for the Knight's Cross but it was not approved. On 18th February 1942, he changed his name and took the name of Tyczka. He was promoted to *Hauptmann* in March 1942 and a few days later was awarded the German Cross in Gold.

In March 1943, he assumed command of the 1st Battalion of the 6th *Fallschirmjäger* Regiment but was soon transferred to the 3rd Battalion of the 2nd *Fallschirmjäger* regiment as acting commander. He returned to Russia, where he saw action near Kirovograd and Novgorodka and again defended against a Russian armoured onslaught. This time for his efforts and leadership he was awarded the Knight's Cross. His troops had taken part in a tough defensive action, in January 1944, against a large enemy attack east of Kirovograd with approximately 500 tanks and three rifle divisions that had gone almost half-way through Tannert's battalion. During this battle, Tannert maintained position with the few remaining men into the evening and maintained his command in the area of Novo-Andrejewka. His actions enabled the regiment to form a new defensive line and to delay the advance of the Russian tanks just long enough until the city of Kirovograd was cleared in an orderly way.

In August 1944, *Major* Tannert assumed acting command of the 2nd *Fallschirmjäger* Regiment and took part in the German defence of Brest, France. On 16th September, in the surrounded city, General Ramcke had recommended Tannert for the Oakleaves and a promotion to *Oberstleutnant*, before the surrender of the fortress. Tannert went into Allied captivity on 20th September 1944. He was later promoted to *Oberstleutnant* but never received the Oakleaves; the award had not been confirmed. He was released from captivity on 28th June 1948.

OTHER AWARDS		PROMOTIONS	
00.09.1936	Armed Forces Long Service Award 4th Class	00.00.1936	Obergefreiter
04.05.1939	Commemorative Medal of 1st October 1939	19.09.1938	Leutnant (Heer)
18.04.1940	Iron Cross 2nd Class	26.06.1939	Leutnant der Reserve (Luftwaffe)
18.05.1940	Iron Cross 1st Class	01.08.1939	Oberleutnant der Reserve
15.07.1941	Wound Badge in Black	01.07.1940	Oberleutnant (active)
14.08.1941	Narvik Campaign Shield	01.03.1942	Hauptmann
25.02.1942	German Cross in Gold	29.08.1944	Major
22.07.1942	Eastern Front Medal	01.01.1945	Oberstleutnant
20.09.1942	Luftwaffe Ground Assault Badge	-----	-----

HANS TEUSEN

(26.07.1917 – 11.02.2011)   *Major*

(Wehrkundearchiv)

Knight's Cross: Awarded on 14th June 1941 as *Leutnant* and Platoon Leader in the 6th Company of the 2nd *Fallschirmjäger* Regiment for actions in the Balkans. He led his platoon during an airborne assault on Corinth Canal where his platoon eliminated an anti-aircraft battery and where seventy-two officers and 1,200 men surrendered to them.

Hans Teusen was born on 26th July 1917 in Salz, Westerwald District, and he joined the 4th Anti-aircraft Regiment in Dortmund as an officer candidate on 1st July 1937. After attending the Luftwaffe Officer Candidate School in Werden he took the parachutist-rifleman course in Wittstock-Dosse before joining the 2nd *Fallschirmjäger* Regiment in November 1939. The following month, he was commissioned as a *Leutnant* and appointed a Platoon Leader with the 2nd Company.

In April 1941, he led his platoon during the airborne assault on Corinth Canal. After jumping, his troops parachuted into position and eliminated an anti-aircraft battery at the southern end of the crossing over Corinth Canal, but were unable to prevent the bridge from being blown up. Nevertheless, his men stormed into Corinth, there his company commander *Hauptmann* Schirmer, ordered him to set out in the direction of Nauplia as the advance detachment. Teusen was wounded during the attack but stayed with his men, and he accepted the surrender of seventy-two officers and 1,200 men. For his leadership and for his part in the victory he was awarded the Knight's Cross.

On 1st October 1941, Teusen became adjutant of the 2nd Battalion of the 2nd *Fallschirmjäger* Regiment and the following month came his promotion to *Oberleutnant*. In March 1943, he took command of the 9th Company of the 2nd *Fallschirmjäger* Regiment and saw action at the Mius River. During a train journey, while on the way back to Germany, the train was attacked and his regiment took part in some heavy fighting at the Volkhov. Then following a brief period in Italy, he returned with his regiment to Russia, where Teusen was severely wounded near Zhitomir. On 1st May 1944, he took command of the 1ts Battalion of the 16th *Fallschirmjäger* Regiment and continued to see heavy action and was awarded the German Cross in Gold. His last command was as Ordnance Officer of the 1st *Fallschirmjäger* Army.

After the war, he joined the *Bundeswehr*, serving in a number of different roles and was promoted to the rank of *Generalmajor* in October 1971. Hans Teusen died on 11th February 2011 in Bad Neuenahr, a town in the Rhineland-Palatinate.

OTHER AWARDS		PROMOTIONS	
31.12.1939	Parachutist Badge	01.10.1937	Fahnenjunker-Gefreiter
15.05.1940	Iron Cross 2nd Class	28.12.1939	Leutnant
28.05.1940	Iron Cross 1st Class	01.11.1941	Oberleutnant
29.04.1941	Wound badge in Black	01.09.1943	Hauptmann
06.11.1942	Luftwaffe Ground Assault Badge	28.04.1945	Major
12.11.1942	KRETA Cuff title	-----	-----
10.09.1944	German Cross in Gold	-----	-----

CORD HERMANN JOHANN TIETJEN

(10.11.1914 – 28.06.2005) *Hauptmann*

Captured by the British on 5th November 1942, Tietjen spent time in various POW camps in Egypt, Canada and England, being released on 11th February 1947. (Wehrkundearchiv)

Knight's Cross: Awarded on 29th May 1940 as *Leutnant* and Platoon Leader in the 5th Company, 1st *Fallschirmjäger* Regiment for action during the Western Campaign. He led his troops during an attack on a Dutch bunker at Moerdijk, at the north end of the key railroad bridge over the Maas River and blew it up.

Cord Tietjen was born on 10th November 1914 in Danzig-Langfuhr, and volunteered to join the Army in October 1936. He was assigned to the 20th Engineer Battalion in Hamburg and the following year he attended the airborne school at Stendal. In April 1938, he was selected to be an officer candidate and transferred to the Luftwaffe.

On 28th January 1939, he was seconded to a special demolition unit at Ahlhorn and in May he was commissioned as a *Leutnant*. He saw action during the Polish Campaign with the 5th Company of the 1st *Fallschirmjäger* Regiment and jumped into Holland in May 1940. He led his platoon during an assault in Moerdijk of a Dutch bunker at the north end of the key railroad bridge over the Maas River and blew it up. However, during the fighting he was wounded in the right knee by a grenade fragment but remained with his men. In recognition of his efforts and leadership, he was awarded the Iron Cross 1st and 2nd Classes on 23rd May, then a few days later he was decorated with the Knight's Cross.

On 1st September 1940, Tietjen assumed command of the 1st Company of the 7th *Fallshirm-Pionier* Battalion and the following month he was promoted to *Oberleutnant*. On 20th May, he led his unit during the airborne invasion of Crete. They landed in Prison Valley south of Kirtomados, and his troops battled against the 8th Greek Regiment. In February 1942, he became commander of the 2nd Company of the *Korps-Fallschirm-Pionier* Battalion and led this unit at El Alamein in the Ramcke Brigade. On 5th November 1942, he was captured by British troops in Egypt and was transferred to Canada and later to England. While in captivity, he was promoted to *Hauptmann*, and he remained in captivity until 11th February 1947. Tietjen died on 18th June 2005 at Arnsberg, North Rhine-Westphalia. He is buried in the local cemetery on Sunderner Street (N101 Grave 87).

OTHER AWARDS		PROMOTIONS	
18.12.1937	Army Parachutist Badge	01.10.1937	Oberschütze
00.03.1940	West Wall Medal	01.01.1938	Gefreiter
23.05.1940	Iron Cross 2nd Class	21.04.1938	Reserve-Offiziersanwärter
23.05.1940	Iron Cross 1st Class	01.06.1938	Unteroffizier
-----	-----	01.10.1938	Feldwebel
-----	-----	07.05.1939	Leutnant der Reserve
-----	-----	03.01.1940	Leutnant (active)
-----	-----	28.10.1940	Oberleutnant
-----	-----	01.03.1943	Hauptmann

ERICH TIMM

(15.02.1913 – 06.10.1997)

Oberstleutnant

(Wehrkundearchiv)

Knight's Cross: Awarded on 3rd October 1944 as *Major* and Commander 12th *Fallschirmjäger* Assault Regiment in recognition for his numerous accomplishments in the defence of Italy. His Knight's Cross was personally presented to him by *Generalleutnant* Alfred Schlemm, Commander of the 1st *Fallschirmjäger* Corps.

Erich Tim was born on 15th February 1913 in Königsberg, Prussia and entered the *Landespolizei* in April 1933. Just over two years later, he transferred to the ranks of the Luftwaffe as a *Leutnant*, serving in the 4th Battery of the 12th Anti-aircraft Regiment. The following year, he became a battery commander in the 32nd Anti-aircraft Regiment in Berlin.

Promoted to *Oberleutnant* in June 1938, he later took part in the invasion of Holland in May 1940 as part of the 7th Air Division and he was later awarded the Iron Cross 1st and 2nd Classes for his leadership during the campaign. In April 1941, he assumed command of the 1st Company of the Parachute Anti-aircraft Machine-gun Battalion and saw action during the airborne invasion of Crete. However, on the very first day of fighting he was severely wounded and he remained away from the action until February 1943, when he took command of the 100th Special Luftwaffe Field Battalion in Russia.

On 1st August 1943, he was appointed commander of the 1st Battalion of the 12th *Fallschirmjäger* Assault Regiment in Italy. He saw further action and his leadership skills and general ability were brought to the attention of *General* Student who recommended that Timm be promoted to *Major*. In October, he was officially

Timm seen here shortly after being presented with his Knight's Cross by General Alfred Schlemm. (Wehrkundearchiv and Author's Collection)

promoted and the following month he became acting commander of the 12th *Fallschirmjäger* Regiment. His leadership skills were needed in January 1944 when his regiment became heavily engaged at the Anzio-Nettuno beachhead where it fought as part of the 4th *Fallschirmjäger* Division. On 16th February, his regiment was part of the German attack – to support the Hermann Göring Division's main attack at Cisterna – to eliminate the beachhead. His regiment broke through the British lines and gained two miles. On 23rd May 1944, Timm led his unit during an attempted counterattack of the flank of the Allied breakout attempt near the town of Velletri. The following month, his name was mentioned in the Official Armed Force Communiqué: "... *west of Velletri our troops fought back against strong enemy attacks ... twenty-three enemy tanks were destroyed and east of Velletri during heavy fighting a parachute assault regiment under the leadership of Major Timm was especially outstanding.*" At the end of August, the 4th *Fallschirmjäger*

Division then took part in defensive fighting near Florence and attempted a fighting retreat. A month later after brutal combat at the Futa Pass, the 12th *Fallschirmjäger* Regiment had been reduced to less than 50% strength. It had done its duty and *Major* Timm was awarded the Knight's Cross for his numerous accomplishments in the defence of Italy.

In January 1945, Timm was promoted to *Oberstleutnant*, but by now the Allied advance across the Po River was relentless and Timm didn't have the equipment or the troops to stop them. On 28th April, he surrendered to Allied forces and became a prisoner of war. He was released from a prison camp in Florence and went home. He later joined the Bundeswehr and was promoted to *Oberst* in February 1961, and retired ten years later – having commanded the Paratrooper School in Augsburg-Gablingen and was Head of the Personal Department of the Army. Timm died on 6th October 1997 in Erftstadt.

OTHER AWARDS		PROMOTIONS	
00.05.1936	Armed Forces Long Service Award 4th Class	01.04.1935	Leutnant der Landespolizei
17.05.1940	Iron Cross 2nd Class	25.07.1935	Leutnant (Luftwaffe)
17.05.1940	Iron Cross 1st Class	03.06.1938	Oberleutnant
05.08.1940	Parachutist Badge	01.06.1941	Hauptmann
15.04.1941	Luftwaffe Anti-Aircraft Badge	01.10.1943	Major
07.06.1941	Wound Badge in Black	01.01.1945	Oberstleutnant
07.10.1941	Luftwaffe Honour Goblet	-----	-----
20.05.1943	KRETA Cuff title	-----	-----
01.10.1944	Luftwaffe Ground Assault Badge	-----	-----

RUDOLF PAUL TOSCHKA

(26.09.1911 – 20.02.1944) *Hauptmann*

(Wehrkundearchiv)

Knight's Cross: Awarded on 14th June 1941 as *Oberleutnant* and Platoon Leader in the 1st Company, 1st Air-Landing Regiment in recognition of his bravery during the fighting in Crete. His platoon destroyed enemy troops near Chania and put a anti-aircraft battery out of action.

Rudolf Toschka was born on 26th September 1911 in Berlin-Wilmersdorf and entered the Brandenburg-Havel Police School as a cadet on 6th October 1931. On 1st September 1933, he became a member of the 6th Company of the *Landespolizei* (State Police) Regiment Göring and was automatically accepted into the General *Göring* Regiment in October 1935. In October 1937, he was assigned to the 2nd Company (Parachute) of the Regiment *General Göring* with the rank of *Feldwebel*. He took the obligatory parachutist-rifleman course in March 1938 and in April was appointed a platoon leader in the 1st Company of the 1st *Fallschirmjäger* Regiment. In February 1940, he transferred to the 17th Company, and in May, took part in the parachute and glider operations against the bridges over the Albert Canal and the fortress of Eben Emael in Belgium. He led his men with great bravery and was awarded the Iron Cross 1st and 2nd Classes and on 20th May was promoted to *Leutnant*.

On 16th July 1940, he was a platoon leader in the 1st Battalion of the 1st Air-Landing Assault Regiment, and in May 1941, took part in the airborne invasion of Crete. Ninety men in nine gliders landed near Chania and their main objective was to capture the anti-aircraft battery's at Suda and Chania and at Malemes airfield. The 1st Platoon, under the command of Toschka, immediately set up its firing position when it landed just south of Chania. He directed his troops with great skill and his platoon destroyed the enemy troops there and the anti-aircraft battery was put out of action. Toschka was seriously wounded during the fighting but would later recover. For his leadership abilities he was awarded the Knight's Cross.

Toschka was promoted to *Hauptmann* in October 1942, and a year later, fully recovered from his wounds, he took temporary command of the 1st Battalion of the *Fallschirmjäger* Assault Regiment and saw action in Russia. On 20th February 1944, he was killed during the heavy fighting in the Anzio-Nettuno bridgehead, Italy. He is buried in the War Cemetery in Pomezia. Grave location: Block L; Grave 13.

OTHER AWARDS		PROMOTIONS	
02.10.1936	Armed Forces Long Service Award 4th Class	01.10.1932	Polizei-Wachtmeister
01.06.1938	Parachutist Badge	01.09.1935	Oberwachtmeister
12.05.1940	Iron Cross 2nd Class	01.10.1935	Oberjäger
12.05.1940	Iron Cross 1st Class	01.04.1937	Feldwebel
18.09.1941	Wound Badge in Black	01.02.1940	Oberfeldwebel
15.02.1943	Luftwaffe Ground Assault Badge	20.05.1940	Leutnant der Reserve
20.05.1943	KRETA Cuff title	01.09.1940	Oberleutnant der Reserve
-----	-----	14.10.1942	Hauptmann (active)

HORST TREBES

(22.10.1916 – 29.07.1944)   *Hauptmann*

(Wehrkundearchiv)

Knight's Cross: Awarded on 9th July 1941 as *Oberleutnant* and *Führer* III Battalion, 1st *Fallschirmjäger* Assault Regiment for actions during the invasion of Crete.

Horst Trebes was born on 22nd October 1916, in Freyburg, a town in the Burgen district of Saxony-Anhalt near the River Unstrut. He entered the Armed Forces as an officer candidate in April 1936 and within two years he had been commissioned as a *Leutnant*. In June 1938, he joined the *Fallschirm* Infantry Battalion in Braunschweig, and in April 1939 it became part of the 3rd Battalion of the 1st *Fallschirmjäger* Regiment under *Major* Richard Heidrich.

In September 1939, Trebes saw action during the invasion of Poland where he was awarded the Iron Cross 2nd Class. He was promoted to *Oberleutnant* in November and took part in the campaign in Holland where he won the Iron Cross 1st Class. In 1941, he saw action as part of the German invasion airborne attack on Crete. Trebes was dropped into Crete along with *Major* Braun and *Oberleutnant* Schächter as part of a battle group from the regimental headquarters which landed at the large bridge due west of Malemes in nine gliders. The battle group had been ordered to seize the bridge over the Tavronitis and set out to attack the anti-aircraft positions due west of the airfield with the support of the 1st Battalion of the 1st *Fallschirmjäger* Regiment. At 11:00 on 20th May, Trebes attacked and rescued a German platoon from the enemy, and took thirty prisoners. Trebes assumed command of the battle group when its commander *Major* Braun had been killed and *Oberleutnant* Schächter had been badly wounded. Trebes led the battle group and attacked the enemy again on 23rd May, then stormed through the enemy lines and captured Hill 107. This amazing feat won him the Knight's Cross.

On 2 June 1941, *Oberleutnant* Trebes drove with four trucks filled with *Fallschirmjäger* to the village of Kondomari where more than 100 civilians were rounded up and executed. *Oberleutnant* Trebes commanded this terrible reprisal action. He returned to Germany where, at a drunken celebration in Halberstadt with a group of *Fallschirmjäger*, the party ended tragically; *Oberjäger* Karl Polzin, a member of the famous *Fallschirmjäger Trupp 4* which had captured Fort Eben Emael, was carelessly shot and killed by Trebes. As the party wound down *Oberjäger* Polzin was drunk and sleeping in the bathroom, Trebes insisted on awakening Polzin by shooting his pistol, unfortunately when he did, he hit Polzin and killed him. Trebes was spared the death penalty probably due to his stature as a Knight's Cross winner as well as his mother-in-law's direct appeal to *Reichsmarschall* Göring.

In January 1942, Trebes was made company commander in the 3rd Battalion of the 1st *Fallschirmjäger* Assault Regiment and saw action in Russia. He was promoted to *Hauptmann* in November 1942 and in March 1944 he took command of the 3rd Battalion of the 6th *Fallschirmjäger* Regiment in Normandy. Trebes was killed near Carentan, South of Saint-Denis-le-Gast, on 29 July 1944, during the fighting in the hedgerows during the breakout of the Allied armies through Saint-Lô. He is buried in an unmarked grave in the Military Cemetery in La Cambe, France

OTHER AWARDS		PROMOTIONS	
00.00.1938	Parachutist Badge	01.04.1936	Fähnrich
13.10.1939	Iron Cross 2nd Class	20.04.1938	Leutnant
00.11.1939	Commemorative Medal of 1st October 1939	17.11.1939	Oberleutnant
23.05.1940	Iron Cross 1st Class	01.11.1942	Hauptmann

HEINRICH "HEINZ" TRETTNER

(19.09.1907 – 18.09.2006)   *Generalleutnant*

(Author's Collection)

Knight's Cross: Awarded on 24th May 1940 as *Major.i.G* and Chief of Operations (Ia) in the 7th Air Division for his part in the planning of the invasion of Holland, he organised the troops, equipment and training.

Knight's Cross with Oakleaves: He became the 586th recipient of the Oakleaves on 17th September 1944, as *Generalmajor* and Commander 4th *Fallschirmjäger Division* for his outstanding leadership during the fighting in Anzio.

Heinrich "Heinz" Trettner was an excellent divisional commander and an outstanding staff officer, in fact he was one of the most successful generals of the Luftwaffe. He was born on 19th September 1907, in Minden, the son of a Prussian officer. He graduated from the Hohenzollern Gymnasium in Düsseldorf and in April 1925 entered the army.

In November 1926, he was attached to the 18th Mounted Regiment and was later assigned to the Infantry School at Dresden and later at the Cavalry School in Hannover. In February 1929, he was commissioned as a *Leutnant* and by 1932 was having flying lessons. He flew with Lufthansa and the Royal Italian Air Force before joining the Luftwaffe in May 1933. He served in various schools as an adjutant and by June 1935 had been promoted to *Hauptmann.* After completing his third training course at the 2nd Air War School in Berlin, he joined the Legion Condor as Chief Personnel Officer, and was adjutant to its commander *Oberst* Wolfram von Richthofen. In September 1937, Trettner was Squadron Leader of the 1st Squadron of K88, the Bomber Wing of the Legion Condor and saw action during the Spanish Civil War. He returned to Germany in January 1938 and started training as a staff officer at the Berlin War Academy.

In July 1938, he was appointed Operations Officer in the 7th Air Division, under *Generalleutnant* Kurt Student and was promoted to *Major* in August 1939. He took part in the invasion of Belgium and Holland in 1940, and was so busy during this time that he failed to take parachute training and had to jump during the invasion without having made any practice jumps. During the negotiations for the surrender of Rotterdam, Trettner was standing with Student when was struck in the head by a stray bullet. In December, he took over as Operations Officer with the 11th Air Corps in Berlin. Later, he was involved in the preparations and planning of the invasion of Crete for which he was awarded Knight's Cross.

In early-1943, now with the rank of *Oberst*, Trettner's headquarters moved to Nimes in Southern France. On 4th October 1943, at his own request, he was given his own command. He was tasked with forming the 4th *Fallschirmjäger* Division. His new command was formed in Italy from the 2nd *Fallschirmjäger* Division and two Italian *Fallschirmjäger* Divisions. It first saw action in January 1944 when it was part of the battle to contain the Allied beachhead at Anzio-Nettuno as part of General Schlemm's 1st Parachute Corps. For the next sixteen months, the 4th *Fallschirmjäger* Division saw action in Italy during the battles of Rome, north of Florence, Rimini, Bologna and in the struggle for the Gothic Line. In July 1944, Trettner was promoted to *Generalmajor,* and in September, he became the 586th recipient of the Knight's Cross with Oakleaves.

In April 1945, his command had suffered many casualties, and was fighting for survival in Verona when he was taken prisoner by the Americans. He was held in captivity until April 1948. After the war, he studied law and earned his diploma in 1956, when he joined the *Bundeswehr* with the rank of *Generalmajor*. He was, until 1959, head of logistics at NATO headquarters in Paris. In February 1960, he commanded the 1st Corps and was later appointed Inspector General of the *Bundeswehr*. He retired from military service in August 1966, with the rank of full General. He died on 18th September 2006, in Munchen-Gladbach, the last surviving general of Hitler's Luftwaffe.

OTHER AWARDS		PROMOTIONS	
02.10.1936	Armed Forces Long Service Award 4th Class	01.11.1926	Fahnenjunker-Unteroffizier
01.04.1937	Armed Forces Long Service Award 3rd Class	01.08.1927	Fähnrich
30.09.1938	Medal for the Spanish Campaign	01.08.1928	Oberfähnrich
01.12.1938	Spanish War Cross	01.02.1929	Leutnant
06.06.1939	Spanish Cross in Gold + Swords	01.02.1933	Oberleutnant
12.05.1940	Iron Cross 2nd Class	01.06.1935	Hauptmann
12.05.1940	Iron Cross 1st Class	01.08.1939	Major im Generalstab
00.05.1943	KRETA Cuff title	01.10.1941	Oberstleutnant im Generalstab
00.00.1943	Parachutist Badge	01.03.1943	Oberst im Generalstab
03.03.1944	Wound Badge in Black	01.07.1944	Generalmajor
00.00.1944	Combined Pilots & Observers Badge in Gold + Diamonds	01.04.1945	Generalleutnant

HERBERT OTTO TROTZ

(11.05.1915 – 31.07.1980)   *Hauptmann*

(Wehrkundearchiv)

Knight's Cross: Awarded on 30th April 1945 as *Hauptmann* and Commander Fortress Grenadier Battalion *Trotz* part of Fortress Breslau for his bravery during the fierce hand-to-hand fighting in the ruins of Breslau.

Herbert Trotz was born on 11th May 1915 in Glatz a city in Lower Silesia and entered the 6th Company of the 7th Prussian Infantry Regiment in April 1933. He trained as a radio operator before joining the East Prussian Air Transport Unit in Seerappen and later Neukuhren. He was promoted to *Oberfeldwebel* in October 1938 and took part in the invasion of Poland.

In November 1940, he was made an Officer Candidate, and in May 1941, he took command of a platoon in the 2nd Company of the 1st Luftwaffe Signals Regiment. Commissioned as a *Leutnant* in March 1941 he was transferred to Russia in June seeing action while attached to a Luftwaffe Signals Company. In May 1943, now an *Oberleutnant,* Trotz was made commander of the 2nd Company of the 203rd Luftwaffe Signals Regiment, and a year later he assumed command of the 2nd Company of the 57th Luftwaffe Signals Regiment. He was twice wounded in Russia, and in April 1943, was promoted to *Hauptmann*.

On 9th November 1944, he was attached to the Switchboard Detachment West of the 4th *Jagddivision* in Metz, and later attended the parachute school in Golsar and Wittstock to make ready for his first parachute jump into action. On 22nd November, he took command of the 10th Company of the 26th *Fallschirmjäger* Regiment. The 3rd Battalion of the 26th *Fallschirmjäger* Regiment, which included his company, was flown in Ju 52s into the surrounded fortress of Breslau in February 1945. Immediately on landing, his company took part in the defensive battles waged in the city. He fought up front with his men and took part in hand-to-hand combat in the sewers and ruins of the besieged city. On the orders of *General der Infanterie* Niehoff, he was appointed commander of a battle group, and in April 1945, took part in some of the bitterest fighting for the city. It was for his leadership and bravery during this time that he was awarded the Knight's Cross on 30th April 1945 – one of the last of the war. On 6th May, after the surrender of Breslau, he was taken prisoner by the Soviets and wasn't released from captivity until 7th August 1949. He died on 31st July 1980 in Bad Meinberg.

OTHER AWARDS		PROMOTIONS	
00.04.1937	Armed Forces Long Service Award 4th Class	01.10.1934	Gefreiter
30.01.1942	War Service Cross 2nd Class + Swords	01.05.1935	Unteroffizier
00.08.1942	Eastern Front Medal	01.03.1938	Feldwebel
03.02.1945	Iron Cross 2nd Class	01.10.1938	Oberfeldwebel
09.03.1945	Iron Cross 1st Class	16.11.1940	Offiziersanwärter
-----	-----	13.03.1941	Leutnant
-----	-----	11.10.1942	Oberleutnant
-----	-----	01.04.1943	Hauptmann

ALEXANDER UHLIG

(09.02.1919 – 01.11.2008)   *Oberfeldwebel*

(Wehrkundearchiv)

(Author's Collection)

Alexander Uhlig during a late-1980s reunion wearing his original Knight's Cross. Note the swastika on the Knight's Cross which was illegal after the war. (Author's Collection)

Knight's Cross: Awarded on 29th October 1944 as *Oberfeldwebel* and Platoon Leader in the 16th Company, 6th *Fallschirmjäger* Regiment for actions near Carentan, Normandy. He led the 16th Company after its commander had been killed and eliminated an enemy attack taking hundreds of prisoners.

Alexander Uhlig was born in Meusdorf, Leipzig on 9th February 1919. He entered the 4th Parachute Battalion of the General Göring Regiment in November 1937, after serving for six months with the Reich Labour Service. In April 1938, after attending his parachutist-rifleman's course in Stendal, he joined the 1st Company of the 1st *Fallschirmjäger* Regiment and took part in the formation of the regiment.

He saw action during the invasion of Poland as a squad leader in the 1st Company of the 1st *Fallschirmjäger* Regiment. His first combat drop took place on 19th April 1940, when he and his company put down near Dombas in Norway. Uhlig and his thirty-five comrades were captured by Norwegian troops but were soon freed. He was then able to take part in the reinforcement of *General* Dietl's 3rd Mountain Infantry Division at Narvik. In December 1940, he joined the flying personnel of the Luftwaffe and joined the 1st Squadron of the Special Purpose Bomber Wing, with which he saw action over Crete.

In November 1942, he became an observer with the 2nd Squadron of the Special Purpose Bomber Wing in Naples and flew supply missions to Africa. In March 1943, he was promoted to *Oberfeldwebel* and in August was awarded the Iron Cross 1st Class. In February 1944 he joined the 8th Company of the 6th *Fallschirmjäger* Regiment and became a platoon leader. In April, he transferred to the 4th Company and two months later his unit moved to Carentan in Normandy, where during the night of 5th June American paratroopers dropped on them. Uhlig took over the 16th Company after its commander had been killed. He and thirty-five of his comrades halted an enemy attack and fired on enemy-occupied buildings with *Panzerfaust* anti-tank weapons and took hundreds of prisoners, including the American battalion commander. For these actions, he was awarded the Knight's Cross. On 23rd July 1944, the commander of the U.S. 90th Infantry Divisions had appealed to the Germans for a ceasefire so they could attend hundreds of their wounded, this was agreed. U.S. medics and army chaplains with Red Cross flags entered no-man's land and were assisted by members of the 6th *Fallschirmjäger* Regiment, whose commander *Major* von der Heydte had ordered the ceasefire.

On 31st July 1944, Uhlig was taken prisoner by U.S. troops and was held in the prisoner-of-war camp "Camp Clark" until February 1946, when he was transferred to Camp 23 in Sudbury, Burton-on-Trent, England. He was considered by the British military to be a potential escapee and was closely watched. Nonetheless, on 22nd April 1947, he did make his escape. He made it to Hull where he was able to stow away on a ship bound for Cuxhaven. By the time his escape had been discovered – by the ruse of having a dummy take his place during the morning Roll Call – he had already reached Germany. He then made his way through the less-strictly controlled U.S. Zone and managed to cross the Soviet lines undetected, and he finally reached his home in Leipzig on 28th April. He is one of the only known German soldiers to have successfully escaped from a prison camp that was located in England.

Once home, he enrolled in the Darmstadt University of Technology and studied economics. He worked for a number of well-known German companies until his retirement in 1984. He lived in Essen until his death on 1st November 2008.

OTHER AWARDS		PROMOTIONS	
07.09.1938	Army Parachutist Badge	01.11.1938	Gefreiter
20.06.1939	Commemorative Medal of 1st October 1938 + Bar	01.08.1939	Oberjäger
11.05.1940	Iron Cross 2nd Class	01.10.1939	Feldwebel
01.03.1941	Narvik Campaign Shield	01.10.1939	Reserve-Offiziersanwärter
28.10.1942	Wound Badge in Black	01.03.1943	Oberfeldwebel
15.11.1942	KRETA Cuff title	-----	-----
22.12.1942	Operational Flying Clasp for Transport Pilots in Bronze	-----	-----
10.01.1943	Operational Flying Clasp for Transport Pilots in Silver	-----	-----
23.02.1943	Operational Flying Clasp for Transport Pilots in Gold	-----	-----
08.06.1943	Observers Badge	-----	-----
01.08.1943	Iron Cross 1st Class	-----	-----

KURT VETH
(01.06.1907 – 27.12.1994)   *Major der Reserve*

In this post-war photograph, Kurt Veth is wearing the Knight's Cross with Oakleaves. According to the historian Veit Scherzer in his book, "Der Ritterkreuzträger 1939-1945" Veth isn't mentioned as having ever been awarded the Oakleaves, although some sources claim the award was won on 30th April 1945. With no mention in the Scherzer book, this author concludes that the Oakleaves was never officially awarded and the only proof is the word of the recipient. (Author's Collection)

Knight's Cross: Awarded on 30th September 1944 as *Hauptmann der Reserve* and Commander II Battalion, 3rd *Fallschirmjäger* Regiment for actions in Italy. He led his company during the Third Battle of Cassino where he took part in the attack on Calvary Mountain.

Kurt Veth was born on 1st June 1907, in Delmenhorst in Lower Saxony, and joined the 63rd Infantry Regiment as a volunteer in August 1935. He transferred to the 90th Infantry Regiment in Hamburg-Wentorf in May 1937, and was commissioned as a *Leutnant der Reserve* in August of the following year. He served as a platoon leader until February 1940, and did not participate in the invasion of Poland.

On 15th February 1940, he transferred to the parachute troops and joined the 3rd *Fallschirmjäger* Regiment. He was promoted to *Oberleutnant der Reserve* in November 1940, and in March 1941, was made Operations Officer of the 1st Battalion of the 3rd *Fallschirmjäger* Regiment. His first taste of action came during the airborne invasion of Crete when he jumped as part of the 3rd *Fallschirmjäger* Regiment in May 1941. He later saw action in the northern sector of the Eastern Front and fought at Leningrad, Wyborg, and Wyborgskaja where he won the Iron Cross 1st and 2nd Classes. He then served a second tour in Russia in 1942-1943, on the Kalinin front as a company commander.

In July 1943, he took part in the German defensive fighting in Sicily as commander of the 2nd Company of the 3rd *Fallschirmjäger* Regiment. Veth repelled a British landing attempt at Agone, and later fought at Catenanuova and Centuripe, Aderno and Maletto. He was wounded three times between 5th August and 11th August but remained at the front. In January 1944, he was promoted to *Hauptmann der Reserve,* and in April, he took command of the 2nd Battalion of the 3rd *Fallschirmjäger* Regiment and continued to see heavy action until he was wounded for the fourth time, and this time he was evacuated to hospital. He returned to see action during the Third Battle of Cassino where his company participated in the attack on Calvary Mountain, which was eventually taken by *Oberfeldwebel* Karl Schmidt in the second assault. Veth was awarded the Knight's Cross for his leadership and effort during the fierce fighting and Schmidt won the German Cross in Gold.

Veth continued to see action in Italy as a battalion commander until the end of the war, and was promoted to *Major der Reserve* on 1st January 1945. He was captured by the Allies in May 1945 but was released the following year. He died in Hamburg on 27th December 1994.

OTHER AWARDS		PROMOTIONS	
00.04.1939	Armed Forces Long Service Award 4th Class	01.08.1938	Leutnant der Reserve
15.05.1940	Parachutist Badge	01.11.1940	Oberleutnant der Reserve
10.06.1941	Iron Cross 2nd Class	01.01.1944	Hauptmann der Reserve
21.06.1941	Iron Cross 1st Class	01.01.1945	Major der Reserve
00.10.1942	Eastern Front Medal	-----	-----
10.12.1942	Luftwaffe Ground Assault Badge	-----	-----
20.05.1943	KRETA Cuff title	-----	-----
27.10.1943	German Cross in Gold	-----	-----
06.08.1944	Wound Badge in Silver	-----	-----
10.04.1945	Wound Badge in Gold	-----	-----

VIKTOR VITALI

(03.04.1920 – 16.01.2012)   *Oberleutnant*

Knight's Cross: Awarded on 30th April 1945 as *Leutnant* and Platoon Leader, 5th Company, 4th *Fallschirmjäger* Regiment for actions during the battles at the Senio, at Santerno and the Gaina, at Quaderna and Idice, Italy. *However, there is no proof in surviving records in the German Archives of such an award. No legally valid award by the Commanding General of the I Fallschirm Corps, General der Fallschirmtruppe Richard Heidrich.*

Viktro Vitali was born on 3rd April 1920 in Vienna, part of the Austro-Hungarian Empire and

Vitali remained in Allied captivity until his release on 13th March 1946, when he returned to Vienna, where he died on 16th January 2012 at the age of ninety-one. He is seen here in a post-war photograph wearing his wartime awards including his Knight's Cross. (Author's Collection)

(Wehrkundearchiv)

now part of Austria. He entered the 19th Anti-aircraft Replacement Battalion in Gotha in June 1940 and was assigned to the 3rd Battery. After various postings to other anti-aircraft searchlight and anti-aircraft artillery battalions, he was sent on a platoon leader's course in Berlin. He later attended another course in Vienna which concerned the 2000mm searchlight and various types of remote control equipment.

From 26th March 1943 until 1st May 1943, he attended a retraining course on heavy anti-aircraft artillery and was assigned to the 1st Battery of the 133rd Heavy Anti-aircraft Battalion. On 15th April, now a *Leutnant*, he joined the parachute troops as a volunteer. He attended the parachutist-rifleman's course in Pont du Mousson, France, on 23rd April and joined the 4th *Fallschirmjäger* Regiment the following month, where he became an operations officer in the regimental headquarters.

In the summer 1944, Vitali and his regiment were transferred to Italy, and from July until September he led the 5th Company in the area north of Cassino and at Lake Trasimeno, at Val di Chiana and at the Arno River. He went on to distinguish himself in the Goten Position, where he fought in the Foglia-Metauro River sector. From November until January 1945, he took part in the German defence of Hill 131 in the Apennines, in the area of Monte Grande. Here he was awarded the Iron Cross 1st Class. He then saw action in the battles at the Senio, at Senterno and the Gaina, at Quaderna and Idice, as well as in the fierce fighting to capture the Po Crossing. It was after his efforts and bravery at this time, that *General der Fallschirmtruppe* Heidrich recommended Vitali for the Knight's Cross. There is no proof that the award was ever officially confirmed; Vitali always maintained that General Heidrich told him that the award was legal. On 3rd May 1945, Vitali was seriously wounded and taken to an SS Field Hospital in Perugia, where he was taken prisoner by the Americans.

OTHER AWARDS		PROMOTIONS	
20.04.1939	Commemorative Medal of 13th March 1938	01.03.1941	Gefreiter

20.11.1942	Luftwaffe Anti-Aircraft Badge	01.05.1941	Unteroffizier
15.08.1943	War Service Cross 2nd Class + Swords	01.09.1941	Wachtmeister
01.09.1944	Iron Cross 2nd Class	01.06.1941	Kriegsoffizieranwärter
21.12.1944	Wound Badge in Black	11.07.1942	Leutnant
11.03.1945	Iron Cross 1st Class	26.04.1945	Oberleutnant

HELMUT WAGNER
(18.08.1915 – 07.06.1944)   *Hauptmann*

(Author's Collection)

Knight's Cross: Awarded on 24th January 1942 as *Leutnant* and Platoon Leader in the 6th Company, 1st *Fallschirmjäger* Regiment for actions during the invasion of Crete. Despite having been wounded a number of times Wagner and a handful of men put out of action three British anti-aircraft positions and Wagner personally destroyed a British tank.

Helmut Wagner was born on 18th August 1915 in Köslin, Pomerania and he entered the Luftwaffe on 1st April 1938 as a *Gefreiter*. A year to the day he was assigned to the 2nd Battalion of the 1st *Fallschirmjäger* Regiment and saw action during the invasion of Poland. He then saw action during the German invasion of Holland, winning the Iron Cross 1st and 2nd Classes.

During the airborne invasion of Crete Wagner and his platoon parachuted into Heraklion airfield. Unfortunately, Wagner was wounded in the foot even before he landed. Despite this setback he fought with great courage. Wagner was wounded five times during the fighting for the Greek island and was part of a small group that managed to put out of action three British anti-aircraft positions. In fact, Wagner was responsible for destroying one of the few British tanks single-handed using grenades. For this action, he was awarded the Knight's Cross – personally pushed through by *Reichsmarschall* Göring after he had read the official account of Wagner's amazing efforts.

Once he had recovered from his wounds he joined was transferred to Normandy where he took temporary command of the 9th Company of the 6th *Fallschirmjäger* Regiment. He was promoted to *Hauptmann* in September; Wagner was a quiet unassuming man who preferred instead to let his actions speak for him. On the second day of the invasion, (7th June) he was killed in the Carentan area by a direct hit by an artillery shell on his dugout. He rests in the Military Cemetery in Orglandes, Manche. (Location: Block 12; Row 10; Grave 384).

OTHER AWARDS		PROMOTIONS		
00.00.1938	Air Warden Honour Award 2nd Class	01.04.1938	Gefreiter	
00.04.1939	Parachutist Badge	00.00.1939	Unteroffizier	
25.05.1940	Iron Cross 2nd Class	01.08.1940	Leutnant	
28.07.1940	Iron Cross 1st Class	01.09.1942	Oberleutnant	
00.00.1941	Wound Badge in Silver	27.09.1944	Hauptmann	
00.00.1942	Wound Badge in Gold	-----	-----	
00.00.1942	Luftwaffe Ground Assault Badge	-----	-----	
00.05.1943	KRETA Cuff title	-----	-----	

ERICH WALTHER

(05.08.1903 – 26.12.1948)   *Generalmajor*

(Author's Collection)

Knight's Cross: Awarded on 24th May 1940, as *Major* and Commander I Battalion, 1st *Fallschirmjäger* Regiment for his contribution to the victory in Norway.

Knight's Cross with Oakleaves: He became the 411th recipient of the Oakleaves on 2nd March 1944 as *Oberst* and Commander 4th *Fallschirmjäger* Regiment for actions in Russia. He took command of the 2nd *Fallschirm-Panzer* Grenadier Division *"Hermann Göring"* in East Prussia in September 1944 and faced a Soviet onslaught. He went onto see action at Arnhem where he helped to stop the enemy paratroopers during the Allied ill-fated Operation Market Garden. In late-1944, he returned to East Prussia and was promoted to *Generalmajor* in January 1945.

Knight's Cross with Oakleaves and Swords: Awarded on 1st February 1945, to become the 131st recipient of the Swords as *Oberst* and *Führer* 2nd *Fallschirm-Panzer* Grenadier Division *"Hermann Göring"* in recognition of his outstanding leadership during the successful attacks against the Red Army in East Prussia.

Erich Walther served the entire war as a parachute officer attached to the Hermann Göring Division and became one of the most highly decorated *Luftwaffe* officers. He was born in the small town of Gordon, Saxony, on 5th August 1903. He joined the Berlin police in April 1924 and in June 1928 was a commissioned as a *Leutnant*. In 1933, he was promoted to *Oberleutnant* and transferred to the *Landespolizeigruppe Wecke* where he served until January 1934 when the Wecke units became known as the *Landespolizeigruppe "General Göring."*

In October 1935, he entered the Luftwaffe as a *Hauptmann* and was appointed company commander in the 1st Battalion of the Luftwaffe Regiment *"General Göring."* In May, he passed his parachute training course and in April 1938 the *"General Göring"* Regiment was redesignated the 1st *Fallschirmjäger* Regiment. At the time of the attack on Poland Walther was assigned as Inspector of Parachute Troops in the Air Ministry. In November 1939, he was made Battalion commander and saw action in Holland and was dropped with his unit near Dordrecht. In May 1940, he fought in Norway in support of the 3rd Mountain Infantry Division, commanded by *Generalleutnant* Eduard Dietl, who personally thanked Walther for his support. For his efforts and his leadership, Walther was awarded the Knight's Cross.

In June 1941, he led the 3rd Battalion in Heraklion during the invasion of Crete, and marched into the city at the head of his troops. In September, Walther saw action in Russia where he was awarded the German Cross in Gold for actions near Leningrad. On 20th April 1942, he was promoted to *Oberst* and in September he helped to form three new battalions to make up the

4th *Fallschirmjäger* Regiment, and consequently led this unit in Sicily and later at Cassino, where his regiment defended well and fought bravely on the hills around the area.

He was awarded the Knight's Cross with Oakleaves for his actions in Russia on 2nd March 1944, and later saw action in East Prussia. Here he was directly subordinated to the Parachute Panzer Corps *"Hermann Göring,"* under the command of *Generalleutnant* Wilhelm Schmalz. He then saw action as commander of a Battle Group at Arnhem and here managed to stop enemy paratroopers during the ill-fated "Operation Market Garden." By early-1945, Walther was running out of troops and supplies, yet he still fought on and was eventually promoted to *Generalmajor*. In February

Walther was kept in the former concentration camp of Buchenwald, where he was forgotten. It also is reported that Walther was treated badly and just left to rot. On 26th December 1947, he died in circumstances that have never been fully explained, but he probably died of malnutrition coupled with very bad treatment, even torture and perhaps even suicide. (Private source)

1945, his leadership was again recognized when he was awarded the Knight's Cross with Oakleaves and Swords. However, by March, his command had been pushed back into the heart of East Prussia, and was later transferred south and ended the war east of Prague, where Walther surrendered to Soviet forces on 8th May 1945.

OTHER AWARDS		PROMOTIONS	
00.06.1937	Parachutist Badge	01.07.1925	Polizei-Wachtmeister
00.01.1938	Police Long Service Award 3rd Class	16.06.1928	Polizei-Leutnant
20.06.1939	Commemorative Medal of 1st October 1938 + Bar	21.03.1933	Polizei-Oberleutnant
02.10.1939	Armed Forces Long Service Award 4th Class	01.10.1935	Hauptmann (Luftwaffe)
18.04.1940	Iron Cross 2nd Class	19.06.1940	Major
26.04.1940	Iron Cross 1st Class	01.01.1942	Oberstleutnant
00.00.1941	Narvik Campaign Shield	20.04.1942	Oberst
00.00.1942	Wound Badge in Silver	30.01.1945	Generalmajor
31.03.1942	German Cross in Gold	-----	-----
00.10.1942	Eastern Front Medal	-----	-----
00.05.1943	KRETA Cuff title	-----	-----

FRIEDRICH-WILHELM WANGERIN

(27.01.1915 – 13.11.2002) *Hauptmann*

(Wehrkundearchiv)

Knight's Cross: Awarded on 24th October 1944 as *Hauptmann* and Commander 3rd Battalion, 16th *Fallschirmjäger* Regiment for actions on the Eastern Front.

Friedrich-Wilhelm Wangerin was born on 27th January 1915 in Berlin. From April to September 1935, he served with the Reich Labour Service in Schwiebus, Brandenburg. In October 1935, he joined the 1st Battalion of the 67th Infantry Regiment in Berlin-Spandau. In December 1939, he was transferred to the 477th Infantry Replacement Battalion in Meseritz and from there he joined the parachute troops.

Wangerin was commissioned as a *Leutnant* in January 1940, and from April to June 1940, he attended the parachutist-rifleman's course at Stendal before being assigned to the 3rd *Fallschirmjäger* Regiment in September 1940 as a Platoon Leader. In April 1941, he was assigned to the 1st *Fallschirmjäger* Replacement Battalion in Stendal, and served as battalion adjutant from December 1941. In April 1942, now with the rank of *Oberleutnant*, he served in a similar capacity with the 5th *Fallschirmjäger* Regiment and from July served as a Platoon Leader.

From November 1942, Wangerin and his regiment saw action in Northwest Africa following the Allied landings there. He served with distinction in Tunisia and was awarded the Iron Cross 1st and 2nd Classes. A year later, still serving with the 5th *Fallschirmjäger* Regiment, but now a company commander, *Hauptmann* Wangerin saw action in the Ukraine, where he remained until February 1944. He then served as director of training in the Schirmer Battalion, and from June, he commanded the 3rd Battalion of the 16th *Fallschirmjäger* Regiment-East, seeing further action on the Russian Front. Here, once again, he fought with great distinction and was awarded not only the Honour Roll Clasp of the Army but in October was awarded the Knight's Cross.

Wangerin was seriously wounded on 27th October 1944 and was evacuated to a hospital in Königsberg, East Prussia, and from there to a hospital in Jüterbog. In April 1945, he returned to action with the *Fallschirm-Panzer-Jagd* Brigade, under *Oberst* Harry Herrmannn and saw action while defending Berlin against the Russians. On 3rd May 1945 he was taken prisoner by British troops and was released in early-1946. He served with the *Bundeswehr* from March 1956 to September 1965, when he retired with the rank of *Oberstleutnant*. Wangerin died on 13th November 2002 in Bonn.

OTHER AWARDS		PROMOTIONS	
00.05.1939	Armed Forces Long Service Award 4th Class	**01.10.1936**	Gefreiter
25.07.1940	Parachutist Badge	**01.06.1937**	Unteroffizier
30.01.1942	War Service Cross 2nd Class	**30.09.1937**	Feldwebel
13.03.1943	Iron Cross 2nd Class	**01.01.1940**	Leutnant
25.04.1943	Iron Cross 1st Class	**01.01.1942**	Oberleutnant
17.05.1943	Wound Badge in Silver	**01.01.1944**	Hauptmann
06.06.1943	Luftwaffe Ground Assault Badge	-----	-----
30.06.1943	Italian-German Campaign Medal in Africa	-----	-----
14.07.1943	KRETA Cuff title	-----	-----
05.02.1944	German Cross in Gold	-----	-----
25.08.1944	Honour Roll Clasp of the Army	-----	-----
09.11.1944	Wound Badge in Gold	-----	-----

HANS-JOACHIM WECK

(22.12.1920 – 22.06.2007)   *Oberleutnant*

(Wehrkundearchiv)

Knight's Cross: Awarded on 30th April 1945, as *Leutnant* and *Führer* 3rd Company, 4th *Fallschirmjäger* Regiment for actions in Italy. *There is no proof in the Federal Archives of the award being approved. No legally valid award by the Commanding General of the I Fallschirm Corps, General der Fallschirmtruppe Richard Heidrich*

Hans-Joachim Weck was born on 22nd December 1920 in Königsberg, East Prussia and joined the 4th Company of the 53rd Flight Training Regiment in July 1940. He was subsequently sent to flying school A/B 120 in Jena-Rödingen. In September 1941, he was named as a wartime officer candidate, and from January 1942, he participated in a parachute weapons course in Weissewarth-Tangerhütte.

Weck completed his parachutist-rifleman course and was assigned to the Luftwaffe Officer Candidate School at Berlin-Gatow in October 1942. In December, he was assigned to the 2nd Company of the 4th *Fallschirmjäger* Regiment as a platoon leader. He saw action during the winter campaign in Russia from December 1942 until March 1943. From July 1943, he saw action in Sicily as a *Feldwebel* with his old regiment. Wounded in December 1943, he fought later on the Italian mainland where he was promoted to *Leutnant* in January 1944 and was once again wounded.

In June 1944, he was named as operations officer of the 1st Battalion of the 4th *Fallschirmjäger* Regiment and was later battalion adjutant. He undertook a series of risky and quiet dangerous reconnaissance and offensive patrols and as a result of his leadership was awarded the Iron Cross 1st Class. On 1st October, he was placed in command of the 3rd Company in the 4th *Fallschirmjäger* Regiment and was wounded for a third time on 22nd January 1945. Weck returned to action on 3rd February and was named as commander of the 3rd Company of his old regiment and took part in the fighting withdrawal to Bologna and from there into the Po Plain, preventing numerous attempts by the enemy to break through the lines with their armour. Weck was recommended for the Knight's Cross and was later presented with the award by *General* Heidrich – the award however was never made official.

Weck was promoted to *Oberleutnant* in April 1945, and on 2nd May, was taken prisoner by the British while still fighting in Italy. He was released on 31st March 1947. He joined the Bundeswehr in November 1957 and served in numerous positions with the new German paratroopers. He retired March 1979 with the rank of *Oberstleutnant*. He then served as a clerk in the German Federal Defence Ministry and was granted the pension of an *Oberst*. He died on 22nd June 2007 in Bonn.

OTHER AWARDS		PROMOTIONS	
13.08.1942	Parachutist Badge	01.01.1940	Gefreiter
29.07.1944	Iron Cross 2nd Class	01.01.1942	Oberjäger
29.09.1944	Iron Cross 1st Class	01.03.1943	Feldwebel
24.11.1944	Wound Badge in Black	01.01.1944	Leutnant der Reserve
03.02.1945	Wound Badge in Silver	01.03.1944	Leutnant (active)
30.03.1945	Luftwaffe Ground Assault Badge	20.04.1945	Oberleutnant

HEINRICH WELSKOP

(08.08.1916 – 07.05.1981)   *Oberfeldwebel*

Knight's Cross: Awarded on 21st August 1941 as *Oberfeldwebel* and Platoon Leader in the 11th Company, 3rd *Fallschirmjäger* Regiment for actions in Crete. During the fighting south of Privolia his company commander had been killed and Welskop took command and stormed a hill near Chania and held back strong counterattacks by the New Zealanders. The Knight's Cross was presented to Welskop by *Reichsmarschall* Hermann Göring.

His war ended in Italy when he surrendered to Allied troops in April 1945. He died on 7th May 1981 in his hometown of Duisburg. (Author's Collection)

(Author's Collection)

Heinrich Welskop was born on 8th August 1916 in Duisburg-Hamborn, a German city in the western part of the Ruhr District in North Rhine-Westphalia. He joined the 1st Battalion of the Regiment *"General Göring"* on 1st November 1937. In April 1939, he was assigned to 6th Company of the 1st *Fallschirmjäger* Regiment and saw action during the western campaign during the battle for Fortress Holland and was decorated with the Iron Cross 1st and 2nd Classes in May 1940.

In August, he transferred to the 11th Company of the 3rd *Fallschirmjäger* Regiment, and in May 1941, was appointed Platoon Leader. He took his platoon into action during the airborne invasion of Crete. His battalion was commanded by *Major* Heilmann and his company was dropped in the middle of the Barren Mountains south of Privolia and had to fight his way through the enemy to the 1st Battalion. During the fierce fighting, his company commander was killed and at first it seemed as though Welskop's platoon was doomed. However, acting on his own initiative, Welskop stormed a hill near Chania which protruded into the enemy positions. He and his platoon became engaged in fierce counterattacks with New Zealand troops. The fighting was close hand-to-hand combat and was bloody. Finally, *Oberst* Heidrich ordered that the hill be abandoned, but the order did not reach Welskop and his platoon who fought on. He held the small salient in the front alone against superior enemy forces, and for this he won the Knight's Cross.

Welskop remained with his regiment during the campaign in Russia, where he was wounded but remained with his men. He later served in Italy where he once again distinguished himself in battle, holding the positions assigned to him.

OTHER AWARDS		PROMOTIONS	
00.00.1938	Parachutist Badge	01.10.1938	Gefreiter
25.05.1940	Iron Cross 2nd Class	01.12.1939	Oberjäger
26.05.1940	Iron Cross 1st Class	01.06.1940	Feldwebel
00.00.1942	Eastern Front Medal	01.04.1941	Oberfeldwebel
00.00.1942	Wound Badge in Black	-----	-----
00.00.1942	KRETA Cuff title	-----	-----

WALTER HERBERT WERNER
(11.07.1917 – 25.06.1997)   *Leutnant*

(Wehrkundearchiv)

Knight's Cross: Awarded on 9th June 1944 as *Feldwebel* and Section Leader in the 1st Company, 1st *Fallschirm-Pioniere* Battalion for actions at Monte Cassino where undertook a number of offensive patrols and drove the enemy from the northern part of the city.

Walter Werner was born on 11th July 1917, in Brand-Erbisdorf near Freiberg in Saxony. He entered the armed forces in November 1938 and spent his first few years in the Luftwaffe as a mechanic. In June 1939, he started his engineer training, serving with support troops in Poland, France, and the Balkans from April to May 1941.

From June to August 1941, he saw action during the summer offensive in Russia. In January 1942, he transferred to the 13th Company of the 1st Supplemental (training) Paratrooper Regiment, before being transferred to the 1st Company of the 1st *Fallschirmjäger* Engineer Battalion. In October 1942, he returned to Russia where he remained until 31st March 1943. He fought with great skill and bravery and his commander noted, *"Werner demonstrates particular capabilities and far-reaching action during combat. As early as the battles at Leningrad and during the Russian campaign of 1942-1943, he excelled through particular courage."* He won the Iron Cross 2nd Class in Russia, and in July, his unit transferred to Italy; where from March 1944 he and his company saw action at Cassino. Here they faced massive Allied bombing, and his engineers repelled numerous attacks in the city. Werner received the Iron Cross 1st Class on 1st April 1944. He continued to see action and was wounded on 4th May, when a rocket exploded. He stayed with his troops and was awarded the Knight's Cross for his bravery and leadership. He was also recommended for promotion to officer rank by *Major* Ernst Frömming, the commander of the 1st Paratrooper Engineer Battalion, who said, *"Werner is recommended for preferential promotion to officer as a skillful and risk-taking engineer platoon leader."* On 22nd August 1944, Werner was commissioned as a *Leutnant*

He was taken prisoner along with his platoon by British troops on 2nd May 1945. He died on 25th June 1997 at Neustadt am Rübenberge. His grave lies at the Cemetery in Hannover. (Section 143, Grave 48).

OTHER AWARDS		PROMOTIONS	
19.06.1941	War Service Cross 2nd Class + Swords	01.10.1939	Gefreiter
00.10.1942	Eastern Front Medal	01.10.1940	Obergefreiter
29.12.1942	Parachutist Badge	01.05.1942	Unteroffizier
25.04.1943	Iron Cross 2nd Class	01.04.1944	Feldwebel
01.04.1944	Iron Cross 1st Class	22.08.1944	Leutnant
00.06.1944	Wound Badge in Black	-----	-----
21.02.1945	Luftwaffe Ground Assault Badge	-----	-----

KARL-HANS WITTIG

(27.07.1918 – 29.12.1984)   *Leutnant der Reserve*

(Wehrkundearchiv)

Knight's Cross: Awarded on 5th February 1944 as *Feldwebel* and *Führer* 11th Company, 1st *Fallschirmjäger* Regiment for action in Russia, where he led his company during the fierce fighting southeast of Orel and in the house-to-house fighting in Nagorno where his company destroyed nine enemy tanks and took sixty prisoners.

Karl-Hans Wittig was born on 27th July 1918 in Seeläsgen (Przelazy), Züllichau, a village in the administrative district of Gmina Lubrza in western Poland, which used to be part of Germany. He joined the armed forces in October 1937 and served initially with the *General Göring* Regiment which later formed the 1st *Fallschirmjäger* Regiment.

He later participated in the invasion of Holland as an *Obergefreiter,* seeing action at Dordrecht and later at The Hague, where he won the Iron Cross 1st Class. He then saw action during the airborne invasion of Crete serving with the 11th Company. He was promoted to *Feldwebel* in October 1942 and transferred to Russia. He led the security platoon on an offensive patrol at Durnewo and when the patrol found itself cut off Wittig led them back to freedom, bringing eighteen prisoners along with captured guns and equipment. During the offensive actions at Velikye Luki, Wittig led the battalion's leading platoon, but the German attempt to relieve the surrounded fortress failed. South of Gribushino, Wittig led his men in a counter-attack, stormed a hill away from the enemy and fought off all attempts to regain it. During the fighting, Wittig was wounded for the fourth time, and was awarded the German Cross in Gold.

He then took part in the fierce fighting south of Stolbetskoye, where his men destroyed four of the eight attacking enemy tanks from close range. Wittig then assumed command of the company after the company commander was badly wounded, stormed a hill and secured a gap in the front southeast of Orel. There he was wounded for the fifth time. On the night of 19th and 20th of February 1943, he led his platoon during the street fighting in Nagorno, here his troops had to fight house by house until they broke the enemy resistance. Eventually, the town was taken by the Germans. During the night attack, nine enemy tanks were destroyed and over sixty prisoners captured as well as large amounts of weapons and other war material. The enemy had lost just over one hundred men. For this Wittig was rewarded with the Knight's Cross.

In 1944, he was promoted to *Leutnant* and transferred to the western front as part of the 5th *Fallschirmjäger* Regiment. In late-August 1944, he was captured near Mons, Belgium, by British troops. He remained a prisoner until early-1948 when he returned to Germany. Wittig died in Nuremberg on 29th December 1984.

OTHER AWARDS		PROMOTIONS	
07.09.1938	Parachutist Badge	00.00.1939	Gefreiter
00.11.1939	Commemorative Medal of 13th March 1938	00.00.1940	Obergefreiter
00.11.1939	Commemorative Medal of 1st October 1938	00.00.1941	Oberjäger
18.05.1940	Iron Cross 2nd Class	00.00.1942	Feldwebel

20.05.1940	Iron Cross 1st Class	00.00.1944	Leutnant der Reserve
01.10.1942	Luftwaffe Ground Assault Badge	-----	-----
00.11.1942	Wound Badge in Black	-----	-----
00.03.1943	Wound Badge in Silver	-----	-----
20.03.1943	German Cross in Gold	-----	-----
20.05.1943	KRETA Cuff title	-----	-----

RUDOLF WITZIG
(14.08.1916 – 03.10.2001) *Major*

Knight's Cross: Awarded on 10th May 1940 as *Oberleutnant* and *Führer* of Assault Group "*Granit*" in the Air-Landing Battalion *Koch* in recognition of his part in the successful attack of the Eben Emael Fort in Belgium.

Knight's Cross with Oakleaves: He became the 662nd recipient of the Oakleaves on 25th November 1944 as *Major* and Commander I Battalion, 21st Parachute Engineer Regiment for his gallantry during the heavy

Rudolf Witzig as depicted in a Willich propaganda postcard. (Author's Collection)

(Author's Collection)

fighting on the Eastern Front west of Kauen. His battalion destroyed twenty-seven enemy tanks.

Rudolf Witzig was born in Röhlinghausen, Wanne-Eickel, on 14th August 1916, and he began his military career as an officer candidate in April 1935. He joined the 16th Pioneer Battalion in Höxter and two years later he was commissioned as a *Leutnant* and served as a Platoon Leader in the 31st Pioneer Battalion. In August 1938, he volunteered for the parachute troops and joined the Parachute Infantry Regiment under *Major* Heidrich. A year later he transferred to the Luftwaffe and in July was promoted to *Oberleutnant* and served with the Koch Parachute Assault Battalion.

In April 1940, he transferred to the 17th Company of the 1st *Fallschirmjäger* Regiment and in May he took part in the capture of Eben Emael fort in Belgium. The assault on the fort was made in gliders, and it wasn't long before it was overrun; within a few minutes fourteen guns had been destroyed. Witzig, who had missed the initial jump, finally arrived at the fort some three hours later and found his men pinned down by enemy fire. He rallied his troops and in one great effort he led them into attack. The Belgian defenders quickly surrendered and Witzig and his eighty-five strong assault group had defeated more than 1,200 men. Only six of Witzig's men had been lost. When he was awarded the Knight's Cross, it was found that he hadn't yet received the two grades of the Iron Cross, a pre-requisite for the award of the Knight's Cross. So he was quickly approved for both grades and they were dated 12th and 13th May respectively.

This was to be his greatest feat which was mentioned in the Official Armed Forces Communiqué on the 11th May: *"The strongest of the fortress Lüttich, Eben-Emael, which dominates the crossings of the Maas and Albert-Canal near and west of Maastrich surrendered on Saturday afternoon. The commanding officer and 1,000 men were taken prisoner. The fort was already rendered defenceless and the garrison pinned down on 10th May by a specially selected unit of the Luftwaffe under the leadership of Oberleutnant Witzig and deploying new combat means. The garrison dropped their arms when an attacking unit of the Army, after heavy combat, established contact with the detachment Witzig."*

Witzig was awarded the Iron Cross 1st and 2nd Classes and the Knight's Cross, all simultaneously, and he was promoted to *Hauptmann*. Later, during the Crete operation, he led the 9th Company of the Parachute Assault Regiment, and was wounded and had to be evacuated to the Luftwaffe hospital in Athens.

On 10th May 1942, Witzig was placed in command of the Corps Parachute Pioneer Battalion and in August of that year he was promoted to *Major*. From November 1942, he and his battalion served in Tunisia and took part in major offensive battles in the northern sector of the front. Here his command was very successful and the success the Luftwaffe had are closely linked with his name. In June 1944, he was appointed commander of the 1st Battalion of the 21st Parachute Pioneer Battalion and at the same time he took command of the regiment. He now saw action on the Eastern Front where, in November, he won the Knight's Cross with Oakleaves. He and his command were again mentioned in an Armed Forces Communiqué on 8th August telling of how his forces had destroyed twenty-seven enemy tanks near Kumele. In December, he was named as the commanding officer of the 18th *Fallschirmjäger* Regiment and he was captured by Allied forces on 8th May 1945.

After the war, Witzig entered the West German Army, the Bundeswehr, with the rank of *Oberst*. He finally retired after twenty-eight years of service in September 1974. He died on 3rd October 2001, in Oberschleißheim, Munich.

OTHER AWARDS		PROMOTIONS		
01.10.1938	Army Parachutist Badge	01.04.1935	Fahnenjunker-Gefreiter	
00.04.1939	Armed Forces Long Service Award 4th Class	00.00.1937	Fahnenjunker-Feldwebel	
12.05.1940	Iron Cross 2nd Class	20.04.1937	Leutnant	
13.05.1940	Iron Cross 1st Class	31.07.1939	Oberleutnant	
18.10.1941	Wound Badge in Black	16.05.1940	Hauptmann	
12.11.1942	KRETA Cuff title	24.08.1942	Major	
01.05.1943	AFRIKA Cuff title	-----	-----	
01.08.1943	Luftwaffe Ground Assault Badge	-----	-----	
17.10.1943	German Cross in Gold	-----	-----	
09.11.1943	Luftwaffe Parachutist Badge	-----	-----	
15.11.1943	Italian-German Campaign Medal in Africa	-----	-----	
07.05.1945	Honour Roll Clasp of the Luftwaffe	-----	-----	

HILMAR KARL ADOLF ZAHN

(06.09.1919 – 08.03.2008)   *Hauptmann*

(Wehrkundearchiv)

Knight's Cross: Awarded on 9th June 1944 as *Oberleutnant* and Commander 5th Company, 1st *Fallschirmjäger* Regiment in recognition of his bravery and leadership during the fierce fighting at Monet Cassino. He was recognized by his superiors as being one of the bravest of the defenders, leading offensive and reconnaissance patrols and undertaking counter-attacks and raids.

Hilmar Zahn was born on 6th September 1919, in Wiesbaden-Rambach, and he served in the German Labour Service in 1937 before joining the 5th Company of the 5th Infantry Regiment in Bad Kreuznach. He transferred to the Luftwaffe in April 1938 and was assigned to the air base at Mannheim-Sandhofen, and in March 1939 he joined the 133rd Fighter Wing.

In January 1940, he was promoted to *Oberjäger* and began service with the 28th Luftwaffe Construction Company and was promoted to *Unteroffizier* the following month. From August 1940 until March 1941, he served in France. From June 1941, he saw action during the invasion of Russia and attended two wartime officer courses and passed his platoon commanders course in Wittstock, at the end of 1941. He was commissioned as a *Leutnant der Reserve* on 20th April 1942. In June, he became a platoon leader in the 5th Company of the 1st *Fallschirmjäger* Regiment and was deployed to Russia in October 1942. On 15th February 1943, while leading a reconnaissance patrol near Aleksejewka, he was wounded in action. He was awarded the Iron Cross 2nd Class in March 1943 and left hospital a few months later, and was assigned to the Paratrooper Replacement Battalion at Stendal. He was then sent to Italy, where he once again became a platoon commander in the 5th Company of the 1st *Fallschirmjäger* regiment.

In June 1943, his battalion commander submitted a special report on Zahn stating, in part that he was a very confident and energetic young officer who had a good education and mentally was very flexible and vivid. He was described as physically robust and above average. He had excelled during battalion operations in the East as a platoon leader, particularly as reconnaissance and assault troop leader. This report did much to help Zahn with his next promotion. In June 1943, he was promoted to *Oberleutnant der Reserve*. In January 1944, he became acting commander of the 5th Company of the 1st *Fallschirmjäger* Regiment and fought at Ortona and Cassino. He received the Iron Cross 1st Class in February, but was severely wounded the following month. The wound became infected and he had to have his right leg amputated. While recovering in hospital, Zahn heard that he had become an active officer, he was no longer a reserve officer, and in May 1944 was made an *Oberleutnant*. On 9th June 1944, Zahn was awarded the Knight's Cross for his bravery and leadership skills during the battles at Monte Cassino, the following week he was promoted to *Hauptmann*.

On 23rd March 1945, now with a prosthetic leg, he returned to command the 5th Company of the 1st *Fallschirmjäger* Regiment and fought near Bologna, before he became a prisoner of war on 8th May 1945. He was released from Allied captivity in Steinach am Brenner, on 30th June 1945. He died in his hometown of Wiesbaden on 8th March 2008 at the age of eighty-eight.

OTHER AWARDS		PROMOTIONS	
00.00.1937	Golden Hitler Youth Badge of Honour	01.11.1938	Gefreiter
06.02.1940	Commemorative Medal of 1st October 1938	01.10.1939	Obergefreiter
22.07.1942	Parachutist Badge	01.02.1940	Unteroffizier
03.03.1943	Wound Badge in Black	01.02.1941	Feldwebel
03.03.1943	Iron Cross 2nd Class	22.08.1941	Kriegsoffizieranwärter
18.02.1944	Iron Cross 1st Class	20.04.1942	Leutnant der Reserve
05.03.1944	Luftwaffe Ground Assault Badge	14.07.1943	Oberleutnant der Reserve
10.04.1944	Wound Badge in Silver	10.05.1944	Oberleutnant (active)
03.06.1944	Wound Badge in Gold	16.06.1944	Hauptmann

OTTO ZIERACH

(26.01.1907 – 12.08.1976)   *Major*

(Wehrkundearchiv)

Knight's Cross: Awarded on 15th May 1940 as *Oberleutnant der Reserve* and Operations Officer (Ia) in the Air-Landing Battalion *Koch* for actions in France. He took part in the aerial assault of the fortress Eben Emael and the four bridges over the Albert Canal. He took an active role in the fighting and in the prevention of the Vroenhoven Bridge from being destroyed.

Otto Zierach was born on 26th January 1907, in Eberswalde near Berlin and he entered the Brandenburg-Havel Police School on 13th April 1928. From April 1929 until April 1933, he served with the *Schutzpolizei* in Berlin and was then transferred to the Wecke Special Purpose Police Battalion as a Police *Oberwachtmeister*. In October 1934, he became a member of the *General Göring* Regiment after the police battalion was renamed. In April 1938, the *General Göring* Regiment was taken into the Luftwaffe and was known as the 1st *Fallschirmjäger* Regiment and Zierach transferred to the 1st Company as an *Hauptfeldwbel*.

Zierach didn't take part in the Polish Campaign, and in February 1940, immediately after the formation of the Koch Parachute Assault Battalion, he became the unit's Operations Officer. Koch had been placed in command of the airborne operations against the fortress of Eben Emael and the four bridges over the Albert Canal. Zierach, as Koch found out, was a capable and knowledgeable assistant whose help and support played a vital role in the unit's success. The battalion staff jumped with Assault Group Beton near Vroenhoven Bridge, and the defenders were prevented from destroying the bridge. It was for this action and his support of his commander that Zierach was awarded the Knight's Cross.

He took part in the airborne invasion of Crete while attached to the Air Landing Assault Regiment. In February 1942, he was transferred to Russia and joined the staff of the Luftwaffe Division Meindl as a special duties officer. From 28th September, he was made temporary commander of the 3rd Battalion of the 1st Luftwaffe Field Division and from there he joined the staff of the II Air Corps, serving as Quartermaster. On 8th January 1944, *Generalleutnant* Meindl sent Zierach to the Luftwaffe Air Warfare Academy in Berlin-Gatow. He returned in April and was assigned to the Staff of the II Parachute Corps, seeing action in Normandy during the bitter fighting on the Ems River. On 8th May 1945, he was captured by British troops and was held until the end of the year. Otto Zierach died on 12th August 1976 in Veserde, Nachrodt-Wiblingwerde.

OTHER AWARDS

02.10.1936	Armed Forces Long Service Award 4th Class
18.12.1936	Army Parachutist Badge
22.05.1939	Commemorative Medal of 13th March 1938
12.05.1940	Iron Cross 2nd Class
13.05.1940	Iron Cross 1st Class
15.08.1942	Eastern Front Medal
-----	-----
-----	-----
-----	-----
-----	-----

PROMOTIONS

01.04.1929	Polizei-Wachtmeister
01.04.1933	Polizei-Oberwachtmeister
01.10.1934	Hauptwachtmeister der Landespolizei
29.02.1935	Hauptwachtmeister (Luftwaffe)
01.04.1938	Hauptfeldwebel
01.10.1938	Reserve-Offiziersanwärter
01.02.1940	Oberleutnant der Reserve
20.05.1940	Hauptmann der Reserve
14.03.1941	Hauptmann (active)
26.08.1942	Major

BIBLIOGRAPHY

Angolia, John R. *For Führer and Fatherland Vol: 1*. San Jose: Roger James Bender, 1976.

Antill, Peter D. *Crete 1941: Germany's Lightning Airborne Assault*. Osprey, 2005.

Dixon, Jeremy *Luftwaffe Generals: The Knight's Cross Holders 1939-1945*. Schiffer Military History, Atglen, PA, 2009.

Dunstan, Simon. *Fort Eben Emael: The Key to Hitler's Victory in the West*. Osprey, 2005.

Ford, Ken *Cassino 1944: Breaking the Gustav Line*. Osprey, 2004.

Kurowski, Franz *Knight's Cross Holders of the Fallschirmjäger*. Schiffer Military History, Atglen, PA, 1995.

MacLean, French L. *Luftwaffe Efficiency and Promotion Reports for the Knight's Cross Winners Vol: 1 and Vol: 2*. Schiffer Military History, Atglen, PA, 2007.

Mrazek, James E. *The Fall of Eben Emael*. New York: Presidio Press, 1991.

Neitzel, Sönke (Editor). *Tapping Hitler's Generals*. Transcripts of Secret Conversations, 1942-1945. Frontline Books, 2005.

Patzwall Klaus and Veit Scherzer *Das Deutsche Kreuz 1941-1945. Geschichte und Inhaber Band II*. Verlag Klaus D. Patzwall – Norderstedt, 2001.

Scherzer, Veit *Ritterkreuzträger 1939-1945*. Scherzers Militaer Verlag, 2007.

Thomas, Franz and Günter Wegmann. *Die Ritterkreuztrager der Deutschen Wehrmacht 1939-1945 Teil II: Fallschirmjäger*. Biblio-Verlag, Osnabrück, 1986.

More Schiffer Titles

www.schifferbooks.com

OPERATION DRVAR
A Facsimile of Official KriegsberichterReports on the Attack by SS-Fallschirmjägeron Tito's Headquarters May 25, 1944.

Branislav Radovic

This book is a text and photographic facsimile of two very rare after action reports by Luftwaffe kriegsberichter (war correspondents) chronicling Operation "Drvar" where German airborne and land forces attempted to capture or kill the Yugoslav communist partisan leader Tito in his headquarters in Drvar, Bosnia & Herzegovina. Includes text in English and German, and over forty rare photographs.

Size: 8 1/2" x 11" • over 40 bw images • 64 pp
ISBN: 978-0-7643-3060-5 • soft cover • $29.99

GERMAN PARATROOPS IN SCANDINAVIA
Fallschirmjäger in Denmark and Norway April-June 1940.

Óscar González

The German conquest of Denmark and Norway in spring 1940 presents an interesting study of joint strategy between ground, air, and sea forces. In this campaign, the Germans placed great emphasis on mobility, speed, and surprise. The Fallschirmjäger of 1940 was a well-trained, highly-motivated force, and their participation in Operation "Weserübung" – the codename for the Wehrmacht assault on Denmark and Norway – is this subject of this book. Among the topics discussed are German paratroop operations (some of the first combat jumps of the war) against the main Danish and Norwegian bridges and aerodromes, the jump on Dombås, behind enemy lines, and also their tenacious resistance on the snow-covered grounds of Narvik.

Size: 6" x 9" • over 160 color/bw images • 192 pp
ISBN: 978-0-7643-3241-8 • hard cover • $45.00

SUMMER OF '42
A Study of German-Armenian Relations During the Second World War.

Levon Thomassian

Despite the overwhelming contributions made by the Armenians to the Allied war effort, it is widely unknown that at least 18,000 served under the Third Reich. After the war, these so-called collaborators were chastised and indiscriminately labeled as traitors by those unable to grasp the complexity of their circumstances. Largely based on archival research, German-Armenian Relations in the Second World War attempts to separate fact from fallacy by examining the complex motives, treatment, and history of these Armenians.

Size: 6" x 9" • over 40 color/bw images • 216 pp
ISBN: 978-0-7643-4045-1 • hard cover • $29.99

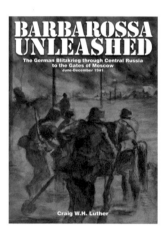

BARBAROSSA UNLEASHED
The German Blitzkrieg through Central Russia to the Gates of Moscow • June-December 1941

Craig W.H. Luther

This book examines in unprecedented detail the advance of German forces through central Russia in the summer of 1941, followed by brief accounts of the Battle of Moscow and winter battles into early 1942. Based on hundreds of veterans' accounts, archival documents and key primary and secondary literature, it offers the most detailed account to date of virtually all aspects of the German soldiers' experiences in Russia in 1941.

Size: 7" x 10" • 220 b/w photos, and 22 color and b/w maps
736 pp • ISBN: 978-0-7643-4376-6 • hard cover • $59.99

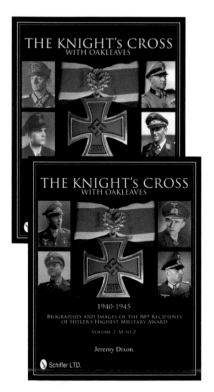

THE KNIGHT'S CROSS WITH OAKLEAVES
1940-1945: Biographies and Images of the 889 Recipients of Hitler's Highest Military Award

Jeremy Dixon

This extensive, two-volume set presents every recipient of the Knight's Cross with Oakleaves, awarded during the Second World War, and presented personally by Hitler from 1940 until 1945. Described inside – and shown with at least one photograph – are each of the 889 recipients from the Luftwaffe, Heer, Waffen-SS, and Kriegsmarine, as well as foreign recipients. This work contains over 1000 photographs, from the author's own collection as well as other private collections. This is first time such a work has been written in the English language and is a must for anyone interested in Germany's highest decoration, as well as anyone interested in the careers of each recipient.

Size: 8 1/2" x 11" • over 1000 bw/color images
Vol. 1 320, Vol. 2, 328 pp • ISBN: 978-0-7643-4266-0
hard cover • $125.00

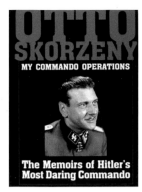

OTTO SKORZENY
My Commando Operations:
The Memoirs of Hitler's Most Daring Commando.

The memoirs of the legendary Skorzeny appear here in its first unabridged English edition. Skorzeny's fame began with the successful raid to free Benito Mussolini from the Gran Sasso, Italy in 1943. His elite commandos surprised Italian guards in a daring daytime raid. Hitler presented Skorzeny with the Knight's Cross for this operation. Not only is this raid explained in minute detail, many of Skorzeny's previously unknown operations in all European and Russian theatres of World War II are given in detailed accounts. Operation Griffin - the innovative use of German Kommandos dressed as American soldiers working behind enemy lines - during the Ardennes Offensive in 1944 is given in-depth coverage, as is Skorzeny's rememberances on the Malmedy massacre. Skorzeny also offers his insights into the mysterious Rudolf Hess mission to England in May 1941, and offers a behind the scenes look at German and Russian secret military intelligence, and the workings of Canaris and Gehlen.

Size: 6" x 9" • 16 pages of photographs • 496 pp
ISBN: 978-0-88740-718-5 • hard cover • $39.99

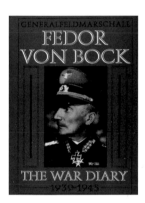

GENERALFELDMARSCHALL
FEDOR VON BOCK
The War Diary 1939-1945.

Klaus Gerbert, Editor and Translated from
the German by David Johnston.

The Von Bock memoirs, which appear here for the first time, allow the reader to see the entire drama of the Second World War through the eyes of one of Germany's most important military commanders. After the attacks on Poland and Western Europe, campaigns he helped bring to a succesful conclusion, von Bock became Commander-in-Chief of Army Group Center which carried out the main drive on Moscow during Operation Barbarossa and brought the Red Army to the verge of collapse in the great battles of encirclement. Hitler relieved von Bock when the German offensive bogged down during the winter of 1941/1942. After he returned as Commander-in-Chief of Army Group South, von Bock was eventually placed in temporary retirement when he critized Hitler's division of forces against Stalingrad and the Caucasus-the road to castrophe began. Army commanders like Hoth, Guderian, Kluge and Paulus served under Generalfeldmarschall Fedor von Bock, while at his side stood his nephew Henning von Tresckow, who led the most active resistance movement against Hitler, and Carl-Hans von Hardenberg, a friend and advisor of Stauffenberg. Their efforts to win over von Bock failed, yet the Generalfeldmarschall tolerated the pronounced resistance sentiments among his staff, and even became privy to the attempted assissination of Hitler on July 20, 1944. This book allows us to reassess Fedor von Bock, whose complex personality is revealed by his diary entries, and by the biographical sketches by editor Klaus Gerbet.

Size: 6" x 9" • 62 b/w photographs • 640 pp
ISBN: 978-0-7643-0075-2 • hard cover • $39.95

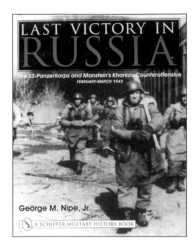

LAST VICTORY IN RUSSIA

The SS-Panzerkorps and Manstein's Kharkov Counteroffensive - February-March 1943.

George M. Nipe, Jr..

This book is the first detailed and comprehensive account of the Kharkov counteroffensive, the operations of the SS divisions and the supporting actions of Armeeabteilung Fretter-Pico and 1. Panzerarmee, and is supported by over 210 photographs and maps. By the end of January of 1943, Hitler's armies had been dealt a series of defeats by the Russians, beginning with the disaster at Stalingrad. Successive Soviet offensives had destroyed the German 6. Armee and annihilated the armies of Germany's Axis allies, Italy, Rumania and Hungary. Germany teetered on the brink of defeat in World War II because the Soviet advance threatened to drive to the Dnepr River and encircle the remaining Germans armies in southern Russia. Stalin and the Russian high command believed that the war could be won with just one more great effort. Accordingly, they planned and launched two offensives, designated Operations "Star" and "Gallop." The focal points of the two offensives included the recapture of Kharkov, the industrial heart of the Ukraine and the destruction of Armeeabteilung Hollidt, 4. Panzerarmee and 2. Armee. Feldmarschall Erich von Manstein entered the picture in late 1942 when he was appointed commander of Heeresgruppe Don. Beginning in February he engineered a remarkable operation that changed the course of the war in Russia. Manstein's counteroffensive destroyed or severely damaged four Russian armies and regained much of the territory lost in January. The troops that played the most important role in the offensive were three divisions of the Waffen-SS. "Leibstandarte," "Das Reich" and "Totenkopf" were combined for the first time into a corps, which was commanded by SS-Obergruppenführer Paul Hausser, the senior commander of the Waffen-SS. "Leibstandarte" and "Das Reich" participated in the defense of Kharkov, along with the elite Army division "Grossdeutschland" supported by three weak infantry divisions. This handful of divisions was attacked by four Soviet armies, but under command of Armeeabteilung Lanz, was able to hold the city for two weeks. On 14 February, 1943 the SS-Panzerkorps and the rest of Armeeabteilung Lanz withdrew from Kharkov under disputed circumstances that involved Hausser and his violation of a direct order from Hitler. Almost exactly a month later, the Germans had recaptured Kharkov and destroyed or crippled the four Soviet armies that had driven them out of the city in February. The divisions that played the key role in Manstein's counteroffensive were the three divisions of the Waffen-SS. While "Leibstandarte" defended the supply base of the SS-Panzerkorps from the entire Soviet 3rd Tank Army, "Das Reich" and "Totenkopf" conducted a complex series of operations that began with a 100 kilometer thrust to the south which saved the Dnepr bridges, thus securing supply lines for the armies of Heeresgruppe Don/Süd. Subsequent operations by the SS divisions drove the Russians away from the rail net south of Kharkov and wrested Kharkov from the Russians once again. During the recapture of the city, there was controversy regarding Hausser's command decisions. Hausser has been accused of disregarding his instructions from superior officers and throwing his divisions into costly combat in the city for reasons of personal and SS prestige, in order to regain Hitler's favor. This study has found that the records of the SS-Panzerkorps and 4. Panzerarmee provide a different explanation for Hausser's actions.

Size: 8 1/2" x 11" • over 210 b/w photographs • 368 pp
ISBN: 978-0-7643-1186-4 • hard cover • $59.95

Schiffer books may be ordered from your local bookstore, or they may be ordered directly from the publisher by writing to: **Schiffer Publishing, Ltd. 4880 Lower Valley Rd., Atglen, PA 19310**
(610) 593-1777; Fax (610) 593-2002 E-mail: Info@schifferbooks.com

Please visit our website catalog at **www.schifferbooks.com** or write for a free catalog.

Printed in China